D0301397

ANNA SEWARD:
A CONSTRUCTED LIFE

To Nigel

Anna Seward:
A Constructed Life
A Critical Biography

TERESA BARNARD
University of Derby, UK

ASHGATE

Published by
Ashgate Publishing Limited
Wey Court East
Union Road
Farnham
Surrey, GU9 7PT
England

Ashgate Publishing Company
Suite 420
101 Cherry Street
Burlington
VT 05401-4405
USA

www.ashgate.com

British Library Cataloguing in Publication Data
Barnard, Teresa
Anna Seward: a constructed life: a critical biography
   1. Seward, Anna, 1742–1809 2. Women poets, English – 18th century – Biography
   3. Poets, English – 18th century – Biography
   I. Title
   821.6

Library of Congress Cataloging-in-Publication Data
Barnard, Teresa
  Anna Seward: a constructed life: a critical biography / by Teresa Barnard.
    p. cm.
  Includes bibliographical references and index.
  ISBN 9780754666165 (hbk)
  ISBN 9780754693468 (ebk)
  1. Seward, Anna, 1742–1809. 2. Seward, Anna, 1742–1809—Correspondence. 3. Seward, Anna, 1742–1809—Friends and associates. 4. Authors, English—18th century—Biography. 5. Women authors, English—18th century—Biography. I. Title.

PR3671.S7Z62 2009
821'.6—dc22
[B]
                                                 2008049798
ISBN: 978-0-7546-6616-5

Mixed Sources
Product group from well-managed
forests and other controlled sources
www.fsc.org Cert no. SGS-COC-2482
© 1996 Forest Stewardship Council
FSC

Printed and bound in Great Britain by
TJ International Ltd, Padstow, Cornwall

Contents

List of Illustrations

Acknowledgements

Many people have helped in my work on this book. I am particularly grateful to Dr Anne McDermott and Dr Diana Barsham for their guidance and encouragement. My research has been supported by the University of Birmingham and the University of Derby and was funded by the Arts and Humanities Research Council, to whom I am also thankful. My thanks are extended to the colleagues and friends who have supported my work and who have provided a constant source of advice, especially Dr Lynda Pratt, Dr Valerie Rumbold, Dr Christine Berberich and Dr Deborah Mutch.

In researching my work, I have drawn on manuscripts and have been given invaluable help from Derby Local Studies Library; Cambridge University Library; the National Library of Scotland; the British Library; the Derbyshire Records Office; the Lichfield Records Office; the Erasmus Darwin House Museum; the Samuel Johnson Birthplace Museum; the National Portrait Gallery; the Tate Gallery; the Beinecke Library at Yale University and the Huntington Library, California. I am particularly grateful to Wendy Atkins for information on Frances Brooke, to Nicola Wright of Eyam Hall for her generosity in providing the history of Major John Wright and to Nicholas Redman for his entertaining anecdotes and for sharing his knowledge and manuscripts on Erasmus Darwin.

Finally, I am grateful to Faye McGinty and Lauren Rowberry, who have constantly motivated and inspired me, as has my mother, Mary Prymaka. My greatest debt is to my husband, Nigel, who has always found the time to listen to me and to read my words. It would have been impossible to complete this task without his patience, good-natured encouragement and unfailing enthusiasm for my research.

List of Abbreviations

Cambridge UL   Cambridge University Library, Cambridge, Cambridgeshire

HL   Huntington Library, San Marino, California, USA

JBM   Samuel Johnson Birthplace Museum, Lichfield, Staffordshire

Lichfield RO   Lichfield Record Office, Lichfield, Staffordshire

NLS   National Library of Scotland, Edinburgh, Scotland

YUB   Yale University, Beinecke Rare Book and Manuscript Library, New Haven, Connecticut, USA

Introduction
'The fame of a lady'

For as far back as her memory reached, Anna Seward's main preoccupation was with the written word.[1] Not a day passed without reading, reciting and, most of all, writing. Her preferred medium was letters. Recording her thoughts daily, she wrote relentlessly, in her bold, forward-sloping handwriting, on literature, politics, religion, science and the arts. Her letters depict her life and work, intertwined in vivid detail. Her poems often take their first shape from her letters. Her literary critiques are in the form of letters sent to her favourite journal, the *Gentleman's Magazine*, as are her essays. Her juvenile journal is in the form of letters to an imaginary friend, 'Emma'. Her only novel, *Louisa*, takes an epistolary form.

She wrote to close friends and literary acquaintances in an extraordinary blend of intellectual and anecdotal narrative. Members of her coterie who met in her blue dressing room at the Bishop's Palace in Lichfield included Erasmus Darwin, Richard Lovell Edgeworth, Thomas Day and her platonic companion, the musician John Saville. Later, when she entered a career as a writer, her intellect, charm and literary authority drew new correspondents towards her, including William Hayley, Helen Maria Williams, Frances Brooke, Walter Scott and Robert Southey. With an over-arching passion for literature, she entered lively debates on contemporary writings and the English classics. Her natural curiosity extended beyond literary awareness; as her circle of friends widened so did her interests, and she wrote to, and about, the leading characters of the day. She wrote of theology to the Catholic poet, Edward Jerningham, of landscape gardening to Humphry Repton, of slavery to Josiah Wedgwood, of war to Robert Fellowes. There is more in the correspondence than the record of an individual life; her letters illustrate what life was like for others, particularly for women. Seward tells stories and anecdotes about her friends' lives and the places they inhabited, painting elaborate little word pictures of who they were, what they looked like, how they lived.

There is a clear distinction between Seward's public correspondence and her private letters. With a confident awareness of the fascinating life she lived, she decided that her correspondence would be her autobiography. Her early life is revealed in her juvenile letters to 'Emma', and, from 1780 onwards, she rewrote the letters which she thought most interesting, copying these into a series of letter books for future publication. Written with elaborate flair, the two collections of letters are the 'official' version of her life, and she carefully assembled them to construct a rounded persona for herself. Her private letters to close friends are more intimate, recording the minutiae and the complexities of her daily life.

At the age of sixty-six, Seward was exhausted after an extensive series of debilitating illnesses. As she laid down her pen for the last time she was confident

---

[1]   Pronounced 'Seeward'.

that her words would be remembered. Writing her final letter to Walter Scott, she explained her frailty: 'Much writing is forbid me, indeed its effect is sufficiently forewarning since the moment I begin to think intensely, the pen falls from my hand, a lethargic sensation creeps over me, I doze'.[2] A few days later, she sank into a coma and shortly afterwards she died.

Before she became seriously ill, she began the process of putting her literary house in order. Sorting through meticulously compiled letter books and writings, Seward prepared her correspondence for publication. She anthologised and indexed her poems, revising her juvenile letters to form the prefatory record of her early life. Embarking on the negotiations for copyright sales and finances, she pursued her carefully organised programme, all with the intention of preparing a lasting memorial before her delicate health finally failed. In the latter years of her life, she wavered between the 'horror of the trouble' of self-publication and the alternative, a posthumous publication.[3] As a single woman without close male relatives, it was out of necessity and usually with apprehension that she handled her own finances, arranged for her publications and negotiated her copyrights. She had battled against the politics of the publishing industry many times in the past and was now physically weakened by illness. Yet, her mind was still sharp and she proposed to leave nothing to chance. She continued with copyright negotiations where she was able and, at the same time, she made rigorous provisions for a posthumous publication, issuing her final, precise instructions through her last will and testament, which she herself drew up and engrossed.[4]

Seward was frank about her autobiographical intentions, writing with her usual self-assurance to her close friend, Anna Rogers Stokes, explaining the anticipated outcome for her letters:

> My long habit of transcribing into a book every letter of my own which appears to me worth the attention of the public, omitting the passages which are totally without interest for anyone but those to whom they are addressed, has already filled several volumes. After my death, at least, if not in my lifetime, it is my design that they shall be published. They will faithfully reflect the unimportant events of my life, rendered in some degree interesting, from being animated by the present-time sentiments and feelings of my heart — at least more interesting than a narrative of past occurrences could possibly prove. To sit down formally to such a task of egotism, would extremely revolt my sensations — and, were I inclined to undertake it, I have absolutely no time.[5]

---

[2]   National Library of Scotland, Walter Scott Correspondence, MS 865, fols 131–32, Anna Seward, 'Letter to Walter Scott' (16 March 1809).

[3]   Huntington Library, San Marino, California, Papers of Edward Jerningham, MS JE 756–80, Anna Seward, 'Letter to Edward Jerningham' [?1801].

[4]   Lichfield RO, Seward Family MSS, D262/1/35, Anna Seward, 'Will and Codicils' (1808–1809). See Appendix III for a digest of the will's contents.

[5]   Anna Seward, 'Letter to Mrs Stokes' (15 June 1797), *Letters of Anna Seward: Written Between the Years 1784 and 1807. In Six Volumes*, ed. by Archibald Constable (Edinburgh and London: Archibald Constable and Company, Edinburgh and Longman, Hurst, Rees, Orme, and Brown, William Miller and John Murray, London, 1811), IV, 362.

If autobiography was considered to be 'a task of egotism', it was certainly not unusual for writers to attempt to manipulate their reputation by means of the epistolary genre. Published letters and epistolary novels were popular and influential, and letter-writing manuals gave all the necessary explanation for skilful self-expression. By making private correspondence public, writers had a far greater measure of control than by placing their trust in a biographer or memorialist, and, naturally, the content reflected a self-constructed subjectivity. The image Seward created for herself in her letters is of the independent, self-sufficient writer, an intellectual who constantly searches and challenges, exploring numerous and varied aspects of culture and society. What she did not anticipate as she sorted and revised the letters that were intended to become the representation of her public life and work was the harsh editing by her literary editors, executors and family after her death.

Anna Seward died at a quarter past six on the evening of 25 March 1809 without realising the publication of her works. In her will, there was a directive for the executors to seek out a locked blue hair trunk in her dressing room at the Bishop's Palace. They were led to the trunk by a maid, and there they found a compilation of her letters, poems and prose writings, tied together with a brightly-coloured silk ribbon. This was her bequest to literary posterity. To the Scottish publisher, Archibald Constable, she bequeathed the exclusive copyright for the copious letter books which recorded her own life and illuminated the lives of her many illustrious friends between the years 1784 and 1807. All else was left to Walter Scott, who had been a trusted correspondent friend for many years.

Scott was to play a significant role in the formation of Seward's posthumous literary reputation. After the will had been read, he wrote to Seward's cousin and executor, the clergyman Henry (Harry) White, about the importance of his task, referring to the bequest as 'a trust so sacred and so delicate'. Seward's lawyer, Charles Simpson, also contemplated the magnitude of the bequest, writing to Scott to outline his responsibility as the conserver of 'the fame of a lady who has placed the rank she is destined to hold in poetry under your care and protection'.[6] Scott requested that no one but White should see the contents of the blue hair trunk until he was able to make his way to Lichfield to examine his inheritance for himself.

As Scott read through the juvenile letters, he was troubled by the anecdotal content and set about excising everything he equated with gossip. With his harsh censorship, he effectively removed the vitality of the letters, taking out stories which told of the young men and women of Lichfield who were attempting, and often failing, to negotiate the intricacies of the marriage market. In terms of publication, Scott left nothing of Seward's thoughts on her own battles against the gendered inequalities of female education and career. What does remain is mostly literary debate, giving a misrepresentation of the image Seward had constructed. Although Scott excised almost two thirds of the correspondence prior

---

[6] NLS, MSS, 865, fols 138–39, Charles Simpson, 'Letter to Walter Scott' (9 April 1809).

to publication, sometimes discarding entire letters, he did not destroy his censored extracts, and these can be pieced back together to reveal a broader chronicle of Seward's early life.

In much the same way as the juvenile letters, the selection of correspondence which Seward had rewritten in her letter books for publication was ruthlessly edited by Archibald Constable, her Scottish publisher. Constable also allowed Scott and several others to scour the letter books for indiscretions, local anecdotes and political comments. They turned their attention to anything, in fact, which was personal or either deprecated the literary establishment or was not considered appropriate from a woman writer. It is difficult to gauge exactly how much of the sharp edge of Seward's writing was removed from the letter book manuscripts, and it is most unlikely that anything of the excised material remains at all. There is evidence of these editing techniques to be found in extant letters written to correspondents such as James Boswell and Walter Scott, which can be compared with the letter book versions to reveal the differences. These are an important source of evaluation to help present a comprehensive picture of Seward's life and writings.

As the letters were picked apart and twisted out of shape by the editors and executors, so was Anna Seward's carefully self-constructed image. Contemporary accounts of her place a forceful emphasis on her beauty and charisma; 'she was a dazzling Creature', wrote Hester Thrale Piozzi.[7] Still beautiful in later life, she charmed Scott and Southey with her deep auburn hair, lustrous eyes and melodic voice. The reaction to her poetry, however, was ambivalent. She first came to public attention with her patriotic poems about national heroes, the 'Elegy on Captain Cook' (1780) and the 'Monody on Major André' (1781).[8] The political turmoil following the British army's humiliating defeat in the American campaigns for independence culminated in the need for a new notion of national identity, and Seward's timely publications encapsulated the national mood. She became the emblematic 'immortal MUSE of Britain', enjoying a brief prominence as one of the leading poets of her generation.[9] Unfortunately for her reputation, these works led to an influx of requests for epitaphs, often from complete strangers. The limited scope of the epitaph form resulted in an accumulation of indifferent verse, and, ultimately, she gave up publishing poems after a career of just sixteen years and turned instead to prose. This is not to say that she did not also write exquisite

---

[7]   Hester Thrale Piozzi, 'Letter to Lady Keith' (31 January 1810), *The Piozzi Letters: Correspondence of Hester Thrale Piozzi 1784–1821*, ed. by Edward A. Bloom and Lillian D. Bloom (London and Toronto: Associated University Presses, 1991), IV, 264.

[8]   Anna Seward, *The Poetical Works of Anna Seward; with Extracts from her Literary Correspondence. In Three Volumes*, ed. by Walter Scott (Edinburgh and London: John Ballantyne and Company, Edinburgh and Longman, Hurst, Rees, and Orme, London, 1810) II, 33–46; 68–88.

[9]   Henry F. Cary, 'Sonnet', In Seward, *Llangollen vale, with other poems*, ed. by Jonathan Wordsworth (London: G. Sael, 1796, repr. 1994).

poems, nor that this was the only motive to end a poetic career, but it was a major contributory cause. She continued to write until she died, although she published very little after the early 1790s.

As many other contemporary women writers found, there were hazards and pitfalls paving the route to the literary immortality which Seward strived towards. Her private life was constantly under scrutiny and subject to disapproval because of her relationship with John Saville, who was married and had two daughters. She and Saville adored each other; their relationship lasted thirty-seven years until his death in 1803. According to unpublished letters, the musician could not afford to divorce his bitter, angry wife, and his conscience would not allow him to live openly with Seward, so they chose an ostensibly companionable but intense relationship. On a different level, representations of her affection for her foster sister Honora Sneyd have become, over time, pejorative expressions of an overwhelming fixation that eventually soured her life. These representations are established on a misreading of the contents of her poetry, rather than on contemporaneous accounts in her letters. It would be wrong to pigeonhole her relationships or her sexuality by twenty-first-century values or by the half-formed truths found in the information in letters which have been heavily edited and censored. The uncensored letters, documents and fragments of private correspondence that I present here provide fresh insights into who Seward was, and these altered perceptions offer new readings of her work.

The independence Seward had battled for in her youth was of paramount importance to her and was not to be modestly concealed. Consequently, her conduct was often perceived as over-assertive, even aberrant. Although she was popular with the reading public, her forthright literary critiques and, paradoxically, her generous praise of her colleague writers frequently attracted open hostility. In literary terms, she considered herself on a level with male writers and made no particular concessions in her judgment of women's writing. A piece of work was evaluated on its merit as good, bad, or indifferent, but was never subject to assessment by the sex of its author. Her entry into more masculine areas of writing – biography, epic, literary dissertations, sermons and paraphrases of Horatian odes – brought more condemnation. Yet her biography of Erasmus Darwin, castigated then and now as 'unreliable', is still used for reference by scholars and historians.[10] Seward was reliable in her continual recording of the lives of others. An unfinished but publishable epic, *Telemachus*,[11] was probably excluded from her posthumous work by Scott because it was considered to be a masculine form.

Seward's father, Thomas, was a minor poet and canon of Lichfield Cathedral, and he had parishes in Derbyshire and Staffordshire. The radical sermons Seward wrote for his curates and ministers were excluded from her posthumous body of

---

[10]   Seward, *Memoirs of the Life of Dr Darwin; Chiefly During his Residence in Lichfield, with Anecdotes of his Friends, and Criticisms on his Writings* (London: J. Johnson, 1804).

[11]   NLS, The Sir Walter Scott MSS, 880, fols 1–71, Seward, *Telemachus: an Epic Poem* [n.d.].

work because they were considered too subversive by her family, who claimed that they were 'nearly the reverse of what that solemn order of Composition should be'.[12] The Horatian odes fared no better. In his 'Biographical Preface' to her poetry edition, Walter Scott voiced the general reaction to them, arguing that as paraphrases rather than translations, they 'could hardly be expected to gratify those whose early admiration has been turned to the original'.[13] Interventions like these have a direct bearing on the representation of Seward's literary production. Without the classical education of her male contemporaries, her idea was to provide graceful paraphrases from what she considered to be pedestrian translations. Such a feminisation of a masculine form was perceived to be disrespectful.

There have been biographies written about Seward which do nothing to dispel the image of the unreliable narrator, amateur provincial poet and domesticated carer of sick elderly parents. The notion of her being forced into a life of semi-retirement, unable to write because of household duties, has become exaggerated as time passes. Walter Scott was the first major biographer, with brief memoirs in his 'Biographical Preface'. His version is filled with inaccuracies which I will dispel during the course of this account. Where scholars and biographers try to examine Seward's life through her published letters, they will always founder because the editing techniques of Scott, Constable and the executors of Seward's estate took away more than they left. Scott wrote in his memoirs that his own purpose for life writing was not vanity, but that he believed it important to record 'all that [the public] are entitled to know of an individual who has contributed to their amusement'. He stresses the words 'from good authority', meaning his own.[14] His concern with the non-interference of his life writings is clear in his manner of drawing large flourishes at the bottom of each page as a safeguard against forgery or the unauthorised insertion of text. Yet his letters were naturally subject to editing, as shown in the brief description of editing technique by his biographer, John Gibson Lockhart, who later had to confront criticism of his impartiality and the accusation that he had 'wilfully distorted the character and conduct of other men, for the purpose of raising Scott at their expense'. Lockhart's response was that he had only removed the passages from Scott's letters that 'would have pained' his readers.[15] Interestingly, Robert Southey revealed that Scott's editing of Seward's manuscripts ensured that his own representation was impeccable.

According to correspondence between Seward's lawyer Charles Simpson and Walter Scott, most of her political comments were removed from the correspondence, making it difficult to estimate what impact her views may have made on the reading public and how this might have affected her reputation. It

---

[12]   NLS, Walter Scott Correspondence, MS 865, fol 133, Henry White, 'Letter to Walter Scott' (2 July, 1809).

[13]   Walter Scott, 'Biographical Preface', *Poetical Works*, pp. xix–xx.

[14]   Walter Scott, *Memoirs of the Life of Sir Walter Scott*, ed. by J. G. Lockhart, 7 vols (Edinburgh, Robert Cadell, 1836), I, 1.

[15]   J. G. Lockhart, 'Preface', in Walter Scott, *Memoirs*, VII, p. xii.

appears that her political opinions towards the end of the century were forceful, as her executors were apprehensive about publishing what Simpson described as 'Political Violence', and he suggested that Scott should repress these observations.[16] Some of her political thoughts, however, escaped censorship, and they reveal ambivalence towards expressing her opinion publicly. Letters were valuable political tools, and Seward evaluated the writings of Edmund Burke, Helen Maria Williams, Brooke Boothby, Thomas Paine and Joseph Priestley among others, writing eloquently and at length about the situation in France in the early 1790s. She still insisted she was not qualified to talk about politics, although she clearly was.

Men who achieved success in the eighteenth century could expect 'great men' biographies which praised their feats. Women lived different lives by different standards; their landscapes of domesticity were difficult to abandon. Writing women were able to express their lives in their own chosen form. For Lady Mary Wortley Montagu, it was a lifelong journal, which was destroyed by her relatives after her death, and her correspondence, which laid out her intellect and literary ambitions. Charlotte Smith wrote the tragedies of her life into her poetry and particularly into her novels. The evangelical reformer and educator, Hannah More, gave her personal ideologies in educational and religious tracts, passing on her moral principles to her female readership. Hester Thrale Piozzi illustrated her own life and relationships in her publications on her good friend Samuel Johnson. Frances Burney wrote her experiences and feelings into her novels, as did the radical Mary Hays. For Seward, correspondence was the definition of her life.

Because Seward's letters were intended as an autobiographical text, she voiced her political viewpoint and her philosophical, scientific, theological and cultural ideals through them. In terms of language and content, the published letters, particularly the later ones, define Seward as an author with a wide and varied interest in the world and not as a recorder of exclusively female experience. By refusing to conform to societal expectations, she was able to subvert conventions. The published letters clearly illustrate this model, grounded as they are in ungendered representations of authorship. By primarily avoiding domestic minutiae and inner thoughts, Seward attempted to present a confident, literary self. It is the uncensored letters, some written privately like her letters to Mary Powys and Dorothy Sykes, some written secretly like letters exchanged with James Boswell, some coded like the 'Cat Letters' exchanged with Erasmus Darwin, that reveal who Seward was.

There are other unpublished letters and manuscripts scattered across the world that open up the life that Seward had attempted to construct and that her editors and executors destroyed. These help piece together the narrative that she began with the juvenile letters. It would be an impossible task to cover all the unpublished letters and manuscripts in this account, and I have chosen the ones that make a good starting point to clear up misunderstandings and to rid literary history of

---

[16] NLS, MSS, 865, fol 140, Charles Simpson, 'Letter to Walter Scott' (1 October, 1809).

the recurring pejorative inaccuracies that began during Seward's life and have continued to the present. From beneath layers of written, re-written, self-edited, edited, truthful or fictitious but certainly never straightforward writings, a different picture of Anna Seward gradually emerges. This is the new account of one of the most significant and compelling figures in the history of writing women.

Chapter 1
'My dear Emma':
The Juvenile Letters, 1762–1768

In October 1762, Anna Seward wrote the first of a series of thirty-nine personal letters to an imaginary friend, 'Emma'. This is the journal of her formative years from the age of nineteen to twenty-five, and in the first of the letters she gives her reasons for wanting to express her thoughts in this way:

> And now, dear Emma, are you not ready to ask your friend wherefore she moralizes thus sententiously, at an age when it is more natural, perhaps more pleasing, to feel lively impressions, than to analyze them? There is a wherefore. I have been called romantic. It is my wish that you should better know the heart in which you possess so lively an interest.[1]

The journal reinforces Seward's literary self-definition by demonstrating her extensive knowledge of literature and contemporary culture. To emphasise empathetic aspects of her personality, she also sets herself up as a moral advisor and counsellor; her compassion for her friends' problems allows her to express intimate reflections on her own life. Over a period of time Seward edited and revised her epistolary journal, anticipating its publication with her poems towards the end of her long and successful literary career. As she worked at her revisions, she added a mature perspective to a collection of youthful anecdotes by fleshing out her thoughts with sophisticated literary critiques and philosophical musings.

When the two letter collections were eventually published after Seward's death, with the juvenile letters as the preface to her poetry edition and the later correspondence as a six-volume set, they had been reduced to a great degree by her editors, executors and family. In the same way, the image of Anna Seward that remains within the correspondence has also been diminished to a one-dimensional, book-obsessed figure. Without the comedy, sorrows and warmth of her anecdotes, the published correspondence still confirms her sharp intellect but certainly lacks her sense of humour, sensitivity and vivacity. Her elevated prose does nothing to help the negative image. She acknowledged that her style was unfashionable but that it suited her, telling the landscape gardener Humphry Repton that both her poetry and prose were 'not much calculated to please the popular taste'.[2] Although drastically edited by Walter Scott, the juvenile letters still contain a credible account of six years of Seward's life. In terms of literary control, it was she, not a biographer, who originally assembled the correspondence, although

---

[1] Seward, *Poetical Works*, vol. I, p. xlvi.

[2] Seward, 'Letter to H. Repton, Esq.' (23 February 1786), *Letters*, vol. I, p. 126.

Scott's editing affected the published composition. Rather than edit out individual names or details in cases of criticism or gossip, he removed whole sections and sometimes complete letters without explanation or annotation. Seward's own editing technique can be seen in a few of her early manuscripts which are not part of the main body of juvenilia, but are clearly first drafts. These take the form of short letters which she later extended into publishable versions.

Seward gives her correspondent, Emma, a level of authenticity, depicting her with her a shy disposition and a brief life history. Emma's deceased mother, she explains in the first letter, had been a close friend of her own mother, Elizabeth, and this was the basis of their friendship, 'They said, when they last met, a little before the death of your excellent parent, "our children will love each other",'[3] she writes. Irrespective of the life history, there is an ambiguity surrounding this absent friend. There are no shared childhood memories. There is a third close friend who appears in the juvenile letters, known only as 'Nanette B—', who also purportedly wrote to Emma before dying suddenly in March 1765. Seward employs the device of temporarily removing Nanette from the scene with a series of 'pressing engagements' which, she confirms, have prevented her from writing to Emma. In this way Seward not only controls the narrative but presents a rounded chronicle for the reader by relating Nanette's story directly to Emma. As a literary construct, Emma is most probably a composite of Seward's friends and her favourite fictional characters, blended to form the ideal intimate confidante as a counterpoise to her own self-constructed image. Later, after Seward had become an established writer, rather than negotiate a literary cul-de-sac when she no longer needed the single confidante, she 'killed off' Emma, who receives just one mention in the adult letters as a friend who died.

If Seward situated herself as both the author and the central heroine of her own anecdotal drama, she offered a forceful denial that any influence came from conventional cliché-ridden fiction. In the first of the letters, she distances herself from her young contemporaries whose feelings and actions, particularly relating to friendship and love, could easily be manipulated by 'inferior' reading material.[4] Although female literacy rates were exceptionally high by the mid-century, interaction with print culture was restricted for many young women. Books were expensive and often difficult to acquire, with a novel costing at least 7s. 6d., and works of history, over a guinea. Circulating libraries were comparatively cheap and were accessible for young women, should they wish to use them. For an annual fee of between ten shillings and one guinea, books on all subjects, from mathematics to botany to philosophy, could be borrowed by anyone who was able to subscribe. Borrowers could easily choose their own self-educational route. The libraries provided sentimental novels specifically for women, and this had the progressively beneficial effect of widening the rate of reading, expanding the

---

[3]   Seward, *Poetical Works*, vol. I, p. xlvii.
[4]   Seward, *Poetical Works*, vol. I, p. xlvi.

output of reading material and thus pushing women to write specifically for female readers.

Seward showed no interest in the majority of fashionable romantic novels, which, in general, emphasised traditionally female qualities such as intuition and excluded the perceived masculine quality of reason. Counteracting this trend, her juvenile letters have themes which emphasise the masculine virtues, and there is more reason than intuition in her literary instruction and moral counselling on love affairs. Aside from a few novels from a mere handful of writers whom she considered superior and which were usually recommended to her or sent by friends, she disapproved of the romance form. 'You must not suppose that I make a practice of reading novels', she informed the Derbyshire poet William Newton when writing to him in praise of Thomas Holcroft's 'exquisite' translation of the French novel *Caroline of Lichfield*.[5] Her attitude conformed to the widespread prejudice against novel-reading which Jane Austen satirised in *Northanger Abbey*:

> – there seems almost a general wish of decrying the capacity and undervaluing the labour of the novelist, and of slighting the performances which have only genius, wit and taste to recommend them. 'I am no novel reader – I seldom look into novels – Do not imagine that *I* often read novels […] It is really very well for a novel.' – Such is the common cant. – 'And what are you reading, Miss — ?' 'Oh! It is only a novel!' replies the young lady; while she lays down her book with affected indifference, or momentary shame.[6]

There is no evidence that Seward read the abundant conduct material, moral guides or women's journals, such as Charlotte Lennox's *Ladies Museum* (1760–61), a typical example of one of the more informative miscellany magazines that helped shape the lives of young women. Preferring literary journals, she sent her later essays, letters, poems, critical reviews, strictures and articles directly to the *Gentleman's Magazine* or the *Critical Review*. As a young woman, she took absolutely no interest in fashion or beauty, and she gently mocked those who did, also making it clear that she had no desire to read about domestic concerns or wifely duties. Her moral models were fictional characters from poems and classic literature, or she followed the example set by strong female friends, such as Anne Mompesson, who was one of her closest advisors and mentors. Seward was sixteen and on a two-month summer visit to her birthplace, Eyam, with her father when she first met Mompesson, who was twenty years her senior and was to become an extraordinary role model for Seward throughout her life. Seward describes her friend as a cheerful, energetic, eccentric, wilful woman of 'repulsive

---

[5]   Seward, 'Letter to Mr W. Newton, The Peak Minstrel' (10 May 1787), *Letters*, vol. I, p. 293; Thomas Holcroft, *Caroline of Lichfield: A Novel*, translated from the French [of Madam de Montolieu], 3 vols (London: G. G. J. and J. Robinson, 1786).

[6]   Jane Austen, *Northanger Abbey; Lady Susan; The Watsons; Sanditon*, ed. by James Kinsley and John Davie (Oxford: Oxford University Press, 2003), p. 23.

exterior'. Mompesson lived on a legacy of £200 a year, farming and cultivating the family estate in rural Mansfield Woodhouse. She had turned down several offers of marriage in order to live an independent life, taking the opportunity to travel to France and Germany with her nephew, who was the Court's envoy to Bonn, and to live in Switzerland for two years with relatives. Seward tells the anecdote of how Mompesson, exasperated by her nephew's dilatoriness in a matter of finance which affected her personally, had travelled entirely alone to Germany at the age of sixty-three in order to settle the matter for herself.[7] Here was a good friend to Seward who understood her family conflicts and the dramas of her early life and in whom she could freely confide. Mompesson was certainly much more of an exciting and feisty mentor than Seward's own mother, who, although caring and kind, was preoccupied with domestic matters and obsessed with card-playing.

In her juvenile letters Seward sought to express a spiritual notion of friendship, believing that it should have stronger bonds than marital love. This echoes Samuel Richardson's observations on the familiar letter as a means of 'displaying the force of friendship', although she set her own rules for this.[8] Threading through the anecdotes is a didactic narrative. She dominates the relationship, informing Emma that she wanted a mutual respect from her, 'more *lasting* bands of union', which would centre on a shared intellect, albeit disproportionate in Seward's favour. What she rejected was a shallow relationship approximating the fleeting 'first-sight friendship' that resulted from 'the giddy violence' of the 'novel-reading misses'.[9] To establish the intimacy of her relationship with Emma, the first letter opens with a lengthy monologue on ideal friendship, which allows Seward to express her private thoughts and feelings on the subject.

In addition to the constructed correspondent there is, undeniably, a prevailing literary influence at work in the juvenile letters. The fiction writers to whom Seward best related in her youth wrote in the epistolary novel genre which dominated the eighteenth-century European literary canon. Among these, the writings of Samuel Richardson, Jean-Jacques Rousseau and Frances Brooke (who was a friend) were her own favourites, and her response to this style is unmistakable. Letters were regarded as the appropriate form for articulation for young women and became the natural vehicle for the self-expression of women writers. The ideal model was Richardson's *Clarissa*, a novel which set the standard for both literary and real epistolary writing. But there were hazards. The letter belonged to a female literary tradition, yet, paradoxically, notions of female virtue still disapproved of this kind of public exposure.

---

[7]   Seward, 'Letter to Rev. T. S. Whalley', 13 November 1798, *Letters*, vol. V, pp. 165–71.

[8]   Samuel Richardson, 'To Sophia Westcomb', *Selected Letters of Samuel Richardson*, ed. by John Carroll (Oxford: Oxford University Press, 1986), p. 64.

[9]   Seward, *Poetical Works*, vol. I, p. xlvi.

When she first began her juvenilia, Seward was fresh from reading Rousseau's *Julie, or the New Héloïse*, and she insisted that Emma 'throw it aside'.[10] She saw the book as an instructional, philosophical work, eminently practical for the typically vain women who had been 'educated in the flutter of high life',[11] but also for the modern male youth, who she believed preferred a sensual life to the 'tender attachment' of sensibility.[12] Rousseau's novel helped her to review her moral values and to set her own conception of love, which is why her closest friends gave her the nickname 'Julia'. She adds an interesting thought on education, stating that her future sons would be given the novel to read to gain a full understanding of the qualities necessary for pure and honest relationships. However, she herself would introduce her daughters to the concept of sensibility, as she thought Rousseau's novel might lead to 'dangerous' levels of exposure.

Through her observations, she aligns herself with the university-educated masculine intellect, capable of an objective reading and analysis of Rousseau without absorbing a harmful excess of sensibility. At the same time, she confirms a close relationship to sensibility by conveying an emotional response to sights and situations through her writing. As Emma becomes the pupil to Seward's teachings, she is able to continue her process of literary self-construction. She describes Emma as recently vulnerable, in recovery from a broken love affair, and advises against reading a book abounding with such 'lavish fuel to a kindling attachment'.[13] Taking the notion of letters as her own system for the expression of inner feelings and using Rousseau's novel and Richardson's *Clarissa* as her templates, the story of her youth progresses, and naturally she needed the empathic female friend, the perfect reader, the intimate confidante and counterpart, to whom she could confess her anxieties. Out of this construction, her private and literary personas emerge together.

At exactly the same time that Seward worked on her juvenile letters, she started to write *Louisa*, a novel with the narrative presented in four verse letters. By employing the medium of verse, she had the freedom to write novelistically without actually producing anything resembling a sentimental novel. She eventually published the work in 1784, correcting her own proofs in Lichfield, and it was an immediate success, running to five British editions and an edition in America. Shortly after publication, an admiring James Boswell told her, 'I am delighted with your Louisa', and he published enthusiastic reviews with short extracts.[14]

Like her juvenile letters, she subjected the novel to later revisions, claiming that she wrote the first section of the poem when she was nineteen but that the manuscript was lost. When she found it again several years later, she completed it and made it ready for publication. There are other interesting parallels with the

---

[10] Seward, *Poetical Works*, vol. I, p. xlvii.

[11] Seward, *Poetical Works*, vol. I, p. xlviii.

[12] Seward, *Poetical Works*, vol. I, p. liii.

[13] Seward, *Poetical Works*, vol. I, p. li.

[14] HL, MS L 1142 (18 May 1784).

juvenile correspondence in this complex, intertextual *mélange* of novel, epic and epistolary verse. To emphasise the work's sensibilities, Seward explains in her preamble that her idea is to describe feelings rather than action. Her intention was to shape a composite character, Louisa, out of her own literary favourites, Pope's passionate 'Eloïsa' and Prior's sensitive 'Emma'. She shaped her character into a strong-minded woman who deals with the complexities and injustices of the marriage market with equal measures of rationality and endurance.

Seward takes possession of the 'Louisa' character as her own creation and her self-identification. She describes Louisa as an affectionate woman with a strong imagination, and, in her juvenile letters, her self-portrayal is similar, with 'lively spirits & warm poetic imagination'.[15] Although Louisa's character is resilient, Seward acknowledges that the modern young reader might find it difficult to identify with her more traditional qualities, such as enthusiasm and compassion. By deliberately choosing unfashionable qualities for her heroine or in creating a heroine who rejects contemporary cultural standards, Seward offers a defence of her own challenges to convention. In her poems and letters, she felt no need to compromise her ethics to popular trends. She believed her work represented a value system that might drift in and out of fashion, but would remain essentially enduring.

Unsurprisingly, Louisa's closest friend is 'Emma', and the relationship is epistolary. In the same way that Seward's life narrative is mediated through her letters to Emma, Louisa's story is recounted through her letters to her own Emma. Both Emmas become receivers and transmitters of information, and, as such, both are the centre around which the narrative gyrates. Both versions, the poem and the letters, provide a vehicle of self-expression for their author, who is also the protagonist. Seward's single status, her childlessness and her relationships with John Saville and her foster-sister, Honora Sneyd, are mirrored in the character Louisa, who retains a virginal quality when her lover's wife dies leaving a child. She willingly adopts the role of the child's mother without having had any sexual contact.

Seward's journalised epistolary form was the ideal vehicle for her self-narrative, and she embedded meticulous autobiographical detail into the letters. Through the well-established modes of journals, diaries, housekeeping books, commonplace books and letters, women were able to express an immediate and personal record of their lives, using a literary or non-literary style. Girls were encouraged in the art of letter-writing, often as a moral exercise as much as one in style and format. The *Observer* warned that by the age of eight, young girls were mature enough to 'leer, ogle, talk French, write sonnets, play with footmen, and go through their exercises in admiration'. To guard against this 'vulgarity' and to focus their minds on approved pastimes, they should be sent to boarding school, maintained the *Observer*. Their main holiday occupation should be writing 'sacred and inviolable'

---

15   NLS, Scott MSS, fol. 33 (June 1763).

letters to their school friends, 'by which means they may carry on an intercourse of thoughts without reserve, and greatly improve their stile'.[16]

The prolific letter-writer Madame de Genlis describes in her memoirs her method of instruction for a friend's daughters: 'each of them was to write to me twice a week and [...] I was to send them back their letters corrected'.[17] Constant practicing and the use of writing manuals removed much of the natural spontaneity, however. Exemplars were readily available in print, for instance, in the published letters of Lord Chesterfield and Madame de Sévigné, and, consequently, ideal 'natural' expression could be practiced and learned quite easily. Seward does not record any participation in this learning process. If she read writing manuals and exemplars as a child, she did not admit to it, and her later reading of 'improving' writings was merely to hone her critical skills and her intellectual evaluation methods.

Seward's early lively writing style was discussed in comparison with her later, more elevated style by Thomas Constable as he edited his father, Archibald's, correspondence for his memoirs. Describing the juvenile letters as 'less artificial' than the later letters, he criticised her mature style and eventual 'inability to use ordinary language'. While acknowledging that her works were admired by many of her contemporaries, including his father and Walter Scott, he believed that they had become unfashionable because of her complicated style of expression. 'I suspect there are few of the notable writers of her day', he argued, 'whose works are now permitted to rest more peacefully upon our shelves than those of Anna Seward'.[18] Interestingly, Thomas Constable had access to the censored sections of the letter books that his father and the other editors rejected, and he found these more fascinating and eloquent than the published versions. He agreed with the censorship because of Seward's forthright criticism of the publishing industry that his family was so much a part of. In his memoirs he gave extensive extracts from the excised sections, stating, 'how easily she could write when she threw down her stilts'.[19] As her later letters were plainly written for publication, it is clear that she focused less on the 'natural' and 'authentic' style of writing of the juvenile letters and more on structure and formality. Unfortunately, her most animated discussions were the main target for deletion by the editors.[20]

---

[16]   Richard Cumberland, *The Observer: Being a Collection of Moral, Literary and Familiar Essays* (London: C. Dilly, 1785).

[17]   Stéphanie Felicité Ducrest de St Aubin, Comtesse de Genlis, *Memoirs of the Countess de Genlis: Illustrative of the History of the Eighteenth and Nineteenth Centuries, written by Herself*, 8 vols (London: Henry Colburn, 1825), vol. VIII, p. 91.

[18]   Thomas Constable, *Archibald Constable and his Literary Correspondents*, 3 vols (Edinburgh: Edmonton & Douglas, 1873), vol. II, p. 12.

[19]   Constable, *Archibald Constable*, vol. II, p. 27.

[20]   Of the thirteen volumes of letters Seward suggested that she left to Archibald Constable, it was agreed between executors and editors that there were only 'five or six Volumes well worthy of the attention of the publick and highly satisfactory to the character and fame of the Authoress'. The remainder was considered to contain too much gossip

The compilation of juvenile letters, dated from October 1762 to June 1768 with a gap of the two years when Emma was supposedly living in Lichfield, is scattered through with the conventionally formal, if non-sequential, features of life writing. Although the letters naturally follow a chronological sequence, Seward makes frequent temporal jumps to provide detailed accounts of her early life and upbringing and, presumably, to deflect attention from the vanity implied in her life writing. Family history, educational background, the effects of childhood on the adult psyche and the cultural pressures and constrictions that were present during her formative years all find a place within the narrative. Although the adult letters complement the juvenile correspondence in many instances by providing additional details of the events and the influences of her youth, their scope is too vast and their censorship too drastic to allow for a similar comprehensive analysis. As the juvenile letters can be read as a comparatively intact journal, they reconstruct Seward's early life, and if much of what she wrote in them presented dubious personal truths, the overall narrative is nonetheless revealing.

For Seward, it was literary significance that was imperative, yet she was not prepared to risk the public censure and ridicule that might attach itself to her reputation should she write her memoirs or publish her journal. When the Derbyshire writer Anna Rogers Stokes suggests that Seward should publish her life, her unease about her future reputation is clear in her reference to a 'task of egotism'.[21] Another friend, the poet and playwright Edward Jerningham, suggested she publish her memoirs, and again her response was to avoid 'internal egotism', stating that it was impossible to 'speak of oneself with any propriety, or grace'.[22] Even for men, overt autobiography usually invited scorn. When the poet laureate Colley Cibber published his autobiography in 1740 he was widely ridiculed and satirised. The critics objected because he had written it himself, making him seem vain, although he showed no false modesty in his part-humorous, part-candid statement of intent: '[H]ere, where I have all the Talk to myself, and have no body to interrupt or contradict me, sure, to say whatever I have a mind other People shou'd know of me, is a Pleasure which none but Authors, as vain as myself, can conceive.'[23] Later critical assessments tended to agree with his sentiments, finding that Cibber had no more 'histrionic vanity' than was acceptable in other men of

---

which, although 'interesting', was 'very injurious to the Character or feelings of living Persons' and the 'Political Violence' was censored on the grounds of being outdated and 'too violent to gratify the worst feelings of Party … when the Subject of attack has gone to his awful responsibility enough to satisfy the most imminent Party spirit if guilty and if Innocent the Calumny falls on the head only of the Inventor'. NLS, MSS, 865, fol. 140 (16 April 1809).

[21]   Seward, 'Letter to Mrs Stokes' (15 June 1797), *Letters*, vol. IV, p. 362.

[22]   HL, MS JE 755, Seward, 'Letter to Edward Jerningham' (22 December 1803).

[23]   Colley Cibber, *An apology for the life of Mr Colley Cibber, comedian, and late patentee of the Theatre-Royal: With an historical view of the stage during his own time. Written by himself* (London: J. Watts, 1740).

fame, such as actors or jockeys,[24] or that his work was no more egotistical than autobiography in general.[25]

Many women writers and poets were able to find more subtle means of self-expression through publishable letters filled with their anecdotes and observations. In 1763, Lady Mary Wortley Montagu's letters were published posthumously, but her personal journals were destroyed by her daughter, Lady Bute, because she considered such spontaneous expression completely inappropriate.[26] In 1790, Seward's friend, Helen Maria Williams, began to write the history of her experience of the French Revolution in *Letters Written in France*.[27] Without the stimulating experience of foreign travel, and with her readers' expectations at the forefront, Seward's contribution to the genre was solely literary.

Fiction, too, plays a minor part in Seward's correspondence with Emma, and some of her anecdotes are obviously heavily exaggerated or even fabricated. Although her dismissive views of most novels ruled out the possibility of setting her life in this form, certain of the letters have rudimentary romantic, novelistic frameworks. Whereas other peers, such as Charlotte Smith and Mary Hays, used the romantic novel genre as a means of self-inscription, Seward's antipathy to this form and her eagerness not to be judged as vain meant her relationship between the literary text and life was only feasible in her poetry and letters. More so than a journal, a letter demands an external reader. Where Seward had reservations about the perceived egotism of publishing an autobiographical journal, the epistolary form was ideal for her purpose of presenting her public identity. It was a less transparent route into the public domain, a camouflaged life-writing venture with fewer connotations of arrogance than an unabashed autobiography. Even James Boswell had misgivings about the personal nature of journals. Though his own journals became such a vital constituent of eighteenth-century life-writing, Boswell articulated his anxiety about the publication of private records in his *Hypochondriack* paper for March 1783: 'A diary, therefore, which was much more common in the last age than in this, may be of valuable use to the person who writes it [...] and yet if brought forth to the publick eye may expose him to contempt.'[28]

---

[24]   'Cibber's Apology', *Blackwood's Edinburgh Magazine*, 8 (January–June 1823), 22–30 (p. 24).

[25]   *Notes and Queries*, 2, 8, (1859), p. 317.

[26]   Isobel Grundy, *Lady Mary Wortley Montagu* (Oxford: Oxford University Press, 1999), p. 626.

[27]   Helen Maria Williams, *Letters Written in France, in the Summer 1790, to a Friend in England; Containing Various Anecdotes Relative to the French revolution; and Memoirs of Mons. And Madame du F—* (London: T. Cadell, 1790).

[28]   James Boswell, 'On Diaries', *Hypochondriack*, 66 (March 1783), reprinted in *Boswell's Column. Being his Seventy Contributions to the London Magazine under the pseudonym The Hypochondriack*, ed. by Margery Bailey (London: W. Kimber, 1951), p. 331.

Biography was not an alternative for Seward's public exposure. Despite her vast assortment of literary friends, each potentially with an individual collection of her letters, there was no comprehensive biography produced on her death and no hint of cooperation in any such venture during her life. Any attempts by literary journals to publish her memoirs met with her fierce disapproval. Where the representation of her image was concerned, she refused requests for anecdotes or portraits. If she did respond to such requests, it was solely to monitor the contents. She explained to Edward Jerningham that she wanted control of these matters, as she was fearful of an appearance of a 'fulsome history of myself, abounding with mistaken circumstances, which I shou'd not only have the vexation to see, but the trouble to contradict'. She was particularly irritated by a portrait in the *Monthly Mirror* which, she told Jerningham, left an unflattering image for posterity, that of a 'Quiz' with a dark, heavy-looking head, instead of depicting her with a more respectful 'air of a Gentlewoman'.[29] Her sanctioned but brief memoirs, written by her cousin Harry White, were published in the *Monthly Mirror* of December 1796. These met with her wholehearted approval: 'I do not wish to say more of myself than is there said, and I am sure I do not know how to say it better'.[30]

Harry White was the cousin and close friend who, as part of her intimate Lichfield circle, understood much of the inner workings of her life, and he was qualified to give the official version of her character. The formal description balances an enthusiastic self-disclosure concerning the anecdotal narrative of the juvenile correspondence. It reveals the same preoccupations with the status of her carefully-crafted reputation that had been troublesome since her youth:

> Enemies she has, both personal and literary, though lasting resentment, except towards experienced *treachery*, she is not capable of feeling: but her sense of injury is too quick and keen, her frankness too unguarded, her attachments too zealous, not to have created enemies. That her friendships have ever been disinterested and steady, those who love her least will not deny: neither will they assert, that pride, ostentation or avarice, mark her character; or that satire or envy embitter her conversation. Though too sincere to flatter, she loves to praise; assumes no superiority over those with whom she converses; never aiming to dazzle the unlettered by any display of knowledge, or to repress their frank communications to *her*, by the mute arrogance of reserve. If impolitely treated, she takes no revenge by retaliated impoliteness, contented with ceasing to seek the society of those whose latent ill-will towards her thus discovers itself. On these occasions she seeks to emulate the love-recorded conduct of Lord Lyttleton's Lucy,
>
>> Who injur'd, or offended, never tried
>> Her dignity by vengeance to maintain,
>> *But by magnanimous disdain.*

---

[29]   HL, MS JE 755, Seward, 'Letter to Edward Jerningham' (17 February 1796).
[30]   Seward, 'Letter to Mrs Stokes' (15 June 1797), *Letters*, vol. IV, p. 362.

When any attempt is made by people of talent, either in small or large companies, to lead conversation upon the higher ground of moral disquisition, or the works of genius, or the now universally momentous theme of the national welfare, she follows that lead with glad alacrity, pleased to assist in tracing the meanders of the human mind, the source of exalted, or of mean actions, and in discriminating the difference and degrees of genius. It is then that she is always found ardent and ingenuous, but impartial. Does her friend publish feebly, and is his work the theme, she tries rather to change the subject than to endeavour to support defect or mediocrity by encomium. Has her foe produced a fine composition, she feels every charm of the page, and brings forward to the observation of the ingenious, every obvious and latent beauty: superior to literary jealousy, the frequent misery of authors, and always distinguishing between the merits of the heart and the head.[31]

Walter Scott's interpretation of Seward's personality in his 'Biographical Preface' cites her as being pointlessly oversensitive to 'injuries real or supposed'. He was also considerably less generous than White in his representation of her literary jealousy, contending that 'the same tone of mind rendered her jealous of critical authority, when exercised over her own productions, or those of her friends'.[32] As becomes evident in Seward's dealings with the publishing industry, this is far closer to the truth than White's affectionately flattering eulogy. It is also irrationally hyper-critical, as Scott was aware that Seward's literary friendships invariably grew out of an admiration of their work. This was how their own friendship had begun. She tended to befriend the writers whose work she enjoyed most, and she could therefore be impartial in literary criticism or in the public defence of their works. 'Truth can never be flattery,' she wrote in her own defence of similar accusations, 'Alas! to the utter incapacity of flattering, even those I esteem and admire, I have, through life, owed the loss of much favour that was, in itself, most desirable to my affections – but sincerity is the first duty of friendship.'[33] Her tendency to speak out assertively on literary topics with little regard for the consequences drew attention to this propensity. Additionally, Scott concealed the fact that, as one of the 'friends', he regularly benefited from her support. She endorsed his writings and attempted to reverse the effects of poor critical reviews in the literary journals.[34]

---

[31]   Henry White, 'Memoir of Anna Seward', in *The Monthly Mirror*, 2 (January and February 1796).

[32]   Scott, 'Biographical Preface', *Poetical Works*, vol. I, p. xxiv.

[33]   Seward, 'Letter to Court Dewes, Esq.' (30 March 1786), *Letters*, vol. I, pp. 147–48.

[34]   In a letter dated November 1802, Scott thanks Seward for her support and influence (NLS, MSS, 854, fol. 24, Scott, 'Letter to Anna Seward' (30 November 1802)). In September 1803, she discusses the poems which Scott sent for her opinion, writing, 'I feel the presumption of criticising your charming poetry, but remember it was your injunction' (NLS, MSS, 870, fols 1–2, Seward, 'Letter to Walter Scott' (September 1803)). When the *Critical Review* published a severe review of Scott's *Marmion*, Seward used her influence with the editor to publish a more flattering critique in the form of a letter: 'I told [Fellowes] my *full mind* concerning the malicious and stupid attack in that work upon your

In all probability there is, in the juvenile letters, an anachronistic blend of early writings with inclusions of reflections from a far later period of her life. This is skilfully merged together. Literary debate and descriptive passages have the sophisticated characteristics and preoccupations of her later writings. The anecdotes of life in Lichfield, however, possess the unmistakable immediate vibrancy of a youthful correspondence or journal, although she probably also emended the majority of these to a certain extent. There are some areas that do not sit comfortably within the monologic format of the juvenile letters, such as supplying the details of her early life to a correspondent who purportedly knows her well. She overcomes these obstacles with replies to (sometimes clumsy) hypothetical questions. Her response, 'Your request that I wou'd minutely describe to you the situation of my native Village, amidst the Peak Sublimities, is too flattering to be forgotten or neglected', provides her with an awkward but accessible entry level into her family history.[35] The expressions 'you ask' and 'you enquire after' surface with regularity throughout the correspondence. Seward was to continue her epistolary autobiography throughout her life, writing to irrefutably real correspondents and relating to actual events, yet these are the imaginative early beginnings. Collectively the juvenile letters assume a monologue, the perfect form to accommodate the narrative of an intellectually ambitious and high-spirited young woman, absorbed with these 'giddy, romantic, happy, hoping' years.[36]

Long before Seward achieved public recognition, she employed her knowledge of the English classics and a regional association with Derbyshire to construct a literary, imaginative and intellectual persona. Her later public reputation related initially to the notion of Britishness. 'We have all heard of Anna Seward, and sighed over her lines on the death of Major André', wrote *Blackwood's Edinburgh Magazine* twenty-five years after Seward's death. The editor recollected the early days of her rapid rise to fame and the effect of her work on the reading public when she first published her nationalistic poems, 'Elegy on Captain Cook' and 'Monody on Major André'.[37] Her immediate acclaim was connected with her contribution to the restoration of a national culture, which Harriet Guest summarises as the 'powerfully doubled language of patriotism and piety rooted in the associations of the place'.[38] With almost certainly less piety than patriotism, together with the desire to articulate Britain's loss of two heroes, one of whom, André, was a

---

last noble poem. I fought the criticism every inch of its ground and made the lists 12 pages in extent, quoting a number of the beautiful and sublime passages. I have transcribed that appeal against the injustice of the *Critical Review* into these epistolary volumes which I have mentioned to you.' (NLS, MSS, 865, fols 126–30, Seward, 'Letter to Walter Scott' (8 August 1808)). Scott excised these sections from the published correspondence.

[35]   NLS, Sir Walter Scott MSS, 879, fol. 71 (1 February 1765).

[36]   Seward, 'Letter to Miss Powys' (13 May 1791), *Letters*, vol. III, p. 55.

[37]   'Reginald Dalton', *Blackwood's Edinburgh Magazine* (January–June 1824), vol. XV, p. 106.

[38]   Harriet Guest, *Small Change: Women, Learning, Patriotism, 1750–1810* (Chicago: University of Chicago Press, 2000), p. 252.

close friend, Seward achieved a remarkable success and was publicly praised by Erasmus Darwin as 'the inventress of the epic elegy'.[39] The use of the epic was a bold decision because, as Lynda Pratt has observed, although the epic was subject to revival in the second part of the eighteenth century, it was generally considered more suited to male writing. 'Contemporary reviewers expressed concern about the "female pen",' confirms Pratt, 'particularly when it was set loose on the epic'.[40]

Before her fame, she emphasised her considerable knowledge of the English poets in order to stand level with her male contemporaries. A higher education was a male prerogative, and without Latin, Greek and the experience of the Grand Tour, her literary expertise was limited in comparison. Although she briefly mentions James Macpherson, the Scottish poet who forged translations of the poetry of Ossian, she writes at length on the English poets in the juvenilia, these being the only ones she felt she could judge with any accuracy.[41] With the construction of a self-educated authority on English poetry, Seward uses her juvenilia to describe her relationship with her rural birthplace to augment her literary persona. She refers to the 'blended society' of her youth, meaning the combination of the rural simplicity of Eyam (pronounced Eem) in Derbyshire and the genteel refinement of Lichfield.[42] She believed this made her a complex person, sometimes volatile and headstrong, sometimes solemn and studious, as she engaged with the characteristics of each place. There is also the tacit recognition of having to provide a justification for not living in London in order to avoid negative perceptions of provincialism. Samuel Johnson had put forward the generally accepted advantages of living in London, confirming that the capital was comparable with people:

> They, with narrow minds are contracted to the consideration of some one particular pursuit, view it only through that medium. [...] But the intellectual man is struck with it, as comprehending the whole of human life in all its variety, the contemplation of which is inexhaustible.[43]

Whatever Johnson's observations, Seward had her reasons for living in Lichfield all of her adult life. Her letters to Mary Powys and Dorothy Sykes reveal the primary reason for this to be her relationship with John Saville. As she continued to shape

---

[39] 'Biographical Sketch of the late Miss Seward', *The Gentleman's Magazine*, LXXIX (1809), I, 378–79 (p. 378).

[40] Lynda Pratt, 'Epic', in *An Oxford Guide to Romanticism*, ed. by Nicholas Roe (Oxford: Oxford University Press, 2005), pp. 332–49 (p. 338).

[41] NLS, Scott MSS, 879; *Poetical Works*, vol. I, p. lxxxiii. Seward confidently discusses the works of Shakespeare, Milton, Johnson, Collins, Mason, Pryor, Dryden, Pope, Butler, Shenstone and Gray.

[42] Seward, *Poetical Works*, vol. I, p. lxvi.

[43] James Boswell, *The Life of Samuel Johnson. Together with Boswell's Journals of a Tour to the Hebrides and Johnson's Diary of a Journey into North Wales*, ed. by George Birkbeck Hill, 6 vols, 2nd edn, rev. by L. F. Powell (Oxford: Clarendon Press, 1964; repr. 1971), vol. I, p. 532.

her identity as a poet, she also wanted to express a close association with her own 'remote situations'. She accentuated an empathy with nature by comparing the isolation and rugged scenery of Eyam to the romantic Scottish landscape. 'I have a natural prepossession in favour of Ossianic scenery;' she wrote to Emma, 'born, and nursed as I was, in the craggy heights of Derbyshire'.[44] This was a preoccupation that surfaced with regularity throughout her life. In her later epistolary conversations with Scott, for example, she takes up the same themes. On her admiration of his description of Flodden's 'high and heathery side',[45] she explains:

> This partiality is the result of those associations of which we have spoken. I was born 50 miles nearer Scotland than is Lichfield and passed the first 8 years of my existence in my native Village, Eyam, amid the eminences of the Peak of Derbyshire. Hence the first scenery which struck upon my infant perceptions, with wonder and transport, is brought back by poetic pictures of wild, incultivate, lonely nature. To the Peak I often returned in Girlhood, and in Youth, after it had ceased to be my home, and on those occasions, daily walked and rode, with my affectionate dear Father, on the high and heathery sides of its mountains.[46]

Seward's descriptions of her birthplace are scattered through her juvenilia, and it is impossible to ascertain if these are part of her original manuscripts or later additions to provide autobiographical detail, particularly of her connection with rural wilderness. Although she distanced herself from Eyam's more primitive aspects, she was able to construct the perfect romantic foil to sophisticated Lichfield. The picturesque village of her childhood incorporated a mix of workman's cottages surrounded by bee-hives and grand but dour mansions built from Derbyshire gritstone. Central to the community and to the landscape was the parish church where her father was rector. However, as the letters to Emma confirm, she did not identify with the Eyam community but remained on the boundary as a knowledgeable outsider. She writes, for example, of its history and reputation as the 'plague village'.[47] Her poem of childhood remembrance, 'Eyam', which

---

[44]   Seward, 'Letter to Emma' (January 1763), *Poetical Works*, vol. I, p. lxvi.

[45]   Walter Scott, *Sir Tristrem: a metrical romance of the thirteenth century; by Thomas of Ercildoune, called the Rhymer*, edited from the Auchinleck MS. By Walter Scott (Edinburgh: Archibald Constable, 1804).

[46]   Seward, NLS, MSS, 3874, fol. 164, Seward, 'Letter to Walter Scott' (10 July 1802).

[47]   When the plague struck in 1666 and the natural reaction was to shut up one's house and flee the area, the villagers, led by their rector William Mompesson, remained to face the outbreak so as to confine the disease to the immediate area. Seward wrote that the nature of the mountainous countryside made it impossible for the villagers to be forcibly interned, 'a regiment of soldiers ... could not have detained them against their will'. They chose to remain and their strategy worked, but at a cost of many lives. Seward supported her historical facts by publishing copies of letters from Mompesson to his children and his uncle which were in her father's possession (Seward, *Poetical Works*, vol. I, pp. clxiv, clxvii–clxix).

corresponds in tone with contemporary works by poets such as Thomas Gray and Oliver Goldsmith, describes her past and her present from within a framework of local history.[48]

Seward was greatly influenced by Gray's 1751 poem, 'Elegy written in a Country Churchyard', and she told her friend Court Dewes that she thought it was 'one of the most perfect poems ever written'.[49] 'Eyam' has clear points of comparison with Gray's poem, and with Goldsmith's 'The Deserted Village', notably in the theme of departed glory, which, in Seward's poem, brings out a forceful expression of individual mourning for her own past. She is particularly concerned with memory. She juxtaposes the imagery of the loss of childhood and her dead siblings with the loss of memory in old age and senility. The passed glory is her childhood in Eyam, and she combines this image with her present concern for her father's illness, particularly his senility. Where Gray's 'paths of glory lead but to the grave',[50] Seward's deserted churchyard path lies derelict, 'rough and unsightly', and leads towards the symbol of her father's lost intellect and reason: the 'blank, and silent' pulpit where he had preached in his prime.[51]

In Goldsmith's narrator's birthplace, Auburn, 'desolation saddens' the now lifeless hub, the green.[52] Similarly, Seward's poet narrator despairs at the sight of 'childhood's earliest, liveliest bliss', the dark, deserted rectory and its green lawns, now overgrown with the 'long, coarse grass' of neglect.[53] When William Duff wrote his influential essay on the origins of genius, he rooted its source in the simplicity of country life, relating to the nostalgic past of Greek antiquity: 'A Poet of true Genius delights to contemplate and describe those primitive scenes, which recall to our remembrance the fabulous era of the golden age'.[54] Seward distances herself from Duff's objective notion of an imagined pastoral idyll. Her narrator evokes the golden age of childhood, but intersperses her play with anguish, shedding tears over the early death of her siblings:

And where my infant sister's ashes sleep,
Whose loss I left the childish sport to weep.[55]

Her illustration of the 'primitive scenes' of ancient local custom is as vivid and poignant as the 'withdrawn' charms of Goldsmith's 'dancing pair' who symbolise

---

[48]   Seward, *Poetical Works*, vol. III, pp. 1–4.

[49]   Seward, 'Letter to Court Dewes, Esq.' (30 March 1785), *Letters*, vol. I, p. 54.

[50]   Thomas Gray, 'Elegy Written in a Country Churchyard', in *The Poems of Thomas Gray, William Collins, Oliver Goldsmith,* ed. by Roger Lonsdale (London: Longmans, 1969), p. 124.

[51]   Seward, *Poetical Works*, vol. III, p. 4.

[52]   Oliver Goldsmith, 'The Deserted Village', in Lonsdale, p. 677.

[53]   Seward, *Poetical Works*, vol. III, p. 3.

[54]   William Duff, *An Essay on Original Genius; and its Various Modes of Exertion in Philosophy and the Fine Arts, Particularly in Poetry* (London: Dilly, 1767), vol. V, p. 273.

[55]   Seward, *Poetical Works*, vol. III, p. 3.

departed youth and fertility.[56] In this case, however, death, not progress, is the master as Seward grieves the passing of her own youth through the depiction of an old Derbyshire parish tradition. The narrator notices the remnants of garlands of white paper roses and white gloves, symbolic of innocence, which were left hanging over the pew of a young man or woman who had died, and she is reminded of transience and decay:

> Now the low beams, with paper garlands hung,
> In memory of some village youth, or maid,
> Draw the soft tear, from thrill'd remembrance sprung,
> How oft my childhood mark'd that tribute paid.
> The gloves, suspended by the garland's side,
> White as its snowy flowers, with ribbons tied.[57]

Although Seward repeatedly refers to the poetic influence of her rural birthplace in her juvenile letters and later correspondence, she rarely visited Eyam as an adult, and she was most careful to dissociate herself from rural poets.[58] She avoided having her poems evaluated by the critics against the works of poets such as Ann Yearsley. When the Lunar Group member, Josiah Wedgwood, suggested that Seward should write an anti-slavery poem, she told him that others had already written on this subject, including Yearsley. 'I cannot prevail upon myself to give my scribbling foes new opportunity of venting their spleen, by speaking to the world of the inferiority of my attempt to that of the unlettered milkwoman's', she told Wedgwood, 'So, I am sure, they would say, were I to write as well as Milton on the theme'.[59]

It was more important for Seward to align herself with the 'educated orders'. She believed that poetry was 'unquestionably the language of nature' and was fascinated by the idea of the presence of 'seeds of poetry' in the minds of people who had not received a formal education.[60] Making a clear distinction between a determined self-educated background like her own and an undeveloped natural poetic ability, she analysed the notion of natural genius. In response to a letter from Richard Sykes, who had written on behalf of a friend to ask her about the best method to learn how to write poetry, she offers an insight into her literary learning experiences. First explaining the instinctive ability to speak in metaphorical language, she gives examples of the words of labourers in the Derbyshire Peak, who spoke to her of the clearing mountain mist as 'the old mountain [...] pulling

---

[56]   Oliver Goldsmith, 'The Deserted Village', in Lonsdale, p. 676.

[57]   Seward, *Poetical Works*, vol. III, p. 4. Some Derbyshire churches still retain the remnants of the flowers and gloves.

[58]   In 1778, Seward wrote to Mary Powys telling her that she had recently visited Eyam for the first time in over eight years. JBM, MS 38/8, Seward, 'Letter to Mary Powys' (4 August 1788).

[59]   Seward, 'Letter to J. Wedgewood, Esq.' [*sic*] (18 February 1788), *Letters*, vol. II, p. 33.

[60]   Seward, 'Letter to Rev. Richard Sykes' (1 October 1793), *Letters*, vol. III, pp. 319–25.

off his nightcap', and Filey Bay fishermen discussing a stormy sea: 'it rolled mountains'.[61] She next provides a detailed structure of how to develop writing skills by observing and memorising the works of 'our best authors', noting the complex methodology needed to achieve technically precise measure and form. She completes the lesson with an instructive summary, almost like a recipe for a poem:

> Lay a fine poem in the chosen measure on your table; read it over aloud; endeavour to catch its spirit; observe its pauses and general construction. Thus, a young poet should compose as a student in painting paints, from the best models, not with servile minuteness, but with generous emulation and critical attention.[62]

Seward's early concentration on English poetry eventually widened out to include a study of the regional (and sometimes dialect) poems of Samwell, Ramsay, Thomson, Scott, Burns and Leydon, which she critiques in her later letters to Scott. Her expert knowledge of the English canon was credited by Scott to her father's influence, which, he stated, was 'rigidly classical', although her intention to develop her expertise in this area was clearly self-determined.[63] Towards the end of her life, she confirmed that over fifty years' focused study of the 'best' English poets gave her the advantage over male scholars, as their classical learning was wider and therefore necessarily diluted. Her close attachment to Eyam waned with time, and by 1778 she was complaining of its lack of culture and its 'insipid conversation'.[64]

From the details given in the juvenile letters, it becomes obvious that Seward was closer to her father than to her mother, and yet she maintained an uneasy relationship with each of her parents. Thomas Seward, as a youth, was portrayed as 'civil and sensible, but a little affected in his expressions'.[65] As an adult he was described as a 'valetudinarian' who was constantly 'mending himself'.[66] As a scholar, he resorted to invective, abusing the book or person who expressed ideas contrary to his own. As a father, he was subject to furious outbursts when anything displeased him. Seward's volatile relationship with him changed and mellowed over the years, particularly after 1780, when his illness began to weaken him, eventually reducing him to a childlike, dependent condition. She was satisfied to accept the added responsibility and independence that this brought her. But when she was young their relationship frequently exploded into violent arguments

---

[61]   Seward, 'Letter to Rev. Richard Sykes' (1 October 1793), *Letters*, vol. III, p. 320.

[62]   Seward, 'Letter to Rev. Richard Sykes' (1 October 1793), *Letters*, vol. III, p. 324.

[63]   Scott, 'Biographical Preface', *Poetical Works*, vol. I, p. vii.

[64]   JBM, MS 38/8, Seward, 'Letter to Mary Powys' (4 August 1788).

[65]   Maureen Spinks, Articles by Peter Braby, 'Letters of a Badsey Family 1735–36', *Vale of Evesham Historical Society Research Papers*, (1971), 111, pp. 66–73. http://www.badsey.net/past/braby3.htm.

[66]   Frank Swinnerton, *A Galaxy of Fathers* (London: Hutchinson, 1966), p. 35.

whenever she challenged him or confronted his authoritarian rules. He certainly admitted to a level of hypocrisy in his treatment of her, telling her that both he and Elizabeth were far too hot-tempered to have set her anything like a good example of the model behaviour they expected from her. Neither possessed 'that Christian Reticence and Meekness which we recommend', and her own fiery personality reflected this.[67]

Very few details of Thomas Seward's life are offered by Anna in the correspondence. Scott briefly sketches his literary achievements in the 'Biographical Preface' with particulars which must have been relayed to him by Anna's cousins, Thomas and Harry White. Unlike Frances Burney, who spent twenty years going back over family papers and letters in order to commemorate her father's life in her *Memoirs of Doctor Burney*,[68] Seward made no attempt to write her father's biography following his death in 1790. On her death, a few words of tribute to him are given in her obituary in the *Gentleman's Magazine*, and these include the following description: 'Mr Seward had graceful manners, great hilarity of spirit and active benevolence.'[69] Most other references to him concern his successful publication of the edition of the works of Francis Beaumont and John Fletcher, and his contribution to literature as a minor poet.[70]

Born in Badsey in the Vale of Evesham in 1708, Thomas Seward was the seventh son of Mary and John Seward (originally John Sheward but altered to avoid confusion with a professional colleague of the same name). Thomas came from a wealthy family background with aristocratic connections: his father was a landowner and the estate management agent to Viscount Windsor. In the conventional manner of wealthy youth, he received his education at Westminster School and St. John's College, Oxford, and two years after his ordination in 1731, Lord Windsor gave him the rectory of Llanmaes in Glamorganshire. At this stage of his career Thomas was not interested in rural life, so in 1735, leaving his problematic and dissension-ridden parish in the care of his long-suffering curate, he moved to the Duke of Grafton's Suffolk mansion, Euston House, to become tutor to the second son, the arrogant and over-indulged Lord Charles Fitzroy. Here Thomas was very much the socialite, enjoying the high life and priding himself on his acceptance by the Duke and his aristocratic friends, such as the Duke of Devonshire of Chatsworth House and Lord Burlington. Yet, he was troubled by his

---

[67]   Lichfield RO, Seward Family MSS, D262/1/5, Thomas Seward, 'Letter to Anna Seward' (12 November 1771).

[68]   Frances Burney, *Memoirs of Dr Burney, arranged from his own manuscripts, from family papers, and from personal recollections*, 3 vols (London: Edward Moxon, 1832).

[69]   'Biographical Sketch of the late Miss Seward', *The Gentleman's Magazine*, LXXIX (1809), vol. I, pp. 378–79.

[70]   *The Works of Mr F. Beaumont and Mr J. Fletcher, Collated with all the Former Editions, and Corrected with Notes by Mr Theobald, Mr Seward and Mr Sympson, etc. and with a Preface by Mr Seward*, ed. by Thomas Seward, Sympson of Gainsborough and Lewis Theobald, 10 vols (London: J. & R. Tonson & S. Draper, 1750).

ambivalent relationship with the difficult pupil and his entourage. He wrote of his concerns to William, the brother to whom he was closest when young:

[I] have no reason to think he dislikes me but I'm no favourite. The Person who seems to share most of his good Graces next to his Horses and Hounds, is one whose chief merit seems to consist in abusing cursing and damning everybody that he perceives my Lord dislikes, according to whom any one that is the least suspected not to be full in the Duke's interest is a d—d Jacobite Rascal. [71]

In her correspondence, Seward mentions her father's eldest brother, Henry, who looked after the family estate and was the custodian of a set of valuable ancestral portraits and sketches by the famous Caroline court painter Peter Lely, including one of her paternal grandmother. It is quite remarkable, however, particularly when taking her predilection for anecdotes into consideration, that she writes nothing of her celebrated Uncle William, who had the extraordinary distinction of becoming known as the first Methodist martyr. Originally a successful City broker in Exchange Alley, William was a kindly philanthropist who worked solidly for the London Charity Schools. He converted to Methodism when he met Charles Wesley in 1738 and became closely involved with the early Evangelistic campaigns when the religion was still very much part of the Church of England. William was killed by an angry mob whilst attempting to preach at Hay-on-Wye. [72]

Thomas and William had been especially close until the time of the latter's conversion. They wrote to each other and visited regularly, and, although nothing specific is known of a rift between them, the dogmatic Thomas strongly objected to sects whose basis was 'Enthusiasting Song'. Neither did he approve of preachers who took their inspiration directly from the Holy Spirit rather than being educated specifically for the ministry through the conventional middle-class route of university and the classics. Following William's conversion to Methodism, Thomas appears to have lost contact with him, or, alternatively, he may have

[71] Spinks, 'Letters of a Badsey Family 1735–36', *Vale of Evesham Historical Society Research Papers*, (1971), 111, pp. 66–73. http://www.badsey.net/past/braby3.htm.

[72] 'The Martyrdom of William Seward', *The Reformer*, July/August 1992, file://A:\ The martyrdom of William Seward.htm; Spinks, 'Letters of a Badsey Family 1735–36', *Vale of Evesham Historical Society Research Papers*, (1971), 111, pp. 66–73. http://www. badsey.net/past/braby3.htm. William Seward was enthusiastic about his evangelical calling and travelled around the country preaching outdoors, offering salvation for all. Methodist preachers were frequently in breach of parish boundaries and found themselves antagonising local squires and rural parsons. They often came up against crowds who were sceptical and even abusive. William encountered aggressive mobs in South Wales and particularly in the border town of Hay-on-Wye, a place noted at the time for its 'wickedness' and 'the great spiritual darkness of the people'. An angry mob gathered and began to throw stones at him, but, standing his ground, he continued preaching. He was hit on the head at close range by a large stone and died a few days later, but first he generously forgave his assailant and requested that the authorities should not punish him. Inscribed on William's memorial stone are the words, 'For me to live is Christ and to die is gain'.

thought him a *persona non grata*. The Eyam parish had a history of intermittent problems with Dissenters, which caused Thomas much anguish. In 1776, his young curate, the short-sighted and profoundly deaf Peter Cunningham,[73] wrote to him with the good news that St. Lawrence's was more crowded than usual because there were no more Methodist preachers in Eyam Chapel. He added that Major Trafford had been appointed as resident magistrate and was proving to be 'a terror to evil doers'.[74] Ten years previously, John Wesley had made the following entry in his journal: 'The eagerness with which the poor people of Eyam devoured the Word made me amends for the cold ride over the snowy mountains'.[75]

Taking into consideration Seward's love of sharing a good story, it is completely out of character for her to ignore this fascinating one, unless she did indeed write about William Seward and was censored posthumously by her family or her editor. It is unlikely that her own marginal prejudice against Methodism would have precluded the story of her uncle's life and tragic death from her writings. It is possible that William Seward's martyrdom for the faith that caused so many problems for her father's parish did not conform to the self-constructed representation of herself and her family, and because of her loyalty, it went unreported.

Thomas Seward took his young charge on the Grand Tour but returned to England when Lord Charles died suddenly in Geneva. He then had an exceptionally brief and unsuccessful spell as a naval chaplain, during which time he never actually boarded his ship. In 1740, he arrived in Eyam, and on 28 April he was formally installed in St. Lawrence's Church, where he was presented by Lord and Lady Burlington. A stipend, which was traditionally generated from the local lead mining revenues, started at £400 a year and eventually rose to more than £700, providing a generous living indeed for a country rector.[76]

In 1741, at the age of thirty-two, Thomas Seward triumphed over strong opposition from his professional superiors, the future Bishop of Lincoln, Dr Green, and of Lichfield, Dr Newton, to marry Elizabeth Hunter, the twenty-eight-year-old

---

[73]   Sometimes written as 'Cunninghame'.

[74]   Peter Cunningham, 'Letter to Thomas Seward' (1776), in J. B. Firth, *Highways and Byways in Derbyshire*, 2nd edn (London: Macmillan, 1928), p. 355.

[75]   John Wesley, 'Journal' (1766), in J. B. Firth, *Highways and Byways in Derbyshire*. 2nd edn (London: Macmillan, 1928), p. 355.

[76]   William Wood, 'The Lead Mines', *The History and Antiquities of Eyam, Derbyshire*, 1842, 1845, 1860, ed. by Andrew McCann. http://www.genuki.org.uk/big/eng/DBY/ Eyam/ Wood/Leadmines.html. By Eyam tradition, every thirteenth dish of ore from the mines was taken by the feudal 'Lords of the Mineral Field'. One penny a dish was paid to the rector, with the addition of a minor tax from the purchaser of the ore. An exceptionally rich vein had been discovered and was profitably worked until it reached the water level and became flooded and completely unworkable. Over a period of fifty to sixty years, this seam alone generated revenue of up to £700 per annum for the rector. Other seams were also affected by the water levels and the revenues decreased, until Seward complained in 1786, by which time she was handling her father's estate, that they were receiving a meagre stipend of £150. 'So sink deeper from year to year, our golden hopes in this watery mischief', she stated (Seward, *Letters*, vol. I, p. 228).

daughter of John Hunter and his first wife, Anne Norton. John Hunter was the uncompromisingly cruel headmaster of Lichfield Grammar School, tutor to both Samuel Johnson and David Garrick. A fearsome sight in his gown, cassock and full wig, he instilled knowledge into his terrified pupils with regular vicious beatings. 'He whipped and they learned', said Johnson.[77] Much later, Johnson would joke that Seward's resemblance to her maternal grandfather was so great that he would tremble at the sight of her. Whether or not Hunter beat his daughter or her sister, Anne, is not known, but over time Elizabeth developed a fierce temper of her own which Seward found particularly easy to provoke. She once described an incident where, as a child, she had been cheeky to her mother. She explained what happened when Elizabeth became angry:

> [...] she looked grave, and took her pinch of snuff first at one nostril, and then at the other, with swift and angry energy, and her eyes began to grow dark and to flash. 'Tis an odd peculiarity; but the balls of my mother's eyes change from brown into black, when she feels either indignation or bodily pain.[78]

The energy in Seward that generated the same phenomenon of darkening eyes when she recited poetry, which Scott describes in his 'Biographical Preface', was an inherited trait. He wrote, 'In reciting, or in speaking with animation, [her eyes] appeared to become darker, and, as it were, to flash fire'.[79] Although a shared mannerism, it was channeled by Seward into a more creative output than by her mother.

In her poem 'Eyam', Seward refers with regret to her little dead brothers and sisters. Elizabeth had suffered a series of infant deaths after she gave birth to Anna on 1 December 1742 and her sister Sarah on 17 March 1744. John, Jane and Elizabeth were born and died shortly afterwards, and there were also two unnamed stillborn infants. As Seward was growing up, first in Eyam and later in Lichfield, Elizabeth placed a high value on domesticity, and, according to Seward, she was 'always occupied [...] by [...] explaining some circumstance of domestic management, or needle-work ingenuity, which she thinks will instruct'.[80] Her favourite pastime was card-playing, and she held several card parties each week. She had no love for writing, be it her own or her daughter's, and a telling indication of her inability to communicate with Anna is found in Elizabeth's letter to her when the former was on an extended visit to London in 1764. She writes:

> I am much obliged to my Dear Nancy for ye many kind and Entertaining Letters she has favour'd me with, which I am sure deserved a more early acknowledgement, under my own hand, but you know how much I dislike writing, therefore hope you will never suffer my silence to give you the least concern.

---

[77]   Christopher Hibbert, *The Personal History of Samuel Johnson*, 2nd edn (London: Pimlico, 1998), p. 11.

[78]   Seward, *Poetical Works*, vol. I, p. cxxi.

[79]   Scott, 'Biographical Preface', *Poetical Works*, vol. I, p. xxiii.

[80]   NLS, Scott MSS, fol. 63 (August 1764).

The letter continues with a word of thanks for a gift of oysters, followed by a more unappreciative request not to send more, as she had 'lost all relish for them'.[81]

The most evocative part of the letter is Elizabeth's main theme, the details of materials, caps, finery and accessories requested by her fashionable Lichfield friends. The negative connotation of being 'fashionable' went against Seward's design for her self-image. In her biography of Erasmus Darwin, she emphasises the writer and philosopher Thomas Day's badge of intellect, his plain clothing. Day refused to wear the conventional gentleman's accessories of fine clothes and powder, and he had such an aversion to 'fashionable ladies', although he was ultimately to marry one, that he embarked on an eccentric educational plan. He adopted two ten-year-old girls from the Foundling Hospital and, under the influence of the writings of Rousseau, who advocated simple manners and republican virtue, he commenced an experiment with female education. His own belief that education for women was flawed in its pursuit of a 'polished society' drove him to attempt to isolate the girls in order to nurture their innocence. Renaming his charges Sabrina Sidney and Lucretia, he took them to France to instruct them in his own standards of virtuous behaviour and spartan living and in literature, science and philosophy. His purpose was to choose the most suitably 'trained' girl to be his future wife. The girls, recounts Seward, refused to conform to his teaching:

> They teized and perplexed him; they quarrelled and fought incessantly; they sickened of the small-pox; they chained him to their bed-side by screaming if they were ever left a moment with any person who could not speak to them in English. He was obliged to sit up with them many nights; to perform for them the lowest offices of assistance.[82]

On their return to England, Day placed the 'invincibly stupid' Lucretia with a chamber milliner and kept beautiful, auburn-haired Sabrina as his favourite potential wife.[83] The experiment failed, as Sabrina was not brave enough for the appalling ordeals Day set for her, crying when he dripped hot sealing wax onto her arms and screaming when he fired pistol blanks at her.

---

[81]   Lichfield Record Office, MS AS17, Elizabeth Seward, 'Letter to Anna Seward' (19 November 1764).

[82]   Seward, *Memoirs*, p. 27.

[83]   Edgeworth, *Memoirs*, vol. I, pp. 217, 178–79, 353. Edgeworth describes Sabrina at thirteen as having a lovely face and curly auburn hair, which appeared all the more spectacular for its lack of fashionable powders and pomades, long eyelashes, expressive eyes and a melodious voice. He states that Lucrezia was 'not disposed to follow his regimen'. Edgeworth also describes his own less severe, although still radical, attempts to follow Rousseau's educational principles a few years later. He and his wife decided to leave their son to the 'education of nature and of accident'. The boy's highly developed sense of independence, his good humour and his bravery pleased his parents, although the results of Edgeworth's experiment appear similar to those of Day's: 'he shewed an invincible dislike of control'. Edgeworth records that when his son was eventually sent to school, he was unable to apply himself to learning, choosing instead a career at sea.

Seward did not approve of Day's techniques but agreed with his principles of simple dress. Early letters indicate that Elizabeth had taught her to make her own clothes. She preferred using plain materials, such as worsted, and she exchanged successful patterns with her friends. She demanded no more of her own clothes other than that they be clean and in good repair. The obsession for hooped skirts and frizzed hair and the time spent by her friends in preparing elaborate gowns for balls and assemblies irritated her. She wrote to Mary Powys in 1777, describing the changing scene in Lichfield: 'Hair-Dressers are running about our streets all morning, and our Misses, the Statues of these frizzing Pygmalions, issue out, in an evening, to the Commerce Table, in the bustle of a *hoop*, and the fragrance of expensive essences'.[84]

Like Thomas Day, but obviously not as extreme, her insistence on an absence of external, frivolous display denotes a concern with internal qualities and strength of character. Elizabeth Seward either did not recognise, or refused to acknowledge her daughter's philosophy and sent out her list regardless:

> Lady Gresley likes ye Gimp for trimming, is much obliged to you for it, and desires you will buy her a white Sattin cloak in ye newest fashion. You'll remember she is rather large over ye Shoulders, therefore don't let it be too little. She would have a Hat or Bonnet, which is most worn, cover'd with ye same Sattin of ye Cloak. She is more Sollicitous to have ye Sattin rich, than ye Trimming, tho' upon ye whole she leaves it to your fancy. Mrs Cobb desires her Cap may be sent by ye first opportunity, but Miss Adey [Sarah's closest friend] would not have hers bought till just before you leave London, as ye fashion may alter between this and that time.[85]

Elizabeth felt nothing but an antipathy towards her eldest daughter's aggressively defended literary ambitions. 'Though an affectionate parent', confirms Walter Scott, 'and an excellent woman, [she] possessed no taste for her daughter's favourite amusements', and, tellingly, Seward offers little information about her relationship with her mother, barely mentioning her in the correspondence.[86]

Elizabeth's second daughter, the fragile Sarah, was much more dutiful and domestic and was described by Seward as having 'elegant economy in the management of pecuniary concerns, & domestic regulations'.[87] Sarah was a small, brown-haired, gentle-natured girl who was more compliant than her sister, and though she also loved reading and discussing literature with a 'delicate, judicious, and awakened' intellect, she was not driven by it.[88] She was far more eager to please her parents than Seward ever was. Most of what is known of Sarah

---

84 JBM, MS 38/7, Seward, 'Letter to Mary Powys' [n.d.].
85 Lichfield RO, MS AS17, Elizabeth Seward, 'Letter to Anna Seward' (19 November 1764).
86 Seward, *Poetical Works*, vol. I, p. vii.
87 NLS, Scott MSS, fol. 33 (June 1763).
88 Seward, *Poetical Works*, vol. I, p. lxii.

comes from Seward's vivid narrative of her proposed marriage to an older man and her sudden death shortly before the wedding. There still survives a copy of a letter Sarah wrote to Mary (Polly) Adey, her 'Bride Maid', just a week before her wedding to Joseph Porter was due to take place. At the time of writing the letter, nineteen-year-old Sarah was in the early stages of a fever. From Seward's description this was most probably typhus, and she died suddenly when it turned putrid a few days later. Sarah described the beginnings of her illness to Polly: 'I have been much indisposed for some Days past with a feverish complaint, which prevented me from writing sooner to You, but I am now, by the help of the Bark [quinine] got tolerably well'.[89] Sarah's death was overwhelmingly distressing for Seward, and she writes at length in her letters to Emma of their relationship, their shared interests and their contrasting characters:

> O! how perfect was our amity! Upon that tender, instinctive affection, which grew with our growth, was engrafted esteem the most established, and confidence the most entire. – One bed! – one heart! – one soul! Even the difference of our dispositions became a cement to our friendship; her gentleness tempered my impetuosity; her natural composure caught animation from her sister's sprightliness; – 'our studies, our amusements, our taste the same'. O heavy, heavy loss![90]

The family had moved to the city of Lichfield on Thomas's promotion to canon residentiary of the city's three-spired cathedral in 1749.[91] Thomas Seward retained the responsibility for the parish church of St. Lawrence in Eyam, in addition to his rectorate of Kingsley in Staffordshire. The tenancy of the Bishop's Palace on the Cathedral Close was available to the Seward family as the bishop lived at Eccleshall Castle and Harley Street in London. The Bishop's Palace soon became

---

[89]   Lichfield RO, Seward Family MSS, D262/1/2, Sarah Seward, 'Letter to Polly Adey' (29 May 1764).

[90]   Seward, *Poetical Works*, vol. I, p. cxxx.

[91]   Lichfield provided the converse, sophisticated aspect of the 'blended society' of Seward's youth. There was a thriving communal social life with balls, card parties, theatre productions and public walks. With a population numbering approximately five thousand, the city was set in a mellow open vale, sixteen miles equidistant between Stafford and Birmingham, and was a bustling staging post on the line of the Roman Icknield Street. The Sheffield historian, William White, described the Cathedral Close as occupying the highest and most attractive part of the town, skirted by 'handsome houses' and separated from the city by the brook which forms Lichfield's 'pool'. William White, 'History, Gazetteer and Directory of Staffordshire' (1881), *Genuki UK and Ireland Genealogy*. http://www. genuki.org.uk/big/eng/STS/Lichfield/Cathedral/ index.html. Here, the traditions were more urbane than in Eyam. The Sheriff's Ride, dating from 1553, celebrated Lichfield's status as a separate county with its own sheriff. The Court of Arraye, an annual assembly dating from the twelfth century, reviewed the local defence forces and was followed by the Greenhill Bower, a carnival holiday (Lichfield City Council, 'Customs and Traditions'. http://www. lichfield.gov.uk/events .ihtml). The customs described continue today.

the centre for Thomas Seward's literary coterie, and his new appointment allowed him to return to Eyam to oversee the management of his parish for two months each summer.

Seward was aware of the historical significance of the Bishop's Palace and of the city of Lichfield. 'It is true I dwell on classic ground',[92] she wrote to Emma, referring to Joseph Addison's 'A Letter from Italy', in which the narrator views the 'immortal glories' he has read of in Roman poetry:

> 'Poetic Fields encompass me around,
> And still I seem to tread on classic ground;
> For here the Muse so oft her harp has strung.[93]

Addison's Roman pilgrimage took him to the seat of the classics, and through her allusion to his letter, Seward establishes a further bond with her own 'classic ground', the English classics. She was specifically fascinated by Lichfield's literary hierarchy: Joseph Addison, whose father, Lancelot, was dean of Lichfield, Gilbert Walmesley, David Garrick, Samuel Johnson, Elias Ashmole and Erasmus Darwin. As the Bishop's Palace had previously been occupied by Walmesley, she was thrilled to relate that his protégés, Johnson and Garrick, had been regular visitors as school-boys. She stated confidently that as she approached maturity, she did not have to 'struggle up to the notice of [her] neighbours from the gloom of an inferior station'. Her father was a gentleman, a scholar and a canon of the cathedral, and so she was able to meet and converse on equal terms with the 'proudest inhabitants of our little city' from an early age.[94]

Thomas Seward educated his daughters at home, giving preference to his gifted eldest daughter, whose predilection for literature was noticeable from an exceptionally early age. Like Johnson, but apparently more willingly, she was made to recite complex poetry as a small child for the amusement of visitors.[95] Thomas had tutored her in poetry from her infancy, and what she absorbed then remained with her, setting her reading criteria and sowing the seeds of her literary ambition. Starting with the Psalms and Milton, he gave her Shakespeare, Dryden, Pope, Prior, Gray and Mason to read. These early lessons set her standards in reading and writing. 'More verses I cou'd *never never* endure,' she told Scott, 'those soulless forms those Apparitions of Poetry: – but Genius, in all its degrees can yet fascinate my spirit, from its Suns to its smallest stars, the strength of the spell increasing with the lustre of the orbs.'[96]

Thomas's attitude to his eldest daughter's education was ambivalent. Though initially enthusiastic, he was gradually overtaken with an anxiety about her

---

[92]   Seward, *Poetical Works*, vol. I, p. lxix.

[93]   Joseph Addison, *A Letter from Italy To the Right Honourable Charles Lord Halifax In the Year MDCCI* (London: H. Hills, 1709).

[94]   Seward, *Poetical Works*, vol. I, pp. lxix, lxxii, lxxiii.

[95]   Seward, *Poetical Works*, vol. I, pp. iv–v.

[96]   NLS, MSS, 865, fols 112–15, Seward, 'Letter to Walter Scott' (18 January 1808).

intellect when he could not halt the literary ambition which he had set in motion. Sarah, however, was her mother's child. At the time of her letter to Polly Adey she was thoroughly domesticated and complacently anticipating the prospect of an arranged marriage to an unseen, prematurely-aged, stooped and wrinkled bachelor over twenty years her senior. Before his marriage to Elizabeth, Thomas's idealistic perspective on female education and self-determination appears forceful and progressive. At the start of his Grand Tour with Lord Charles Fitzroy, he had met and fallen in love with a wealthy young woman called Miss Pratt. Her qualities of charm and intellect inspired him to compose and dedicate a poem to her, 'The Female Right to Literature'.[97]

Seward considered that this poem had an exceptional importance to her father's memory and to her own development, and she left the manuscript to Walter Scott to publish with her own poems, giving the following firm instructions in posthumous directions to the publisher:

> The compositions in this quarto manuscript must be *preceded* by a Poem anonymously published in the second Vol. of Dodsley's Miscellany, 1st Ed: page 295, and intitled '*The Female Right to Literature*'; – add '*By the Revd Thomas Seward*' – add also – 'Written at Florence about the year 1735, and addressed to Miss Pratt, afterwards Lady Cambden'. [98]

Protecting her father's reputation, she was careful to point out to the publisher that an explanatory note must be added to the foot of the first page to confirm that Thomas Seward was unmarried when he wrote the poem and that he was on his travels with Lord Charles Fitzroy. Seward was not a great enthusiast of her father's writing, which tends to be didactic and can be pedestrian. She described him as 'a scholar, though perhaps not a deep one, and a very tolerable poet'. This verse, however, pleased Seward, and she was eager to revive a few of his other poems after his death.

In his poem, Thomas's seemingly progressive views on female education, which are in opposition to 'custom's rapid tide',[99] are somewhat tempered by his belief in the necessity for all women, whether intellectuals or not, to comply with the conventional rules of female virtue: femininity, obedience and 'soft innocence and virgin modesty'.[100] The implied condition of childlike simplicity suggests, in turn, a naïve dependency and an absence of self-determination. In the mid-century, the role of women was subtly changing. There were new opportunities to engage with literature and to be able to confront established ideas through study. Thomas's

---

[97] Thomas Seward, 'The Female Right to Literature, in a Letter to a Young Lady from Florence', in *A Collection of Poems by Several Hands: compiled by Robert Dodsley*, with a new introduction, notes, and indices by Michael F. Suarez (London: J. Dodsley, 1782; repr. London: Routledge/Thoemmes, 1997), pp. 309–15.

[98] NLS, Scott MSS, fol. 2 [n.d.].

[99] Thomas Seward, 'The Female Right to Literature', p. 309.

[100] Thomas Seward, 'The Female Right to Literature', p. 314.

poem is consistent with the notion of inner beauty being seated in intellect, but was clearly not a fixed reflection of his views on further education for women. Much later, his youthful ideals changed dramatically when he was confronted with the prospect of a daughter who challenged her cultural role. She was an intellectual and therefore possibly unmarriageable. Though he endorsed the notion of female education, he enforced strict ground rules when it applied to his own family.

It is both difficult and fascinating to try to understand Seward's intention that her father's poem should be used in the forefront of her own poetic works. During her youth she had many fights with Thomas over freedom of choice in religious and intellectual matters and particularly in her choice of partner. In this instance, in giving way to his stance on female education, she is also endorsing his view of feminine virtue. This may have been acceptable when she was an impressionable child, but it is difficult to imagine that, as an assertive mature woman in control of her career and finances, she would give quite as much credence to her father's opinion. Yet, Thomas Seward did at least offer his daughters literature as their educational right when they were children, even if he retracted at a later date. He enhanced their early years with selective reading materials, very much against Elizabeth's wishes. For this, Seward must have been grateful, although the choices she made and her literary achievements were hers alone.

An extract from a poem that Seward wrote in 1786, 'Epistle to Nathaniel Lister, Esq. Of Lichfield', shows her generosity of spirit towards her father and the extent of the value she placed on what she obviously believed to be his progressive views. Because her own career eclipsed his, she wanted to rank him with the Lichfield literati:

> The Female Rights shall flourish long;
> That song, with generous disdain,
> Which breaks the sullen pedant's chain,
> Forg'd our aspiring sex to bind
> From ranging the high tracts of mind,
> Where Fancy's flowers, and Learning's fruit,
> On every side, luxuriant shoot; –
> [...] Source of my Life, it will not prove
> A vain essay of filial love,
> Here, if a right thy daughter claim,
> To rank with theirs thy honour'd name,
> Whose silver lyre's harmonious sound,
> Made lovely Lichfield classic ground.[101]

Thomas Seward's poem did not 'flourish long'. Regardless of her instructions for its inclusion in her poetry edition, Walter Scott rescinded 'The Female Right to

---

[101] Seward, 'Epistle to Nathaniel Lister, Esq. Of Lichfield', *Poetical Works*, vol. II, pp. 333–47.

Literature', together with Thomas's other poems that Seward wanted published. He excluded it on the grounds that he needed to limit the size of the volumes.

Thomas's ideas of teaching centred on literature, not on the science that he recommends in his poem for Miss Pratt, or on modern or classical languages. These would all have been well within his competence of teaching and within Seward's capability of learning. He certainly had an interest in science, as James Boswell mentions his amateur study of the strata of earth in volcanoes.[102] French, music, drawing and embroidery were the basics of education for most girls, unless, like the poet and translator Elizabeth Carter, for example, a father's liberalism included equality of education for all his children. In Carter's case, his own scope extended to teaching his daughter Latin, Greek, Hebrew, Arabic, modern languages, geography, history and astronomy, which eventually led to her earning a considerable amount of money for her translations of Epictetus. Yet, apart from Elizabeth Seward's forte of embroidery, these subjects were not part of the Seward sisters' early education. This implies that before leaving them to their own devices, Thomas taught them theology, numeracy, how to read and to appreciate poetry, how to write and how to perform party-trick recitations. Although altogether polite accomplishments, these subjects are by no means excessively liberal. By omitting the conventional drawing room accomplishments from their education he was encouraging them away from the traditional female role, and had he included languages and science, it would be easier to believe his educational ideology to be enlightened. It cannot have been a comfortable experience for Seward when she first managed to obtain a copy of Rousseau's *Julie* and had to tolerate her younger foster-sister Honora Sneyd's translation from French into English. Honora had attended Mrs Latuffier's day school in Lichfield for two years and was fluent in French, translating effortlessly as she read.

Honora Sneyd came to live with the Sewards when her mother died when she was just six years old and her father was unable to care for her and her seven siblings. She was fostered by Thomas and Elizabeth and was instantly adored by the thirteen-year-old Anna and by Sarah, who was then twelve. Seward took on the responsibility for Honora's literary education. Having been forbidden to write poetry when she reached the age of sixteen, she was able to alleviate some of her own frustrated literary ambitions by teaching the child and inspiring in her the love of literature. She describes the start of her fascination with Honora in her poem 'The Anniversary', which recounts their first meeting when she and Sarah returned from a Sunday evening walk:

---

[102] Boswell, *Life of Johnson*, vol. II, pp. 467–8. Boswell writes: 'Mr Seward mentioned to us the observations which he had made upon the strata of earth in volcanoes, from which it appeared, that they were so very different in depth at different periods, that no calculation whatever could be made as to the time required for their formation. This fully refuted an anti-mosaical remark introduced into Captain Brydone's entertaining tour, I hope heedlessly, from a kind of vanity which is too common in those who have not studied the most important of all subjects.'

O! hast thou seen the star of eve on high,
Through the soft dusk of Summer's balmy sky,
Shed its green light, and in the glassy stream
Eye the mild reflex of its trembling beam?
So look'd on us, with tender, bashful gaze,
The destined charmer of our youthful days;[103]

Honora's health was extremely fragile, and when she finally succumbed to tuberculosis, dying in 1780 aged twenty-nine, Seward was painfully distressed, more so because of a long estrangement between the two. She celebrated a vision of youth and promise through a series of poems and sonnets dedicated to Honora. She returns, for the most part, to the youthful imagery of the 'destined charmer' and their days spent together, reading and sewing.

Female literacy amongst the middle classes was exceptionally high in the mid-century, and most little girls were taught at home by their fathers or brothers, with the main emphasis placed on moral improvement. Periodicals, newspapers and journals gave girls access to political and cultural debate. Translations of classical texts promoted virtuous behaviour. If Eyam was relatively isolated from the outside world, print culture found its way through. Life in a remote locality did not prevent Seward from getting hold of virtually any book she wanted to read, even at such an early age, and she helped herself to books from her father's library. Although Scott tells us that her taste was influenced by her father's preferences, this gives a false impression, as she found great pleasure in reading all kinds of past and contemporary poems, drama, carefully selected novels and many other works. She does, however, clearly state the standard she preferred for poetry in an ongoing epistolary debate on the subject with Walter Scott:

My feelings differ to yours on the subject of Verse. Nothing of it charmed me in early life, which does not and in equal degree, charm me *now*. This unvarying taste is, I believe, owing to my Father having, even in my infancy, set it high, by putting first into my hands, not our minor, but our first-rate Poets, Shakespeare and Milton, Dryden, Pope, Prior, Gray and Mason. [...] Genius, in all its degrees, can yet fascinate my spirit, from its Suns to its smallest stars, the strength of the spell increasing with the lustre of the orbs – Yes, from the *Heroic Ballads*, the *Lay*, and *Madoc* of this period, to the *Peacock at home*. You have doubtless seen that beautiful little sparkler.[104]

When Thomas Seward died in 1790, he had been seriously ill for ten years, falling progressively into physical and mental incapacity. As his last surviving close female relative, Anna organised care for him during his long illness without restricting her travels or engagements in any way as he was nursed competently by the Bishop's Palace servants. Her situation and her father's had now reversed. For the first time, she was in control of her life and in charge of the efficient running of

---

[103] Seward, 'The Anniversary. Written June 1769', *Poetical Works*, vol. I, p. 73.
[104] NLS, MSS, 865, fols 112–15 (13 January 1808).

the household. She successfully managed her literary career. She was responsible for her own financial affairs and for Thomas's, and now she also had effective control over his life. To emphasise this, she infantilised him, referring to him in a kindly way as her 'aged nurseling'. During the years of his illness, Seward was at her most prolific until she eventually stopped publishing poetry in the early 1790s. Before then, however, Thomas was a powerful will for Seward to overcome, and the juvenile letters illustrate his aggressive tendencies and attempts to control his willful daughter's future.

Where most children were brought up on nursery rhymes and fairy tales, Seward was aware that her early literary education and her ongoing self-education had a more complex foundation. This difference was an ever-present energy that shaped her life and formulated her self-worth, and it finds forceful expression within the anecdotes of her juvenile letters.

Chapter 2
Anecdotes:
The Juvenile Letters

'By the way, I smile to think how little the ensuing circumstances wou'd deserve the name of anecdote', Anna Seward wrote to Emma in August 1763.[1] She was twenty years old and sketching out the stories of her friends' lives in Lichfield. What is also apparent is that through the medium of the letters, she constructs an anecdotally-framed self-portrait which exposes her struggle for independence and authorship. Voicing the anxieties she encountered during her troubled negotiations with convention and the marriage market, she presents herself as an intellectual and sensitive young woman, capable of advising her close friends on every subject from literature to love. Although she joined in the social events, she was primarily a great observer. By watching Lichfield society from a position on the periphery, she stood apart from her contemporaries, recording what she saw. Despite the tribulations of entering adulthood, this was clearly an intoxicating time for her, when she was surrounded by the people she loved most: her sister Sarah, her foster-sister Honora, and friends Nannette, John André and John Saville.

Over the course of the correspondence, stories are told of Emma's relationship with Captain L—, Nannette's brief but disappointing liaison with a wealthy red-haired, pock-marked boy, known only as N—, Sarah's impending marriage to hunched and wrinkled Joseph Porter and Seward's own relationships with 'polished and interesting'[2] young Captain Temple and with the distinguished, middle-aged country gentleman from Eyam, Major John Wright.

Each of the anecdotes is built around a central concept, some of which relate to class and wealth, while others are a negative expression on the institution of marriage. All the anecdotes reflect Seward's attempts to identify and make sense of her role in life. Alternating narrative themes of love, intellect and independence sustain a dialogue with the conventional manners, morals and formalities adopted by polite society. The main characters who inhabit Seward's juvenile letters are rounded and well defined, complete with physical descriptions and histories. Her own persona is portrayed as resolute in her consistent attempts to nurture and preserve her intellect. Tensions spark across the anecdotes when she turns to the forceful themes relating to parental control, which ignited her own self-conflict between independence and obedience. She reveals her instinct for rebellion when she is under pressure to conform to the domestic values imposed by her mother.

---

[1]   NLS, Sir Walter Scott MSS, 879, fol. 42 (August 1763).
[2]   NLS, Sir Walter Scott MSS, 879, fol. 4 (November 1762).

Seward's exposition of the marriage market shows up the powerlessness of young women facing marital partnerships of ruthless inequalities. For most of her female friends there was little choice. For her male acquaintances, marriage options were controlled by the authority of inheritance. Among the wealthy middle classes, a man tended to select a wife who would enhance his future prospects, and his choice could be controlled by his financial benefactor, be that his father or a childless relative. The threat of disinheritance and a life of poverty was a powerful persuasion to adhere to family strategy in these matters. Time and again, the anecdotes emphasise the notion of love taking an equal or lower precedence with financial matters.

With the juvenile letters intended as the record of her early life, Seward clearly set for herself a high literary standard based on Samuel Johnson's writing paradigm. This is obvious in her later revisions and most probably applies to her first lively anecdotes. 'No poetry is more lavish in the use of imagery and metaphor than the prose of Samuel Johnson', she told Emma, aligning him with Milton to assert, 'Their pens always remain in the higher latitudes of abstract ideas, of ornamented and figurative language'.[3] Whether founded on fact or reconstructed from the imagination, the letters are eloquent and expressive, and the anecdotes are interspersed with sophisticated literary debate and philosophical musings.

In thus contriving to leave a specific imprint on eighteenth-century literary history, Seward did not anticipate Walter Scott's censorship, which left her juvenile letters fragmented. Although Scott claimed his Border ballads as a 'personal and regional heritage', he was uncomfortable with the idea of too deep a concern with posterity and with 'handing down personal vices and follies' in the form of posthumous fame. His enduring association with place and his desire to unite himself with a noble and heroic past was influenced by his grandparents' stories, ballads and legends of Border skirmishes. He insisted that he preferred to take the rewards whilst alive. 'Let me please my own generation. The anticipation of their neglect or censure will affect us very little', he wrote to Seward, explaining his view that as taste changes with time, the reading public would soon forget their heroes.[4] The popular 'lives and letters' format did not appeal to Scott. Although Seward makes clear in her 'posthumous' letter, dated July 1807, that she wanted her poems and juvenile letters published in separate volumes, he did not follow her instructions and arranged for the letters to precede the poems in the first volume, having first discarded the majority of the anecdotes.[5]

---

3   Seward, 'Literary Correspondence', *Poetical Works*, vol. I, p. lxxv.

4   NLS, MSS, 854, fol. 15, Scott, 'Letter to Anna Seward' (1808).

5   NLS, MSS, 870, fol. 14, Seward, 'Posthumous Letter to Walter Scott' (17 July 1807). Seward specifically mentions her preference for the poetry edition to be in the same format as Warburton's edition of Pope's works: 'To those Metrical Volumes [her complete collection of published and unpublished poems] I wish the juvenile Letters may be added; succeeding the poetic volumes as in Warburton's Edition of Pope's Works'.

Scott's own literary biographies were not all comprehensive, and he did little original research on the majority of them.[6] His *Life of Dryden*, which he was compiling when he first met Seward in Lichfield, draws repeated attention to writing out of financial necessity. When he published *Dryden*, he confronted the hostile criticism from the *Edinburgh Review* critic Lord Francis Jeffrey with apparent good humour, but his subsequent comments to Seward revealed his anxiety. In his correspondence with her, he appears ambivalent about writing for financial reward. Although he hinted that he wrote solely to provide for his family, and because of this he wanted to produce work 'easily and unambitiously', he also told Seward that a financial legacy in 1802 made his writing more 'a matter of amusement than an object of emolument'. His main concern was not to be perceived as 'a gentleman-author'.[7]

If Scott was empathic with the chosen subjects of his literary biographies, identifying closely with their financial and creative circumstances, he had little common ground with Seward. This accounted for the indifferent editing and publishing techniques of her works. He perceived Seward as wealthy and privileged, which, of course, she was. There were no disruptions to her writing life other than managing her finances, travelling and receiving visits from friends and admirers of her work. It is telling that Scott circumvented the private, intimate details of his subjects' lives. He evaded mention of personal issues, such as Dryden's unhappy marriage, indicating a sensitivity that accounts, in part, for his severe censorship of Seward's anecdotes. Through his editing techniques, he essentially removed the vibrancy from the letters, leaving, for the most part, literary debate which is only occasionally broken by a lively sketch.

Ironically, this division purged from the letter collection the very narrative that was most probably based on original juvenilia. Some of the published letters are so fractured that they make little sense, as in its entirety the collection has continuous themes and links which provide a rounded history. It is now difficult to respond to the edited letters or to the one-dimensional, conservative character that remains at the forefront of the narrative. Although Samuel Johnson encouraged James Boswell to 'give us as many anecdotes as you can',[8] Scott's disapproval of the fashionable trend for anecdotal writing is made clear in his 'Biographical Preface', where he offers justification for his heavy editing:

---

6   Walter Scott, *The Works of John Dryden: Now First Collected in 8 Volumes, Illustrated with Notes Historical, Critical and Explanatory and A Life of the Author*, 8 vols (London: William Miller; Edinburgh: James Ballantyne, 1808); *The Works of Jonathan Swift: containing additional letters, tracts, and poems not hitherto published; with notes and a life of the author*, 19 vols (Edinburgh: Archibald Constable, 1814); *The Life of Napoleon Buonaparte, Emperor of the French*, 9 vols (Edinburgh: Archibald Constable, 1827); *The Lives of the Novelists* (London: Dent, 1825).

7   NLS, MSS, 854, fol. 15, Scott, 'Letter to Anna Seward', 1808; Scott, 'Letter to Anna Seward', July 1802, in Lockhart, *Life of Walter Scott*, I, p. 352.

8   Boswell, *Life of Johnson*, vol. III, p. 358.

> In publishing the correspondence, every thing is retrenched which has reference to personal anecdote. I am aware that I have not consulted the taste of the age; but nothing less important than the ascertainment of historical fact justifies withdrawing the veil from incidents of private life.[9]

Later, he was to carp to Joanna Baillie that Seward's correspondence was, in general, overly 'sentimental' and that he had 'a particular aversion at perpetuating that sort of gossip'.[10]

Seward's letters to Emma confirm her view that the circulation and publication of anecdotes was a practice that was perfectly well accepted by the literary establishment and the reading public. As a young writer with a strong awareness of what constituted 'important' literature, she believed that her own anecdotes might have appeared as immature and insignificant, hardly even worthy of the description 'anecdote', to the 'wise, middle-aged Gentry, whose feelings must be stimulated by *events* ere they can be strongly interested'.[11] This was because her subject matter included descriptions of young women's thoughts and feelings, with details of the kind which included blushing cheeks and rattling tea-cups in the unexpected presence of a lover. Yet there are numerous descriptions of events that are insightful and that are decidedly representative of their time.

Seward justified her intimate chronicles and her preoccupation with relationships and lovers, asserting that the 'quick sensibilities of youth often give to the most trivial incidents a deep and lasting importance'.[12] There was a proviso; she believed that the anecdotal form must be expressed with eloquence if it was not to lose its value, and she was always quick to point out and criticize poor writing. Good writing, she stressed, has 'that grace of style, that vivacity and happiness of manner in narration, which gives interest to trivial communications, while it throws added lustre upon those which are in themselves striking and important'.[13] If her own anecdotes appeared frivolous or did not describe the lives of important people as her later letters did, they were intended to appeal to human interest.

Much later, in 1795, when writing to Samuel Johnson's friend the anecdotist William Seward,[14] she put forward her own long-established view that Johnson's prose style was the exemplary model for this form of writing. William Seward had sent her a copy of his own publication, *Anecdotes of Distinguished Persons*.[15] Wanting Seward's honest opinion on his anecdotes, he lied to her, telling her they

---

9   Scott, 'Biographical Preface', *Poetical Works*, I, p. xxxviii.

10   Scott, 'Letter to Miss Joanna Baillie' (18 March 1810), in Lockhart, *Memoirs of the Life of Sir Walter Scott, Bart.*, vol. II, p. 277.

11   NLS, Sir Walter Scott MSS, 879, fols 42–43 (August 1763).

12   NLS, Sir Walter Scott MSS, 879, fol. 43 (August 1763).

13   Seward, 'Letter to William Seward' (17 May 1795), *Letters*, vol. IV, pp. 53–54.

14   William Seward was a distant relative, who pronounced his own name 'Suward'.

15   William Seward, *Anecdotes of Some Distinguished Persons: chiefly of the present and two preceding centuries. Adorned with sculptures*, 8 vols (London: Cadell & Davies, 1795–1796).

had been written by a friend. Her response was typically forthright, although wounding to the anecdotist's vanity. She found his subject matter absorbing, she told him, but was concerned that the anecdotes were poorly written and that this made them appear trivial. Samuel Johnson should be the benchmark, she explained, as he 'shows us the possibility of giving, by the graces of language, an exquisite charm to many observations and descriptions, which, without those verbal graces, would disgust by their want of essential importance'.[16] Johnson himself recognised the worth of fragments of life expressed through anecdotes. He advised Hester Thrale Piozzi to write down all the anecdotes and observations that she had either heard or had made herself, and all the scraps of information which she found interesting and worth accumulating. The ensuing six volumes of *Thraliana*, which were not published until 1942, are a remarkable store of edifying and witty chronicles that provides an effortlessly accessible wealth of information about her circle and era.[17]

The personal nature of anecdotes was controversial as, for the price of a book, readers could purchase intimate details of the famous. Private lives were laid open to public scrutiny, and, as Scott emphasised to Joanna Baillie, not everyone wanted confidential information to be made common knowledge. When James Boswell published his journal of his Hebridean tour with Samuel Johnson, he had deliberated on the wisdom of printing it as a journal giving personal details about his travelling companion.[18] His alternative was to revise his narrative into a conventional format, but he chose the anecdotal option, believing that everything concerning Johnson was valuable. As there was such a considerable fascination with all aspects of Johnson's life and particularly with his remarkable conversations and succinct aphorisms, the progress of his tour of the Hebrides was followed in the press with immense interest, and his own contemplative publication on it was highly successful.[19] Readers were avid for more, and though Boswell delayed the publication of his journal until after Johnson's death, its indiscreet and humorous record of private conversation and opinion made it just as compulsive as it was disturbing. Public reaction to the journal was neatly summarised by Sir William Forbes: 'I have been amused at it, but should be very sorry either to have been the author or the hero of it.'[20]

---

[16] Seward, 'Letter to William Seward', 17 May 1795, *Letters*, vol. IV, 53–54.

[17] Hester Lynch Thrale, *Thraliana: The Diary of Mrs Hester Lynch Thrale (Later Mrs Piozzi) 1741–1821*, 2nd edn, ed. by Katherine Canby Balderston, 2 vols (Oxford: Clarendon Press, 1951), vol. I, [1776–1809], p. xi.

[18] James Boswell, *The Journal of a Tour to the Hebrides with Samuel Johnson, LL.D* (London: Charles Dilly, 1785).

[19] Samuel Johnson, *A Journey of a Tour to the Western Isles of Scotland in 1773* (London: Hamilton, Adams & Co, 1786).

[20] Adam Sisman, *Boswell's Presumptuous Task: Writing the Life of Dr Johnson* (London: Penguin Books, 2001), p. 111.

The repercussions of making Samuel Johnson's private conversations public included a reaction to his tactless comments and to Boswell's own lack of sensitivity in reporting them. Seward had a horrified fascination with the representation of Johnson, delighted to read about his 'stalking like a Greenland Bear, over the barren Hebrides', but was shocked by his inconsiderate comments on Elizabeth Montagu's scholarly writing, which she considered to be 'ingenious and able'.[21] She took the trouble to reprimand Boswell, telling him that he should have suppressed the passage:

> The only omission cou'd I have *much* desired in these valuable records of Doc[t]. Johnson – that M[rs]. Montague [*sic*] might have been spared the mortification of knowing his injustice to her talents – .[22]

Through Seward's precocious intellect and the privileged position of growing up in literary company, together with her self-identification with the 'classic ground' of Lichfield, she developed strong views on what constituted literary excellence. As Thomas Constable had noted when preparing his father's memoirs, her juvenilia and censored anecdotes had a simplicity that her later letters lacked. The shift to an elaborate style in her correspondence at the start of the 1780s is clearly intentional and relates to her status as a published poet with a new circle of friends. Whatever the value of autobiographical and biographical anecdotes as a record of vanished lives, Scott clearly did not appreciate the genre. Referring to Seward's later correspondence, he claimed to have a personal horror of seeing himself in the letters, laid bare and 'advertised for a live poet like a wild beast on a painted streamer'.[23] He was not convinced that Seward's self-constructed persona in her narrative should be left intact.

It is the unpublished manuscripts that give the unrestrained version of Seward's life narrative, and her anecdotes have a value to cultural history. Embedded in her discourse is her interesting approach to issues of class, the imagery of women, and her preoccupation with the defence of her own intellect. She writes, for example, on the ephemeral nature and vulnerability of beauty in the story of an acquaintance, the beautiful, vain Harriet D—:

> The gift of Beauty is a *dangerous* gift, a great temptation to neglect the attainment of more enduring *graces*. It gives us consequence which costs no pains to acquire; and empire which calls for no exertions to maintain. But short is the duration of these honors, & of this glory – and then where are the resources to supply the place of perpetual homage? Where are the Affection and Esteem, which might fill the void that is left by vanished adulation?[24]

---

[21]   Seward, 'Letter to Mrs G —' (27 August 1785), *Letters*, vol. I, p. 81.

[22]   Yale University, Beinecke Rare Book and Manuscript Library, Letters of Anna Seward, MS 2473, fol. 769, Seward, 'Letter to James Boswell' (7 March 1786).

[23]   Scott, 'Letter to Joanna Baillie' (18 March 1810), in Lockhart, *Life of Walter Scott*, vol. II, p. 277.

[24]   NLS, Sir Walter Scott MSS, 879, fol. 51 (February 1764).

This is how Seward sets the scene for her anecdote about Harriet, who casually exploits her privileged background and beauty by tormenting young admirers rather than using her intelligence for worthier causes. Like many of the censored anecdotes this one takes on an instructive tone as she gives vignettes of her contemporaries, describing their appearance and characteristics in detail, while simultaneously revealing their weaknesses and, consequently, drawing attention to her own sophistication and maturity. Seward employed the conventional device of using initialled names for most of her protagonists, only occasionally providing names of neighbours or acquaintances when it suited her own purpose to identify a character. In such instances, the names are written above the initial as though added later during revisions.

Seward begins her anecdote with her customary opening to introduce a specific topic: 'You enquire after...', in this case, 'the Miss D—s', a trio of wealthy but unpleasant sisters who regularly attended the same Lichfield assemblies and balls as Seward and her circle. Not only does Emma apparently 'enquire after' the sisters, but she also wants to know about their 'dispositions, and manners', which gives Seward the opening to relate her anecdote in full.[25] As she tells a story concerning the middle sister, Harriet, and her mistreatment of her latest admirer, a small, fat soldier, Seward challenges the conduct of wealthy, high-ranking but uneducated young women. The would-be suitor provided the evening's entertainment as the object of Harriet's amused contempt. Much to the malicious delight of her sisters and friends, who laughed behind their fans at her antics, she treated him like a servant, making him dance every dance and fetch her lemonade and biscuits in the intervals until he was completely exhausted. Seward felt little sympathy for the soldier, explaining to Emma that he had once been her own friend but had now abandoned his old circle in his pursuit of the wealthy young woman. As Seward and her friends watched, believing his red-faced distress to be largely self-induced, he struggled to carry out Harriet's demands. However, Seward is more judgemental about Harriet's conduct. She criticises the arrogance which developed out of personal vanity with a warning on the transient nature of beauty: 'she builds the superiority in which she too visibly exults upon the sandy foundations of flattery'.[26]

In her anecdote, Seward dismisses the two unnamed sisters with brief descriptions, depicting them as ugly and boorish – one short and squat with a large scowling face, the other ill-mannered enough to upset the formalities of the minuet with her inappropriate laughter as she 'tittered and tottered' through the dance.[27] Harriet's appearance and character are intricately drawn, however, and Seward initially finds several points of comparison with herself before placing her in direct opposition, thus accentuating her ideology on the image of women. Harriet was of a similar height and build with comparable outgoing qualities and, Seward notes

---

[25] NLS, Sir Walter Scott MSS, 879, fol. 48 (February 1764).

[26] NLS, Sir Walter Scott MSS, 879, fol. 51 (February 1764).

[27] NLS, Sir Walter Scott MSS, 879, fol. 50 (February 1764).

specifically, without a formal education. She pays particular attention to Harriet's carefully contrived negligence in dress, using the imagery as an indicator of her individualism, but more importantly of her lack of vitality. Unusually for a young woman of her status, the dress is 'put on in such a careless style' and is fashioned from 'such *clinging* materials [...] and so *few* in number'.[28] The mid-century fashion for the upper ranks of women called for an exaggerated silhouette, with tight bodices, hooped skirts and high powdered, frizzed hair. Seward equates the flimsiness of Harriet's dress with the concealing draperies on a Grecian statue. While her natural shape is revealed, the imagery is still of a lifeless statue, destined to 'crumble away', as will her youth and beauty.[29]

By identifying Harriet as privileged with every opportunity to educate herself, but as choosing to waste her 'bright abilities', Seward reveals her own values: the mind takes precedence over the body.[30] The pressures placed on young women to behave modestly and decorously extended to their intellect and to their dress. Learning was encouraged, but there were restrictive boundaries to be observed. On one occasion, Erasmus Darwin had advised Seward to curb her impulse to join in conversation, explaining that good listening was a 'more captivating accomplishment' for women than skilful debate.[31] Needless to say, she ignored him. Periodicals such as the *Lady's Magazine* advised women of the standards expected of them, although the content matter gave out conflicting information. They displayed a considerable preoccupation with fashion, making light of it yet linking it with virtue in articles that were usually written by men.[32] The magazine's first editorial informed its readers that its primary intention was educational, that it intended to 'render your minds not less amiable than your persons'. It also considered external appearance to be 'the first inlet to the treasures of the heart', capturing the attention of its readers with a series of patterns and plates.[33]

In her juvenile letters, Seward did not seek to define herself by fashion, and there is no evidence that she read women's periodicals. She emphasises her own indifference by drawing attention to her contemporaries' fashion sense. In one letter, for example, she mocks the way Emma has her hair dressed in preparation for a ball in London: 'You perused my last letter under the operation of the Frissuer [*sic*]; that *high Priest* at the altar of *Fashion*! [...] My internal sight recalls the interval, and presents you to me, invested with all the mystic insignia of a Goddess.'[34] As she imagines the progress of the 'Goddess', with hair primped

28   NLS, Sir Walter Scott MSS, 879, fol. 48 (February 1764).
29   NLS, Sir Walter Scott MSS, 879, fol. 51 (February 1764).
30   NLS, Sir Walter Scott MSS, 879, fols 50–51 (February 1764).
31   NLS, Sir Walter Scott MSS, 879, fol. 47 (January 1764).
32   Jennie Batchelor, 'Re-clothing the Female Reader: Dress and the *Lady's Magazine* (1770–1832)', *Women's History Magazine*, 49 (2005), 11–21 (p. 19).
33   The *Lady's Magazine*, 1 (August 1770), p. 170.
34   NLS, Sir Walter Scott MSS, 879, fol. 14 (January 1763).

and powdered for the ball, she leads into thoughts on her own image, which she constructs as far more cerebral, yet still sociable:

> I love Music, Dancing, and Theatric Representation, yet, wou'd I not resign for a constancy, the power of commanding many hours in every week, which I might pass in the retirement of intellectual cultivation, to enjoy those more tumultuous pleasures, even beneath the splendour of a coronet [...] I have no ostentation, and am too genuinely proud to waste my ambition upon Equipage, or personal Precedence. Genius, and Virtue, are the only human distinctions to which I look *up*. Health, Competence, Friendship, and Leisure, form the boundaries of my desires.[35]

This is not to say that she had no vanity about her appearance. Like Harriet, Seward had an individual style. In contemporary physical descriptions, her distinctive long red hair is mentioned frequently, and so it would appear that she did not 'frizz' or powder it but allowed it to fall free and natural. Seward told Emma of a letter she had received from London which described the appearance at a ball of a red-haired woman who was daring enough to go without powder, which was not 'correct'.[36] A man in the company wrote a spontaneous poem dedicated to 'Rubrilla', giving the 'illustrious red' various classical, regal and nationalistic associations, from the Golden Fleece to the blood of war heroes:

> Red was the golden Fleece, which Jason bore,
> In love's gay triumph, from Colchian shore.
> Britain's red flag commands the subject Main,
> In every heart Rubrilla's streamers reign,
> Thro' Seas of blood undaunted Heroes fly,
> And steep their laurels in that glorious dye.[37]

Clearly impressed by the woman's audacity and the poetic response to her natural beauty, Seward passed on the extensive verses to Emma, labeling them 'spirited and classical'.[38] It would not be difficult to imagine that this anecdote, with its ambiguous source, was based on one of Seward's own experiences that she preferred not to relate in the first person out of concern for the 'more enduring *graces*' of her constructed image.

There was an opportunity for Seward to expand on themes of honour, the inequalities of marriage, and the arbitrariness of love with an anecdote she gives about a duel. Instead, she fails to explore the complexity of such issues and sets up the extraordinary account as a testimony to her literary imagination. The anecdote reads as though written as a synopsis for a novel or a short story, and it has a strong suggestion of fabrication about it. She may have based it on actual events, yet she

---

[35] NLS, Sir Walter Scott MSS, 879, fol. 16 (January 1763).

[36] NLS, Sir Walter Scott MSS, 879, fol. 79 (August 1767).

[37] NLS, Sir Walter Scott MSS, 879, fol. 80 (August 1767).

[38] NLS, Sir Walter Scott MSS, 879, fols 79–81 (August 1767).

provides no substantiating evidence to confirm the story's authenticity. Although the main protagonist is ostensibly an acquaintance who is referred to as 'Mr B—' and is known to both Seward and Emma, she offers no physical description or historical background as she does with her other carefully defined characters, such as Harriet. He is introduced as the subject of ongoing gossip: 'You know how often you, & I, have lamented Mr B—'s ill-starred attachment to the fair, the sacrificed Mrs L—', and as the events described take place over a period of several months but are narrated in their entirety, there is a discrepancy in the anecdote's attention to fact.[39]

The subject matter does not lend itself to Seward's verse, and her frequent and openly-expressed negative opinions on the novel genre would discount the publication of anything below the standard of her poetical novel, *Louisa*. Seward's anecdote tells of marital possessiveness and codes of honour in B—'s love for beautiful Mrs L—. A mutual friend, described as a 'coxcomb', makes fun of the situation, and, to preserve his honour, B— challenges him to a duel, which takes place by the house of an eccentric, wealthy widow. When Mrs L— hears that B— has been seriously wounded, she collapses and dies. B—, however, is nursed back to health by the wealthy widow, who aids his recovery and reconciles her own loss in the manner of a Rousseau heroine, by 'mingling her tears with his' and sharing the 'melancholy luxury of mutual woe; of speaking, during whole hours to each other, of his lacerated friendship, & her widowed love.'[40] Eventually, the pair marry.

In contrast to the other anecdotes, Seward writes in the historical present tense and describes the events in a strangely abrupt narrative voice, using simple language and shortened sentences. This may give the story an energetic immediacy, but it also produces the effect of improvised narrative which points out the deviation from her customary flowing narrative:

> Our Friend receives a bullet in his side. The Servants at the Villa, alarmed by the report of the Pistols, run to the place of action, where the unfortunate B— lies bleeding on the ground. One of those Servants hastens back to inform his Lady. She desires the wounded Knight may be brought to her House. She summons the most celebrated Surgeons. His wound is thought dangerous during several days. She watches over him with a Sister's tenderness.

> Rumor of the duel, & its apprehended consequences, reaches the hapless Object of *real* commiseration. Terror, suspense, restraint, the impossibility of obtaining that hourly intelligence, which *such* a sad state of mind demands, bring on *fever – delirium – death*! She dies on the very day, that her Friend is pronounced out of danger.[41]

---

[39]   NLS, Sir Walter Scott MSS, 879, fol. 76 [n.d.].

[40]   NLS, Sir Walter Scott MSS, 879, fol. 77 [n.d.].

[41]   NLS, Sir Walter Scott MSS, 879, fol. 76 [n.d.].

In comparing this anecdote with the others, particularly the well-crafted ones concerning her sister's marriage and her own affair with Major John Wright, both of which confirm her literary skills, the discordant story of the duel appears to be an abandoned attempt to appropriate popular romantic modes.[42] If her strategy was to experiment with ideas for a novel in the guise of a letter, her lack of concise detail or analytical comment and her unusually laconic narrative suggest she did not develop her thoughts any further than a vague outline.

Seward briefly engages with the notion of marital possession in her depiction of the relationship between L— and his wife by implying that it is the husband's jealousy that instigates the duel. Her thoughts and reasoning on the morality of duelling are left hanging, although in later published correspondence she expressed strong opinions on the subject. In a letter to Thomas Percival, written in response to receiving a present of a selection of his publications, she identifies public acceptance of duelling as 'fashionable society caressing the murderer'.[43] She complains to Percival that he should have taken the opportunity in his tract to apportion blame to the surgeons who attend duels and the men who act as seconds, as they are the ones who allow the crime to be perpetrated. Although prohibited, duelling was widespread among the upper classes. A man was prepared to defend the reliability of his word, or indeed any aspect of his own honour, with his life if necessary. Authors such as Richard Steele and Samuel Richardson drew on the theme to express their own views. Steele's outlook on duelling in his strictures and essays in the *Spectator* infiltrates his comedy, *The Conscious Lovers*, through his sensitive character Bevil Junior. Bevil Junior 'traps determined courage into reason' by refusing to fight a duel with Myrtle.[44] His conciliatory reasoning leads Myrtle towards a reversal of his principles of masculinity: 'your friendly conduct has convinced me that there is nothing manly but what is conducted by reason and agreeable to the practice of virtue and justice.'[45]

Like Steele, Richardson takes a literary stance on the morality of duelling. Clarissa's posthumous letter to her cousin, William Morden, is an expression against premeditated violence as she requests his restraint after her death, appealing not only to his morality, but also to his sense of justice and his legal duty:

---

[42]   The plot of the duel anecdote follows the distinguishable features of the romance quest-myth which have been delineated in Northrop Frye's theory of the romance genre: the conflict, the death, the disappearance of the hero and, finally, the reappearance and recognition of the hero. Northrop Frye, 'The Mythos of Summer: Romance', reprinted from Northrop Frye, *Anatomy of Criticism: Four Essays* (Princeton: Princeton University Press, 1957), in *Modern Genre Theories*, ed. by David Duff (Harlow: Pearson Education, 2000).

[43]   Seward, 'Letter to Dr Percival of Manchester' (29 June 1803), *Letters*, vol. VI, p. 90.

[44]   Richard Steele, 'Epilogue', *The Conscious Lovers*, in *Restoration and Eighteenth Century Comedy*, ed. by Scott McMillin, 2nd edn (New York: Norton, 1997).

[45]   *The Conscious Lovers*, 4, vol. I, p. 364.

Remember, my dear cousin, that vengeance is God's province; and he has undertaken to repay it; nor will you, I hope, invade that province [...] Duelling, sir, I need not tell *you* who have adorned a public character, is not only a usurpation of the Divine prerogative, but it is an insult upon magistracy and good government.[46]

Seward, who would have been familiar with Steele's and Richardson's views, shows no interest in developing her own thoughts through this medium, finishing the letter abruptly without her customary closing words and with her signature scored through. As she offers no analysis other than that she thought B— deserved a better fate than marriage with an eccentric widow, the clipped narrative does not sit comfortably with the other anecdotes and has all the appearance of a literary synopsis that has been dropped into the collection as an afterthought. The story of the duel is conspicuous as the singular unsatisfactory, if enthusiastic, shift in the series of juvenile letters. Seward's experimentation with romantic storytelling is brushed aside as she returns to her customary self-reflective preoccupations in the subsequent anecdotes, and Scott, unsurprisingly, had reservations about publishing it. While anecdotes such as this remain unexplored in our assessment of Seward's work, misrepresentations can alter our perception of her. The published juvenilia omit her energetic, if sometimes immature, writings, but these provide evidence of her vivid imagination.

The complexity of courtship and marriage negotiations is expressed through anecdotes about Seward's friends and her sister in far more detail than in the story of the duel. Aside from the 'public walk', the winter season of balls and assemblies offered the ultimate, glamorous meeting place for young and old alike. Separate rooms were set aside for card parties and refreshments, with the main assembly room turned over to the orchestra and the dance. The evening began with minuets, which, although intricate and requiring concentration, allowed for conversation and even prolonged flirting. These were followed by country dances. Complex formalities accompanied the dancing, particularly the country dances where the men and women were ranged in rows opposite each other. As in life, the wealthy upper classes took precedence in these rows of dancers.

Among the strict codes of behaviour, there was a more intimate etiquette to negotiate. Seward uses her anecdotes to express how young women and, frequently, young men were manipulated towards unwanted courtship and marriage by financially motivated families. She writes vividly, for example, of her friend Nannette's abortive courtship by Mr N—. Framing her story with a clear disdain for the pursuit of wealth, for 'grown children pursuing their *gewgaws*',[47] and for vanity, she tells Emma how N— arrived at a ball one evening, suddenly and dramatically transformed from the gauche boy of their acquaintance into a confident, fashionable youth. Primed by his family to ignore Nannette and pursue a wealthy heiress, he had been 'dress'd with birth-night finery', wearing a blue

---

46   *Clarissa*, p. 1444.
47   NLS, Sir Walter Scott MSS, 879, fol. 16 (January 1763).

silk coat trimmed with silver braiding, a solitaire and an impressive bag-wig.[48]
With N—'s coming of age came a sense of duty to his parents and the fear of
disinheritance. As in the case of Seward's character Eugenio from *Louisa*, a
father's demands took precedence over a son's wishes, and the family prosperity
dominated his marital options. But N— gained nothing from his new clothes
and new confidence as he was rebuffed by the heiress and later by the infuriated
Nannette.

Seward briefly addresses the reversal of gender stereotypes in the relationship
between husband and wife when she relates a further disturbing account of parental
control over a son's choice of marriage partner. There is the handsome Mr H—,
who complains that his parents forced him at nineteen to marry 'a rich and ugly
old Virgin', a bullying woman who had lived at his house since his childhood. She
was cruel to him, beating him regularly until she realised she had become sexually
attracted to him.[49] He considered himself to be quite fortunate, he joked, as his wife
had asthma and was unable to visit polluted London with him for the three month
'season' each year. This left him free to revert to an untroubled, irresponsible
bachelor existence. Not all young men were able to adapt to such situations and
turn them to their own advantage, as disappointed young N— discovered when his
courtships of both Nannette and the heiress failed. The account of the anecdote left
Seward feeling disgusted; 'right glad was I when the hour of retiring came, & right
glad I now am to quit the subject', she told Emma.[50]

As the anecdotes progress, Seward builds on the notion of parental and
societal manipulation to express her own views of the marriage market. What
is ostensibly the story of Sarah Seward's arranged marriage, her sudden illness
and her death also functions as a strong critique of the conventions of marriage.
The story is told in great detail and is, in part, published with the letter extracts in
the poetry volumes. As these are the most eloquent and poignant passages of the
juvenile correspondence, it is not surprising that Scott chose to publish some of the
descriptive narrative. It is also predictable that he disregarded Seward's forthright
appraisal of the state of matrimony and her clear hostility towards her future
brother-in-law's instinct for control. The censored sections reveal her attempts to
analyse her own feelings on marriage, 'spinsterhood' and the problematic notion
of becoming an 'old maid', when faced with the prospect of the unalterable,
claustrophobic nature of her sister's loveless partnership.

Seward approaches this subject through an anecdote with a central theme of
the objectification of women. She describes how fifteen-year-old Sarah attracted
the attention of a neighbour, referred to as Mr B—, who was a collector of fine
painting and sculpture. Although he was initially 'tender, and animated' towards
Sarah, he did not offer marriage, as he had been persuaded by his family to believe
that an impediment in his estate made it necessary for him to marry into wealth.

---

[48]   NLS, Sir Walter Scott MSS, 879, fol. 16 (January 1763).
[49]   NLS, Sir Walter Scott MSS, 879, fol. 72 (February 1765).
[50]   NLS, Sir Walter Scott MSS, 879, fol. 22 (January 1763).

Sarah's distress at this information was aggravated by the news that B— had suddenly married a young woman who was not particularly wealthy or intelligent. Seward explains to Emma that B— was obsessed by a replica of the famous statue of the Venus de' Medici which he had inherited from his brother. Considered to be the standard for female beauty, the statue came to represent his paradigm of perfect womanhood. Once it was in his possession he no longer considered the slender Sarah to be suitable wife material.

Seward becomes the narrator of a dark fable of marital subordination and possession as she repeats a story she has heard from a friend. B— was not at all in love with his wife, but he married her because of her exact likeness to his epitome of womanly perfection, the Venus. It was at a dinner party attended by a large company of guests that B— was struck by the woman's resemblance to his sculpture, and, in full view of the company, he put her through the humiliating ordeal of physically comparing her with the Venus in order to appraise her as a wife: 'he persuaded her to suffer her waist, throat, and ancles, to be measured, with those of the Venus; & that the proportions of each, allowing for the superior *height* of the Lady, proved exactly the same.'[51] After the party, Seward writes, he obtained his '*breathing* Statue'. Once Sarah had recovered from her disappointment, Seward teased her about the slender limbs that had lost her a suitor. Yet, the notion of the breathing statue juxtaposed with the image of the perfect and silent woman who is no more than a possession darkly suggests the marital subordination and control which provoked so much anxiety in Seward.

As the story of the Venus is repeated from gossip, it appears independent of the narrator which, in turn, makes her own reflections on independence all the more intense. She describes how Sarah asked her parents to help find her a husband, believing that her own judgement in men was flawed. At the same time, Lucy Porter, who was a distant relative of the Sewards, was looking for a suitable wife for her brother, Joseph, a forty-year-old bachelor with a forty thousand pound fortune, who lived in Italy.[52] Sarah's lack of self-determination is clear in her unreserved compliance with the match-making process. Likewise, Joseph's absolute faith in his sister's choice of wife and his agreement to marry Sarah 'blindfold' gives him an initial appearance of vulnerability. Seward contrasts her own independent spirit, her 'warm, poetic imagination', with her sister's 'smiling gravity' as she points out that although it was customary in such arrangements to approach the elder sister first, Lucy Porter passed her over because of her intellect and her perceived lack of household skills.[53] The docile, domesticated Sarah appeared to be a more attractive proposition for this middle-aged merchant.

---

[51]   NLS, Sir Walter Scott MSS, 879, fol. 36 (June 1763).

[52]   John Hunter (1674–1741), Seward's grandfather, married Lucy Porter (1690–1768) on the death of his first wife, Anne Norton, who was Seward's grandmother. The Lucy Porter (1715–1786) mentioned here by Seward was Hunter and Porter's granddaughter.

[53]   NLS, Sir Walter Scott MSS, 879, fols 32–33 (June 1763).

Despite the negative connotations attached to the position of the unmarried elder sister, Seward claimed to be grateful for once for her lack of interest in household skills and 'inferiority in many of the female graces'.[54] This condition precluded her from the selection process, thus avoiding the embarrassment of an outright refusal of the proposal. Horrified at the concept of being trapped in a loveless relationship, especially with an older man, she was even more sickened that her little sister should give serious consideration to the proposal for no more compelling reasons than a comfortable life and the notion of parental duty: 'That this dear Creature shou'd think forty thousand p^{ds} a price worth a moment's deliberation, for her *virgin liberty*!' Although Sarah lived in material comfort and expected a three thousand pound inheritance on her parents' deaths, she would not be persuaded against the marriage, even accepting that she would make an obedient wife ('I believe I can perform my duty'), on condition that she did not find Porter physically repulsive.[55]

At this stage, Seward begins an unemotional evaluation of her personal outlook on marriage. She juxtaposes her resolute thoughts on independence with Sarah's desire to exchange parental control for marital submission. Prompted by her sister's experience, she concludes that marriage should not be the inevitable consequence for herself, or for other young women in similar comfortable circumstances, if a sense of self-determination could overcome a sense of duty. It was only love, she believed, that could possibly compensate for the 'train of cares, pains, anxieties, & submissions' that frequently shadowed marriage.[56] Using the concept of physical health, Seward contrasts Sarah's gentle conformity with her own robust determination to control her life. Early in the anecdote, morbid imagery in her terminology, with matrimony described as 'the *grave* of Love',[57] Sarah depicted as 'angelic', and Porter as the ageing 'time-worn Pilot' on 'dangerous Seas',[58] suggests an impending tragic ending. Later, Seward is more explicit, taking up the same theme to insinuate Sarah's fragility with the words 'This dear child will not live',[59] which contrast sharply with her own 'lively spirits'.[60]

Seward was aware that a resilient mentality was necessary when choosing independence above marriage. The average age for a first marriage in the eighteenth century was twenty-six, and though many women were satisfied to remain unmarried, there were negative connotations attached to the notion of the 'old maid'. Seward found a measure of self-justification in her unorthodox opinions by reporting Emma's concurrence with them. 'How I love you for saying you admire the motives by which [Sarah] is induced to incline to this proposal',

---

[54] NLS, Sir Walter Scott MSS, 879, fol. 33 (June 1763).

[55] NLS, Sir Walter Scott MSS, 879, fol. 38 (June 1763).

[56] NLS, Sir Walter Scott MSS, 879, fol. 34 (June 1763).

[57] NLS, Sir Walter Scott MSS, 879, fol. 37 (June 1763).

[58] NLS, Sir Walter Scott MSS, 879, fol. 38 (June 1763).

[59] Seward, 'Literary Correspondence', *Poetical Works*, vol. I, p. cxvii.

[60] NLS, Sir Walter Scott MSS, 879, fol. 33 (June 1763).

she writes, 'yet tremble for her happiness shou'd she accept it!'.[61] The principle of 'Independance' emerges several times in the letters of this period, with implications of financial subsistence, celibacy and self-determination. Without a substantial 'hereditary Independance', the notion of choice could be nonexistent and most young women's dreams of marrying solely for love could prove to be impossible to realise. The same independence forms a 'steady anchor, on which to lean in the Harbor of Celibacy shou'd the Bark of Love be blown back by the Storms of Disappointment'.[62]

Where women either chose or were forced by circumstance to remain unmarried without the 'anchor' of financial security or the possibility of employment, their dependency was less a form of resistance to marriage and motherhood than a perceived aberration that placed them in a purposeless existence, as a 'spinster' on the margins of the community. Like many women, Seward's friend Anne Mompesson preferred to use the married title to avoid the negative connotations of her single state. Seward deliberated on the evils of either condition, the irrevocable nature of a loveless marriage and the dependency of spinsterhood, writing:

> I told [Sarah] she was an angelic Creature, adding 'I hope thou wilt be able to *love* thy prim Batchelor in sober, Matron-like fashion. It will, I conclude, be his *inevitable* Misfortune not to inspire thee with *passion*, but, the irrevocable ceremony passed, it will be his *fault* if he does not gain thy *affection*.'

> Yet O! Dearest Emma, that word '*irrevocable*'! –Well! However plentiful the *numbers*, I wonder there are not yet *more* old Maids, ambling, & bridling over the dim, unvaried plains of Celibacy.[63]

Unsurprisingly, Sarah Seward chose not to follow the route of the 'old maid'. As she doubted her ability to find happiness in any other way than a conventional marriage, her preference was for life with an older stranger. It was some consolation to Anna that she was to accompany her sister to Italy, where Porter intended to spend alternate years. Given the impending changes to her life with Sarah's absence, the marriage would at least facilitate her own ambitions to travel to Europe without having to the pay the price of losing her independence. Seward presents Sarah as potentially disabled by marriage, trapped and helpless by her husband's authority. 'My wings [...] will not be cropt', she wrote to Emma, 'I can fly back again when I please. But Sarah, my dear Sarah! she must be borne back by permission, and in a cage! a golden one, 'tis true, but still a cage'.[64] Despite her first impulse to mock the figure of prematurely-aged Porter, she gives a vignette which leaves no doubt about her view of the cruel inequalities of the intended relationship. She compares the image of the short, stooped merchant, whose only merits are

[61]   NLS, Sir Walter Scott MSS, 879, fol. 41 (August 1763).
[62]   NLS, Sir Walter Scott MSS, 879, fols 34–35 (June 1763).
[63]   NLS, Sir Walter Scott MSS, 879, fol. 38 (June 1763).
[64]   Seward, 'Literary Correspondence', *Poetical Works*, vol. I, pp. cxxiii–cxxiv.

good teeth and general cleanliness, with ethereal, intelligent and sensitive little Sarah, whose mortal fragility is at risk from the 'harshness of authority, and the impenetrability of selfishness'[65] of the physical world. Seward was convinced that her dear little 'Sally' would not survive the physicality of marriage. Her allusion to sexual relations, with an equivocal use of the word 'consummate', emphasises Sarah's innocence and her vulnerability, 'This child seems angel before she is woman; how consummate shall she be if she should be woman before she is actually angel!'.[66]

Sarah overlooked Porter's disagreeable personality traits, writing to Polly Adey at the end of May 1764, explaining her feelings for her fiancé with an uncanny premonition of catastrophe:

> You, who have a Heart capable of rejoicing with transport at the Felicity of your Friends, will I am sure feel a most lovely pleasure in the completion of an Event which promises so much happiness to all our Family: for my own part I am almost asham'd to own even to Polly Adey, how entirely Mr Porter has possession of my Heart, I blush to think how quick a progress He has made in so short a period yet the tenderness & affection He has express'd for me, His desire of doing every thing that can be conducive to mine, & my Relatives happiness, & the fair Character He bears will surely justify the soft confession. I cannot but reflect with amazement on the wonderful alteration of my Sentiments! I, who used to expatiate on the pleasures of Celibacy, who almost abjur'd Matrimony, am about to precipitate myself into Hymeneal Chains, I have all the reason to believe they will prove the soft the Silken Bands of Love, yet I have still many apprehensions, I fear something will happen to cast a gloom over these so promisingly happy Prospects, for experience daily evinces this sad truth.[67]

Sarah died of typhus shortly after writing her letter to Polly. To alleviate some of the pain of her loss Seward took comfort in sentimental recollections of the past, yet, apart from anguished outpourings in her letters to Emma, she found it difficult to establish a source of comfort in her immediate surroundings. Elizabeth Seward showed little emotion at first as she kept herself busy with the funeral arrangements, but then she suffered a nervous collapse. She kept Honora with her and sent Anna to stay with relatives in Nottinghamshire and from there to the Rectory at Eyam. Her father provided no emotional support at all. In common with most of the older men of Seward's acquaintance, Thomas Seward would not indulge in the sentimental reminiscence that she needed. She found this to be an unnatural trait. The devastating effects of the death of a close relative were not, for her, reducible to a concept of masculine or gentlemanly constraint. When writing her memoirs of Erasmus Darwin, she commented forcefully on the physician's moral insensibility

---

[65] Seward, 'Literary Correspondence', *Poetical Works*, vol. I, p. cxvii.

[66] Seward, 'Literary Correspondence', *Poetical Works*, vol. I, p. cxvii.

[67] Lichfield RO, Seward Family MSS, D262/1/2, Sarah Seward, 'Letter to Polly Adey' (29 May 1764).

when he displayed no emotion on the suicide of his least favourite son, also called Erasmus, in 1799.

Darwin's self-discipline habitually suppressed any outward show of emotion, and he tended to criticise conspicuous grief. Both Boswell and Johnson agreed that it was the female prerogative to grieve. In a discussion about the sudden death of Harry Thrale, who was Henry and Hester Thrale's only son, Boswell remarked that Hester had so much to think about, she would soon forget it. 'No, Sir,' replied Johnson, 'Thrale will forget it first. *She* has many things that she *may* think of. *He* has many things that he *must* think of.' Boswell concluded that this is what kept men from brooding over grief, the contrast between 'the different effect of those light pursuits which occupy a vacant and easy mind, and those serious engagements which arrest attention'.[68] The male tendency to repress feelings supported Seward's determination to remain single, as she feared that a husband would insist she suppress her own emotional range. Her comments about the harmful effects of absorbing an excess of sensibility from Rousseau's *Julie*, together with the sound guidance that she offered to her friends, confirm that she found a symmetry between reason and the spontaneity of sentimentalism in both writing and life.

Aside from the letters to Emma, Seward was able to locate two other sources of consolation at this time, the first in the form of her poem 'The Visions',[69] which expresses the organic energy for renewal in the physical environment as a source of solace. The second was in the figure of an old friend from Eyam, Major John Wright, whose comforting presence recalled the nurturing landscape of her childhood home. 'The Visions', which was published as the juvenile poem that opens Scott's edition of her poetry, was written on the terrace walk of the Palace garden a few days after Sarah's death. The poem features the dialogue between the poet-narrator, who defines herself as the mourning visionary, and two apparitions. The first rises from the grave to evoke Despair, and the second, the more compassionate Patience, emerges from the night woods to lead the mourner towards a healing spiritual interaction with nature.

The poem opens with the narrator reminiscing about her dead sister, whom she calls 'Alinda', as she walks through her familiar 'smiling' landscape, finding comfort in the innocent, soothing sounds of the natural world and the refreshing sight of the trees, fields and streams illuminated by the evening sun. The fragile relationship between the physical environment and the notion of solace is destroyed by a sudden change in the weather, which alters the mood from guarded optimism to cold, deep gloom as beauty's transience is accentuated. A shadowy spectre, Despair, appears from the ground to reveal to the narrator a future life of prolonged grief. Despair rejects the notion of the immortality of the soul: 'Where is she now? [...] within the narrow cell.'[70] Rejecting the healing power of nature,

68	Boswell, *Life of Johnson*, vol. II, pp. 468–69.
69	Seward, 'The Visions, An Elegy', *Poetical Works*, vol. I, pp. 1–9.
70	Seward, 'The Visions', vol. I, pp. 4, 57.

she attempts to establish the premise that rural innocence is illusory, as all matter must deteriorate and die:

'See'st thou this rose? Its gay, its crimson glow
'Faded and gone, and all its fragrance fled!
'This sullied lily, once with breast of snow,
'Was the chaste glory of its verdant bed.[71]

The tone of the poem lightens as night falls, the winds drop and the stars slowly emerge. Here the imagery shifts and changes with an optimistic comparison of the transient splendour of nature with life. A compassionate vision, Patience, appears and promises that after the night 'lenient' Time will lead Cheerfulness, the 'fair child of day', to 'chace each dark and deadly shade'.[72] She reminds the narrator that the natural world has the divine power to restore its own vitality through the cyclic continuation of the seasons, yet the bitter but healing winter must first be endured before Spring's celebration of nature's renewed life force:

'Medicinal, tho' sharp, the blended woe, –
'Thou, who hast been most happy, bow resign'd!
'For man no more unfading roses blow,
'Winter lays waste his year, and grief his mind.

'But Heav'n, that sends abroad the breath of Spring
'T'expand the foliage, and disclose the flowers,
'Shall to the sorrowing mind sweet comforts bring,
'And warmly renovate its fainting powers.[73]

Turning from the natural scene, the narrator's thoughts move to the immediate necessity of coping with her parents' grief. In as much as Patience guides the narrator towards thoughts of returning to an innocent state of nature, it is the self-generated awareness of her parents' anguish that emerges and opens up the way towards her own healing process. She acknowledges that her own presence cannot atone for 'Alinda's' absence:

O! she was all parental Hopes desire,
To gild declining life with softest light;
Ill can my frailer mind's impetuous fire,
Compensate her mild soul's eternal flight.[74]

The narrator undertakes to find within herself a compensatory love to 'shed some bless'd relief' on their old age and to encourage the same in their foster daughter,

---

[71]   Seward, 'The Visions', vol. I, pp. 3, 41–44.
[72]   Seward, 'The Visions', vol. I, pp. 6–7, 106, 107, 110.
[73]   Seward, 'The Visions', vol. I, pp. 6, 92–100.
[74]   Seward, 'The Visions', vol. I, pp. 8, 141–44.

the 'transplanted flower', Honora.[75] In response to her renewed sense of hope and revival, the narrator addresses Honora, moving into a celebration of the child's warmth, intuition, empathy and particularly her youthful resilience, which she likens to the life force of the returning Spring:

> Thy tender accents, on my grief-chill'd soul
> Fall, like the vernal breath on wintry bowers,
> When, from the fleecy clouds, that lightly roll,
> Silent and mild descend the sunny showers.[76]

Through the poem, Seward acknowledged that she was not the ideal daughter. Her 'impetuous fire' was no counterpart for her domesticated sister's 'softest light'.[77] If Sarah's role was to care for her parents in their old age whether or not she was married to Porter, Seward was prepared to substitute herself and carry that particular burden. This was the immediate, poetic response to life's misfortunes. In reality, her frequent and violent conflicts with her parents brought more disunity than compensation. There were also problems in locating Honora as her own sister substitute: 'Thy love, my dear Honora, shall revive / The joys that faded o'er Alinda's urn.'[78] She created for herself a dependency that was to be shattered when Honora married Richard Lovell Edgeworth in 1773 and moved to his estate in Ireland.

Unexplored areas of Seward's life include her brief relationships with Major John Wright and Captain Temple, both of which are recorded in her juvenilia but subsequently removed by Scott. The engaging narratives give information about her unsatisfied desire for romance with an 'interesting Cara Sposa'.[79] The episodes are not exactly in line with Seward's ideal literature or with the affairs of her favourite great lovers in literary history, such as Abelard and Eloïsa, and Henry and Emma. Although she situates herself as the object of unrequited love at the mercy of her father's decisions, in both cases she is ultimately thankful for his disapproval and intervention, as the relationships do not fulfill the 'daydreams' and 'tender hopes' that she writes of in her first letter to Emma.[80] As Seward progresses through the anecdotes about her two prospective lovers, the duality of her nature, which she chose to express through landscape, resurfaces in her representations. The solid, comforting presence of Wright unites with the Eyam landscape, while the more elusive Temple flits between the cities of Lichfield and London.

The anecdotes about Wright are written with clarity over the course of three letters to Emma. Soon after her sister's death, Anna had travelled to Eyam with her father. His parish of St. Lawrence was left in the charge of his curate, Peter

---

75   Seward, 'The Visions', vol. I, pp. 9, 151.

76   Seward, 'The Visions', vol. I, pp. 9, 161–64.

77   Seward, 'The Visions', vol. I, pp. 8, 41, 42.

78   Seward, 'The Visions', vol. I, pp. 9, 167–68.

79   NLS, Sir Walter Scott MSS, 879, fol. 66 (August 1764).

80   NLS, Sir Walter Scott MSS, 879, fol. 3 (October 1762).

Cunningham, and Thomas visited for two months each summer, occasionally accompanied by Seward, who enjoyed the familiar magnificent countryside and meeting up with her old friends, such as Anne Mompesson, Anna Rogers Stokes from nearby Dronfield, and the poet William Newton, the 'Peak Minstrel'. She wrote to Emma that she anticipated mixed feelings on this particular return to her birthplace: the consoling 'mournful sweetness' of homecoming and the despair of loss.[81] It was here that Seward was reunited with a long-standing family friend, a retired army officer and respected justice of the peace, Major John Wright. She indicated to Emma that Wright fell deeply in love with her quite early in her stay and that she was flattered by the attention of a sophisticated older man. The series of anecdotes that gives an account of the situation as it developed is intricately detailed, yet a number of the historical facts Seward provides are not consistent with the recorded history of the Wright family. The anecdotes are a sustained account of Seward's continuing self-construction as an independent young woman, with the factual errors and exaggerations transforming them into romance narratives. As they follow directly from the story of Sarah and deliberations on the state of marriage, there is an element of self-analysis which brings Seward's life choices clearly into view.

As the second son of the 'esquire' of the village, who was also called John Wright, Major John Wright was born in 1724 and had eight siblings. Together with his widowed sister, Elizabeth Trafford, he was responsible for the estate management, or 'housekeeping', of his ancestral home, the imposing grey stone Eyam Hall. Seward wrote to Emma that because of his father's extravagances and his large family, his patrimonial property was depleted and he derived his income mostly from the cash he had raised from the sale of his army commissions. His only hope of prosperity, she claimed, was as the heir presumptive to an elderly man, his father's cousin Colonel William Wright, who, in turn, waited for the inheritance of the nearby Great Longstone Hall estate and a thousand pound annuity from a thirteen-year-old boy, Thomas Wright, who was 'weak, deformed and consumptive' and was not expected to live.[82]

Seward's justification for Wright's lack of money, and therefore his unsuitability as a marriage partner, is vague. She reiterates the theme of financial dependence on the impulse of relatives, giving the improbable explanation that he did not inherit the Longstone estate because the old Colonel considered him to be insufficiently 'servile' and consequently left the full legacy to Wright's younger brother.[83] The Wright family records, however, show that both the Eyam and Longstone estates were highly profitable and that Major Wright's father inherited them in 1761. If John Wright inherited nothing, it was for the sole reason that his father outlived him and, accordingly, he had no claim to the family fortune. His prospects, however, were excellent. Scott decided to remove the story of Wright's courtship from the

[81] Seward, 'Literary Correspondence', *Poetical Works*, vol. I, p. cxxxv.
[82] NLS, Sir Walter Scott MSS, 879, fols 55–59 (August 1764).
[83] NLS, Sir Walter Scott MSS, 879, fol. 58 (August 1764).

published version of the letters, as Seward makes reference to Joseph Porter's insidious attempts to 'controll' her now that he no longer had Sarah.[84] Also, as Wright's prominent status in Derbyshire society would have made him easily identifiable, the publication of the account was potentially troublesome for Scott, as the family might have objected to Seward's disclosure of the more sensitive side of her suitor's nature. Seward had anticipated Scott's actions and had crossed through all references to 'Major Wright', replacing them with the still identifiable Major W—.[85]

Though he had not seen Seward since her birth, Wright had met Sarah when she visited Eyam in 1762, and he was now able to offer sympathy to Seward and comfort her by encouraging the sentimental reminiscences she craved. Seward wrote that Wright had last seen her when he was a young soldier of twenty and had cradled her as a baby in his arms at the Rectory.[86] Now a stout forty-year-old bachelor, he became infatuated with her, but she held him off as she did not reciprocate his feelings. In most respects, they had little in common. He was an essential part of the Derbyshire countryside, his family seat being one of the oldest in the area, and he had a dependable, protective presence, which Seward describes variously as 'majestic', 'brave' and 'military'.[87] Wright was not a man of letters, however, and neither was he a patron of the arts; as a soldier, he 'read Men', not books.[88] He loved fox hunting, which Seward despised, and she thought he drank too much wine. Yet she was flattered by 'her Major's' obsessive attention, consoled by his compassion. Clearly she did not disapprove of his interest in her, but she intended to retain control of the situation, and her strategy was to encourage a

---

[84] NLS, Sir Walter Scott MSS, 879, fol. 58 (August 1764).

[85] Seward states that John Wright received his ensign at sixteen and acted as aide-de-camp to General Howard. The Wright family history shows that at fifteen he was ensign in Henry Ponsonby's Regiment of Foot. In 1742 he was a first lieutenant and by 1751 he was adjutant to Colonel Lord Louden, eventually becoming captain and major. In 1760 he was serving as an aide-de-camp, possibly to General Howard, in the Seven Years' War in Germany. He then became aide-de-camp to General Burgoyne, a commander of the British forces in the American War of Independence (information from Nicola Wright of Eyam Hall, December 2004). As the summer visit that Seward describes was in 1764, and she states that John Wright was retired from the army, there is a discrepancy with the dates, as the War of Independence took place from 1776 to 1783. Seward explained to Emma that Wright had received his commission as ensign from the Duke of Devonshire at nearby Chatsworth House at the young age of sixteen. After a series of military engagements, his bravery was rewarded with a promotion to major. There is an inconsistency in the dates Seward gives, which indicates that her account was not written at the specified time but was included later when dates and details were half-remembered or were deliberately changed to suit the dramatic effect of the anecdote. NLS, Sir Walter Scott MSS, 879, fols 55–59 (August 1764).

[86] NLS, Sir Walter Scott MSS, 879, fol. 63 (n.d.).

[87] NLS, Sir Walter Scott MSS, 879, fols 60, 62 (August 1764).

[88] NLS, Sir Walter Scott MSS, 879, fol. 55 (August 1764).

close, platonic friendship. This was inevitably hopeless, as the ex-soldier was not by any means a man of sensibility.

The following words, in which Seward evaluates Wright against Joseph Porter, describe her attempts to avert his attention from her. She was clearly attracted to the concept of idealistic romantic love more than the reality of a physical relationship:

> Major W— is nearly Mr Porter's age – but O! the difference! Time has scarcely injured his fine Person, his manners are easy, and graceful. He delights to remind me often of our *only* interview, previous to this fortnight's acquaintance in the first three hours of my Life [when he held her in his arms] – & he said, last Night, as we were riding home, by moonlight, from a visit at a couple of miles distance, 'Ah! If I cou'd hope that dear little circumstance was a presage'! – He paused; – & I immediately observed to him the fine effects, produced by the pale light of the moon-beams, playing partially on the Rocks, and contrasting their dark and massy shades.[89]

By deflecting Wright's advances with a hasty demonstration of her intellect and her poetic sensibility, she moves the conversation away from her bodily presence and towards the concerns of her mind, taking emotional pleasure in the romantic effects of moonbeams on the landscape.

She returns later to the same theme of light illuminating the landscape with a symbolic description of the early morning sun as she leaves Eyam on her return journey to Lichfield. This time, she is the source of light to Wright's landscape as she realises that his grief on her departure is far greater than her own. 'It is gratifying to perceive that we have the power of diffusing beauty and the soft spirit of pleasure over every surrounding object', she writes, continuing with an elaborate depiction of the morning scene where the early sun's 'lustres illumined the dewy Mountains' and the rocks 'seemed on fire'.[90] This use of symbolism strengthens the self-image of her spiritual nature against Wright's solid physicality.

The affair came to an abrupt end when Porter jealously reported Wright's behaviour to Seward's father, who intercepted his secret love letters and threatened to disinherit her in favour of a nephew if they persisted with the relationship. Wright conceded defeat. Seward was clearly drawn to men who were unsuitable as prospective husbands, as they tended to be either impoverished or already married, indicating that she needed a spiritual relationship of the kind she would achieve later with John Saville. Quite early in the Wright anecdotes, she confirms that she was confused about physical love, stating, 'I have not seen the man with whom I did not prefer the idea of a *distant*, to that of a *near* Union'.[91] Her need to control led her to test her lovers' endurance in the face of parental opposition. If, like Wright, they were not passionate about her, or, like Temple, unable to persevere

---

[89] NLS, Sir Walter Scott MSS, 879, fol. 53 (July 1764).

[90] NLS, Sir Walter Scott MSS, 879, fol. 57 (August 1764).

[91] NLS, Sir Walter Scott MSS, 879, fol. 59 (July 1764).

and overcome obstacles, she lost interest in them altogether. To gain her respect, a man had to meet her own standard of defiance. Saville met this criterion, matching her own disregard for reputation, family pressure and general disapproval. What Seward does not mention during the course of the Wright anecdotes is the fact that Major John Wright had an illegitimate son, John Mower, whom he openly acknowledged and supported. This made him an eminently inappropriate choice for a husband, and certainly the image did not fit with her self-construction, which is why she altered Wright's financial situation to suit her own purposes.

Before the Wright episode took place, Seward writes of her intermittent affair with the 'grave and pensive' young soldier, Captain (later Colonel) Temple, who was stationed for a time in Lichfield before moving to London.[92] For reasons unknown, Temple has come down through history as 'Taylor', and this causes confusion in previous accounts of Seward's life.[93] Disclosing her intimate feelings to Emma, Seward talks of her 'scarlet fever', a reference to the red uniform of the soldier. 'An epaulet on the shoulder, & a black ribbon in the hat, have not yet lost all their power over your Friend', she wrote.[94] Drawn to his story of unrequited love for a young woman above his own class, Seward found herself sympathising with his lost cause until, that is, he whispered to her, 'The object alter'd, the desire the same'.[95]

Without declaring his love openly or asking Seward to write to him, Temple left town with his regiment. Over two years later, following Sarah's death and the brief romantic interlude with Major John Wright, Seward wrote to Emma that she had met Temple by chance in London. The sudden reunion revived their love. Seward coaxed him into revealing his affection for her, and the pair became engaged. She wrote to Emma that she had found the perfect companion, 'the Lover, the indulgent husband, the animated Sharer of my intellectual pleasures'.[96] However, she offers the most meagre of information in the juvenile letters, as once more, apparently, Thomas Seward was not impressed by Temple's financial situation, and he refused to give his permission for the marriage. Temple disappeared without making any attempts at a challenge, which led Seward to believe that his love was not enduring. Many years later, in her published letter books, she gives a little more information about this relationship in a short series of letters to Colonel Temple's wife, who

---

[92]   NLS, Sir Walter Scott MSS, 879, fols 3, 4–6, 10–11.

[93]   E. V. Lucas's biography, *A Swan and her Friends* (1907), and Hesketh Pearson's biography, *The Swan of Lichfield* (1936), both have Temple as 'Colonel Taylor'. Margaret Ashmun's *The Singing Swan* (1931) has the tentative 'Mr T. (Taylor?)'. In the juvenile letters, Seward refers to him as 'Captain T—' and in her later published correspondence as 'Colonel T—'. It is a letter to her cousin Harry White and, most particularly, her unguarded comments to a close friend, Mary Powys, that confirm his name as Temple, although, unfortunately, she does not give his forename (JBM, MS 38/25, Seward, 'Letter to Mary Powys' (n.d.)).

[94]   NLS, Sir Walter Scott MSS, 879, fol. 3 (October 1762).

[95]   NLS, Sir Walter Scott MSS, 879, fol. 3 (October 1762).

[96]   NLS, Sir Walter Scott MSS, 879, fol. 70 (February 1765).

was curious about the poet her husband held in such high regard. From the tone of the letters, it is obvious that Seward was uncomfortable corresponding with the woman. Her writing time was valuable, but Mrs Temple was persistent. Seward wrote to her cousin, Harry White, who was forwarding her correspondence while she was on holiday in Wales, 'I never received [the letter] which Mrs Temple complains of my not having answered. Surely another correspondence with a stranger is not to be added to my epistolary labours.'[97]

The letters to Mrs Temple outline not just Seward's relationship with Captain Temple, but also, most extraordinarily, her brief affair with the 'extremely lovely' Cornet Richard Vyse, which lasted a mere few weeks. If this affair, together with assorted marriage proposals, lacked sufficient importance to deserve reference in the juvenile letters, it took on a far greater significance when reported to Mrs Temple:

> I had proposals of marriage from several, whom my father wished me to approve, but such sort of overtures, not preceded by assiduous tenderness, and which expected to reap the harvest of love, without having nursed its germs, suited not my native enthusiasm, nor were calculated to inspire it. I had known what it was to love, to all the excess of the sentiment; and the sweetness and vivacity of the impression, though obliterated by ingratitude, was not forgotten.[98]

Why did Seward find it necessary to relay this intimate information to a stranger so many years after the events had taken place? It is significant that she was travelling through Wales at this time, tucked up comfortably against the cold November winds in her chaise, with an exhilarated Saville galloping alongside on his horse. They stayed in lodging houses and at the homes of relatives and friends as they explored the rugged coastline and mountains. Two days of their holiday were spent at the 'fairy palace' of Eleanor Butler and Sarah Ponsonby, the celebrated 'Ladies of Llangollen'. The Irish elopers were freely accepted in literary circles as either lesbian lovers or Sapphic friends, yet were maligned in the popular press for the very same reason. Because of her single status, Seward needed to deflect similar accusations against herself, and anecdotes about lovers confirmed her heterosexuality. Mrs Temple's correspondence provided the ideal timely vehicle for this.[99]

---

[97] Seward, 'Letter to the Revd. H. White' (30 August 1795), *Letters*, vol. IV, p. 97.

[98] Seward, 'Letter to Mrs T—' (2 March 1796), *Letters*, vol. IV, pp. 178–79.

[99] There is an interesting footnote to Seward's account of Mrs Temple's endeavours to engage in a correspondence with her. A letter to Mary Powys, which dates from the 1770s and was not intended for publication, gives a full, unvarnished account of the relationship with Temple and the subsequent events, including Mrs Temple's insidious confidence trickery. This letter describes how Temple was in financial difficulties due to his guardians' mismanagement of a £5,000 inheritance from his deceased parents. He and Seward were secretly engaged in 1764 following their meeting in London, but Thomas Seward intercepted their love letters and ended the affair. Temple disappeared to France for

In a comparison of the two different representations of Seward, the first in the Temple anecdotes and the second in the published correspondence, the significant change is in the personal information about Seward's way of thinking. In place of animated expressions of private thoughts and feelings, Scott published a small section of a letter to Emma about Temple's financial losses and Seward's apparent docile compliance with her father's wishes to end the relationship. In his 'Biographical Preface', he explains the reasons for his discretion, that the 'lessons which she taught her own heart [...] must be witheld from the public, lest, even at this distance of time, the incidents to which they relate might injure the feelings of any concerned in them'.[100] He makes the judgement that she was able to observe 'prudence, self-denial, and submission to parental authority' in her dealings with Temple.[101] This gives Seward the surface appearance of a submissive, dutiful daughter rather than the spirited and independent rebel of the original manuscripts.

Much of Seward's defiance grew out of resentment at being misunderstood, and this is revealed in her anecdote about Mary Hammond Cobb, known as 'Moll', a firm friend of Elizabeth Seward and a well-known figure around Lichfield. Outspoken and opinionated, Moll Cobb lived at the Friary with her husband and her niece, Polly Adey, who was Sarah Seward's best friend. In the juvenile

---

six years, returning in 1770 with 'renewed hope'. There was, again, an accidental meeting in St James's Park, which distressed Seward greatly, as she was reminded of the full force of 'parental opposition' to virtually all the plans she had ever made for herself. She instructed the female friend who accompanied her to meet privately with Temple and tell him that after he left for France in 1765, she had met someone else. Temple made his formal farewell and Seward never saw him again.

When Seward received the letters from Mrs Temple, she made some enquiries and found that Temple was working abroad and his wife had been, in his absence, the kept mistress of a disreputable 'libertine' named Franks. Shortly afterwards, the woman and one of her daughters suddenly barged into Seward's blue dressing room. They had little or no money and had found lodgings in Lichfield with Seward's old servant, Molly Clarke. Although Seward felt a little sympathy for this new, unwanted friend, her patience wore thin when it became obvious that she was attempting to inveigle her way into Seward's home and life with a form of emotional blackmail. Mrs Temple resorted to deceitful stories about her husband's continued obsessional admiration for his old love, complaining that this had compromised her own happiness over many years. Seward was not fooled, however. '[She believes] she might be able to acquire influence over my mind, and supplies from my property,' she told Mary Powys, 'together with a probability of establishing her self and her daughters in my family during Colonel Temple's long absences.' Unable to break down Seward's resistance to her claims, Mrs Temple left the area and, it was reported, constantly gossiped and spread rumours about her, even resorting to sending her poison pen letters signed 'Caliban'. Her eldest daughter also made trouble by publishing one of Seward's poems, coincidently an elegy addressed to Richard Vyse, and publishing it under her own name (Johnson BM, MS 38/25 [n.d.]).

[100]   Scott, 'Biographical Preface', *Poetical Works*, vol. I, p. viii.
[101]   Scott, 'Biographical Preface', vol. I, p. viii.

anecdotes, Moll is represented as the metaphorical mouthpiece of the Lichfield community, the sum of parochial prejudice who frequently expresses outraged sentiments against the notion of female intellect. Although not illiterate, Moll disliked poetry, and her reading was limited to novels, plays and, she claimed, Johnson's *Rambler*, although Seward doubted this because of the poetic imagery, metaphorical allusion and recourse to Latin and Greek.[102]

Moll's love of cards and gossip and her selfish nature irritated Seward, but she admitted to an admiration of her spontaneous, fearless wit that could defeat even the most intellectual of beings. Samuel Johnson denigrated this aspect of Moll's nature, asserting, 'How should Moll Cobb be a wit! Cobb has read nothing, Cobb knows nothing; and where nothing has been put into the brain, nothing can come out of it to any purpose of rational entertainment.'[103] If Samuel Johnson despised Moll Cobb's lack of intellect, Seward maintained that he loved her for her 'impudence', but mostly for the convenience of her chaise, the quality of her food and her flattering attention which made him a regular visitor to the Friary. Seward commanded respect from her immediate circle of friends and from Erasmus Darwin, the friend who encouraged her writing when her original enthusiast, her father, had decided that she was completely talentless and wanted to see her settled with a wealthy husband. Her literary prowess was a target of private hostility from her mother, who could see no purpose for it and did not recognise Seward's efforts to find a balance between the expression of her intellect and the accomplishment of domestic duty. Of course, it was impossible to unlearn what she had already absorbed or to revise her feelings of difference from her contemporaries. While she outwardly maintained the kind of inconspicuous literary pride that was advised by her father's muse of *The Female Right to Literature*, she secretly expressed confidence in her self-worth to Emma. She was eventually to move towards an open challenge to parental authority, but first came the demeaning prospect of Moll Cobb's daily tests.

Taking it upon herself to test Seward's knowledge at their every meeting, which was most days, Moll Cobb made the regular comment that Seward's intelligence was well below standard. This humiliating experience at the hands of a woman who was hardly literate, with far less intellectual capacity than her well-read victim, is expressed in an anecdote about the negative reactions to Seward's intellect. The anecdote symbolises Seward's uneasy relationship with her literary talents, which parallels a similarly troubled relationship with her mother. She wrote to Emma in February 1763, describing the extent of her humiliation. After remarking that very few of her friends and acquaintances outside her close circle suspected that her intelligence was in any way superior, she continues:

> Nay there is a Lady, a Mrs Cobb, considered, let me tell you, one of the Belle-Esprits of our City, who, from her intimacy with my Mother, from daily

---

[102] NLS, Sir Walter Scott MSS, 879, fols 26–27 (February 1763).

[103] Seward, 'Letter to Mrs Hayley' (2 October 1793), *Letters*, vol. III, pp. 330–31.

opportunities of sounding my abilities [...] pronounces my Understanding rather
below than *above* the common standard. You know how I am allow'd to have
ingenuity in my needle-works; that I invented upon catgut [a type of gauze used
in embroidery], a nearer imitation of fine point lace than has yet been seen.

Lately, in a crouded Company, of which this Personage was one, somebody
observed that Doc. Darwin said Miss Seward had genius. 'Genius!' exclaimed
the Belle-Esprit, '– why *yes*, she is a *catgut* genius, – that's the sum total, I
fancy.'[104]

Beneath the sarcastic measure of Seward's words there is an underlying tone of
grinding frustration, particularly as she was unable to convince her mother that
she was capable of creativity in both writing and embroidery. From within the
boundaries of modesty and obedience, a confused and angry young woman who
was in conflict with her parents and with cultural demands had at least an outlet in
her letters to Emma, if she lacked a public voice at this stage.

She resumes her monologue to protest against the way people can be so
easily led and that very few have the capacity to gauge talent for themselves, a
sentiment repeated many times in her later condemnation of literary critics. 'The
Lichfieldians listened to their Oracle, & had implicit faith in its decree', she told
Emma. Unlike Moll Cobb, Elizabeth Seward expressed no recognition at all of
'genius' in Seward's conscientious attempt to excel at domesticity. In response
to this attitude, Seward launches a decisive counter-attack on her mother's lack
of intellect, her self-importance and misplaced belief in her own proficiency at
household management:

[M]y Mother, who with a benevolent heart has a naturally strong understanding,
tho' wholly without imagination, and apt to be a little too pompous about trifles;
– who thinks herself and has persuaded her neighbours to think her a pattern of
economy without practising any of its most useful exertions; when you reflect
that this, my Mother, upon the strength of my having committed the sin of
rhyming, chuses to suppose me wholly incompetent to domestic economy, &
has never discovered any thing about me to *balance* deficiencies, which yet I
have the vanity to believe imaginary.[105]

She also throws out a challenge at the concept of masculine authority, despondently
accusing her father of underestimating her literary talent. With the independence
of maturity, Seward was able to build on the strength that developed out of these
and future conflicts and to reject the balance between duty and personal preference
that she had no choice but to endure in her youth.

A letter filled with contemplative musing on the view from the terrace of
the Bishop's Palace, accompanied by thoughts of literary regeneration, closes
the juvenile correspondence to Emma. Walter Scott chose to censor the entire

---

[104]   NLS, Sir Walter Scott MSS, 879, fols 25–26 (February 1763).

[105]   NLS, Sir Walter Scott MSS, 879, fol. 26 (February 1763).

letter, which leaves the published narrative without adequate closure. Seward's concluding words were intended to be the following:

> Summer is in her full pride. I write to you from the Terrace. Honora sits by me, reading. The evening is sultry. We drink tea here, to catch the tardy breeze. You know we call it our green Parlour. The dear bason of a Valley, upon which it looks, was never more lovely. The umbrage, that contains its little encircling Hills, has not yet exchanged the bright green for that duskiness, which will steal upon it in a few weeks. The watry mirror, in its bosom, is glassy clear, and reflects the Trees upon the bank, & the Villa near the edge.
>
> Its fairness makes me ashamed of this defaced and ill-scribbled Epistle. The practice of writing *well* is lost with me. How soon do our bad habits become fixed, while the energy of our good ones is so apt to melt away.[106]

With her independence, her intellect and her circle of friends, she should have had everything to look forward to. However, the equilibrium was set to change radically during the course of the following decade, when she faced a prospect that threatened uncertainty and disappointment. Then, optimism was replaced with despair and, like Thomas Warton, she was forced to take comfort in different sensations, such as those that lead to the delights that 'absence drear has made': the pleasures of melancholy.[107]

---

[106] NLS, Sir Walter Scott MSS, 879, fols 85^v–85^r (June 1768).

[107] Thomas Warton, 'The Pleasures of Melancholy', *Miscellanies and Collections, 1660–1750. A Collection of Poems* (1763), p. 217, line 186. http://lion.chadwyck.co.uk.

Chapter 3
'A free Agent':
The Powys and Sykes Letters,
1770–1780

On the evening of 14 March 1772, the Bishop's Palace was the scene of a large dinner party hosted by Elizabeth and Thomas Seward. Anna Seward was at the table, helping to entertain the company, and among the many guests was their neighbour and good friend, Erasmus Darwin. During the course of the evening, Darwin seized the attention of all present by cruelly repeating a piece of scandalous gossip about Seward's music teacher, John Saville. Darwin voiced the rumours that had been circulating around Lichfield about Saville's unfaithfulness with his pupil. For the previous two years, Mary Saville had been accusing her husband of infidelity, and Seward was the object of her anger, but Elizabeth and Thomas had given no credence to the rumours until now. To Seward's distress and horror, Darwin continued that he knew a Mr Baskerville who had sold his wife and he half-jokingly pronounced that he 'fancied Saville wou'd be glad to do the same'.[1] He said that he had always thought Saville to be a worthy man but that now he thought he should be 'horse-whipt' for his behaviour and so should his wife.

The following Monday morning, Seward sent off an angry but dignified private response to Darwin in which she complained about his disloyalty, making it clear that she intended to live her life without the interference of family or friends: 'For my own part, I am a free Agent, and will be so, of an age to think and act for my self.'[2] As she had always considered Darwin a close friend, she was astonished that he could act so callously towards her. She let him know that he had created the most bitter conflict between herself and her parents, who chose to believe the physician rather than trust the word of their daughter. If her father forbade Saville to visit her at the Palace, she feared the rumours would be seen as truth by all.

---

[1] Cambridge UL, MS DAR 227. 3: 24, Seward, 'Letter to Erasmus Darwin' (16 March 1772). This was not Darwin's friend, John Baskerville, the celebrated atheist type-setter from Birmingham, but may possibly have been a relative of his. Divorce by 'wife-sale' was an unofficial ritual prevalent amongst the poor of large cities, being predominantly widespread in the west of the country. Based on a cattle-market sale, but with mutual consent, a husband would place a halter around his wife's neck and then lead her to market to be sold, ostensibly to the highest bidder who was usually a pre-arranged purchaser (Porter, *English Society in the Eighteenth Century*, p. 31).

[2] Cambridge UL, MS DAR 227. 3: 24, Seward, 'Letter to Erasmus Darwin' (16 March 1772).

She knew that her independence was reliant on her future inheritance but did not consider that it should be conditional upon her submissive obedience:

> It is not in my nature to submit to unreasonable controul, [she told Darwin] and I shou'd prefer freedom, with the barest necessaries, to all the luxuries of affluence without the right of chusing my own Friends, and acquaintance, and that of passing my time as I like best.[3]

The letter to Darwin contains a lengthy description of the nature of Saville's unhappy marriage to 'an irreclaimable Vixen' who spread poison and innuendo about her husband, and who alleged that Seward had destroyed their marriage. She explains how Saville confided in her and her sympathetic reaction to his misery and how she was able to offer him comfort and support. Despite her lengthy protestations about the innocence of their relationship and the damage to her reputation by the insidious gossip, Seward intimates that ultimately, her reputation was of less importance to her than her friendship with Saville:

> Friendship is justly said to be the balm of ev'ry woe. Saville has often declared our kindness and company, the freedom with which he cou'd speak all his sorrows, and all his consolations to us, was the greatest of his few blessings, and almost made amends for ev'ry disappointment, and for myself, I have found a satisfaction in lessening the cares, and adding to the comforts of that worthy creature which I wou'd not exchange for the applause of a generally misjudging world. How often have I heard people blamed for their *virtues*, and others commended for things which are a disgrace.[4]

Erasmus Darwin's disclosure about her secret relationship with Saville forced Seward into making serious decisions about her uncertain future. She chose to continue her now-forbidden relationship with Saville and to brave the negative reactions of family, friends, neighbours and the rest. The optimism of the carefree days of her juvenile years was wiped away as she entered a bleak period of confusion, tedium and lack of direction. Her moral reputation was seriously damaged. Her parents threatened her with disinheritance. Friends and neighbours shunned her as a 'fallen woman', and her expectations were darkened by the image of life as an 'old maid'. Aspirations to a career as a published author began to fade. Religion lost its solace and she suffered a crisis of faith. She found that she was unable to reconcile the notion of a providential God with the lifetime of punishment she believed, at the time, to be her fate. As she attempted to cope with this lost middle period of her life, she was beset by health problems. All the disappointed hopes

---

[3]   Cambridge UL, MS DAR 227. 3: 24, Seward, 'Letter to Erasmus Darwin' (16 March 1772).

[4]   Cambridge UL, MS DAR 227. 3: 24, Seward, 'Letter to Erasmus Darwin' (16 March 1772).

of these unfulfilled years are voiced in a series of letters to two loyal friends, the empathic Mary Powys and the moralising Dorothy Sykes.[5]

Very little has been written about Anna Seward's life during the 1770s, as she did not keep her copy letter books during this period and therefore documentary evidence is scarce. But, importantly, the few surviving letters from the time indicate that by the end of the decade, she was looking back on the most turbulent period of her life. Her two most valuable relationships, those with John Saville and Honora Sneyd, were put under intense pressure, and she found that the repercussions were, for a time, overwhelming. As she was adjusting to her parent's fury and general contempt, her foster-sister Honora married Richard Lovell Edgeworth and moved to his family estate in Edgeworthtown, Ireland, in the summer of 1773.

Unsurprisingly, Thomas Seward banned Saville from the Bishop's Palace and ordered his daughter not to see or speak to him again. Although Seward's relationship with Saville was temporarily disrupted, it remained strong on both sides. Honora, too, remained loyal. After her marriage to Edgeworth, she kept in close contact for several years with letters and visits, but there was an unexplained estrangement, probably instigated by her father, Edward Sneyd, and communication ceased. The chilly, damp climate and marshy conditions at the Irish estate did not suit her fragile health. Ravaged by tuberculosis, Honora died in 1780, aged just twenty-nine.

For much of the decade, Seward was both bored and dejected: 'My heart was aching with misery from the undue and arbitrary exertions of parental sway – to that exerted by Mr Sneyd, I ow'd the loss of my Honora.'[6] The resolve with which she handled these two personal crises, and the train of events which followed, set the precedent for managing future battles. By sheer tenacity and determination, and disregarding the criticism directed at her, she survived the difficulties which assailed her. Just as importantly, she began to fill the gaps left by Honora's departure and Saville's temporary absence with writing, concentrating on her correspondence, yet also finding the resolve to defy her parents and write the poetry for which she is best known. By the end of the decade, with a healthy portfolio of poems, she had moved on to pastures new, winning a prestigious poetry competition.[7] Then she began to publish her work, rightly confident in its success. In the meantime, as she entered a bleak period of uncertainty about her future, she found herself stifled by life in Lichfield, estranged from her parents and shunned by neighbours and acquaintances, apart from a very few close friends. In disgrace, and with her moral reputation in shreds, she still supported Saville's brave challenge to his employers, the church authorities.

---

[5]   The Johnson Birthplace Museum, Collection of autograph letters of Anna Seward to Joseph Sykes and his wife Dorothy, MS 35; 'Letters to Mary Powys', MS 38.

[6]   JBM, MS 35/1, Seward, 'Letter to Dorothy Sykes' (May 1773).

[7]   Seward sent an entry to Lady Anne Miller's Bath-Easton annual poetry competition at some time between 1778 and 1779. Her entry, 'Invocation to the Comic Muse', took first prize (Ashmun, *The Singing Swan*, p. 71).

In the circumstances, she behaved with great dignity. Events did not undermine her confidence, but fed her determination to control her own destiny. She wrote letters to her friends, more out of boredom and with a sense of confessional divulgence than from literary ambition. In this way she was able to unburden the anxieties and fears of what she considered to be the worst years of her life onto her two close friends, Mary Powys and Dorothy Sykes. In a series of mainly incomplete, unpublished letters which span the entire 1770s, it is possible to piece together in precise detail the events of these tumultuous times and the mental anguish that Seward experienced during her progress through the decade, towards her career as a writer. The importance of the two collections of letters is that they enlighten a previously unexplored period of her life. Their contents stand in stark opposition to the buoyant juvenile letters and to the polished mature correspondence, and they also tease out the links between her associations and her poetry of the time.

To date, the progress of Seward's life during the 1770s, together with speculation about her sexuality, has been the subject of vague conjecture by writers and scholars. The Powys and Sykes letters invalidate much of the guesswork of the various hypotheses. A common assumption that Seward stopped writing poetry at the age of sixteen, when her parents first raised an objection, is rooted in Walter Scott's 'Biographical Preface' to the poetry edition:

> Poetry was prohibited, and Miss Seward resorted to other amusements, and to the practice of ornamental needle-work, in which she is said to have excelled. Thus rolled on time for nearly ten years – When it is considered that her attachment to literary pursuits bordered even upon the romantic, the merit of sacrificing them readily to the inclination of her parents, deserves our praise.[8]

It is possible that Scott was given misleading information about Seward's early life by her family and executors. There is evidence in an exchange of letters between Scott and Charles Simpson, the family lawyer, after her death that he had little knowledge of her background. 'I could hardly be expected to produce much biography', he wrote to the lawyer.[9] No doubt Scott relied on Seward's cousins and executors, the White brothers, for his information, and his short 'Biographical Preface' is evidence of his lack of research. In her early youth, Seward worked hard to achieve excellence in both literary and domestic spheres, and it is clear from the censored sections of the juvenile letters and her literary output that she continued writing poetry. Accounts of her life written in the Powys and Sykes letters confirm that by the 1770s, there was no attempt whatsoever to find a compromise to please her parents or anyone else; there was no ready 'sacrifice' whatsoever.

The received stereotype of the young Anna Seward as a dutiful, self-sacrificing daughter contentedly embroidering or mending lace, eventually trapped in Lichfield and devoting all her time to the care of sick elderly parents is far from accurate. Rather than taking care of her parents, she was looking after her father's

---

[8]   Scott, 'Biographical Preface', *Poetical Works*, vol. I, pp. vii–viii.
[9]   NLS, MSS, 9609, fol. 8, Scott, 'Letter to Charles Simpson' (27 June 1810).

business affairs, which occupied much of her time. While her father lived, she was a business woman administrating his financial portfolio of stocks, shares, bonds and monies, to which she later added her own profits and properties. She was a successful professional writer who handled her own copyright negotiations and publishing contracts. Her life was not one of feminine employments, but of varied, complex activity that frequently trespassed on masculine territory.

In contrast to the artful contrivance of the juvenile letters, which encompass the 1760s, and to the literary scheme of the published correspondence, which covers the years from 1784 to 1807, the Powys and Sykes collections of letters are from a time when Seward was writing prolifically but clearly had no expectations of a literary career. The letters are evidently not written for publication. They are not part of her letter books, which she did not begin until 1780, nor are they part of her other organised manuscripts. Their provenance is the recipients' own collection. With no self-conscious gloss, these letters are very different indeed from the ones that were published. There is little literary reference, and the uncharacteristic lack of attention to style, grammar and punctuation marks them as private letters to intimate friends. The letters from the later part of this collection are more eloquent and stylised, with critiques of her colleagues' work. She writes to Mary Powys, for example, of the 'Genius' in her friend Helen Maria Williams' poetry, but that her sponsor, Elizabeth Montagu, 'wants critical ability' and she proceeds to critique the poem herself.[10] But the earlier correspondence has a spontaneous effect, dashed off complete with the 'blots and blunders' of a busily-writing young woman who does not have enough time to mend her broken pen.[11] Unlike the earlier juvenile correspondence, she reveals the true names or nicknames of friends, such as 'Po' for Mary Powys and Dick for Richard Vyse, which she would normally conceal or change in a letter designed to be read by a wider audience. Interestingly, she nearly always speaks of John Saville simply as 'Saville'.

Her subject matter is remarkably personal by the standards usually associated with her. There is no literary persona constructed here. These two bundles of correspondence have a refreshing clarity and a greater verity, as the letters which were designated for publication were written and rewritten with a studied awareness of their ultimate readership. And, of course, their content was devalued by the heavy editing and the censorship. Conversely, the Powys and Sykes letters articulate the minutiae of life that is not present in the published letters. Seward writes of her rheumatism and of worse illnesses and forwards the remedies she has discovered. She discusses needlework and encloses patterns. She complains that her mother wants her pretty little white 'dogess', Loo, sterilized. She grumbles about the pretentious 'Macaronis and Fops' who waste her time on their frequent visits to her. She reflects on the 'accidental advantages' of wealth and pronounces that the love of money is an odious thing. She describes the shock of seeing her cruel uncle beat her Aunt Martin and little cousin, Nancy. She relates the story of

---

10   JBM, MS 38/14, Seward, 'Letter to Mary Powys' (c. 1784).
11   JBM, MS 35/6, Seward, 'Letter to Dorothy Sykes' (21 March 1775).

her young pupil Marianne, Dorothy Sykes' eleven-year-old daughter, for whom she designed a programme of home tuition before the child's entry into a local boarding school. Most significantly, she explains the extent of her love for John Saville and Honora Sneyd, while she discloses her feelings of anger and sorrow at the consequences of the events which took place in the early part of the decade.

The low point began very early in the decade with a warning letter from Mary Powys, who had heard that Seward's relationship with John Saville had been noticed by his wife, Mary. The gossipmongers were already spreading disapproval, repeating Mary Saville's insults and allegations. Mary Powys was Honora Sneyd's cousin, a life-long friend and correspondent who remained unmarried and who lived first at the Abbey in Shrewsbury and later moved to Clifton, Bristol. It was now 1770 and Seward was twenty-seven. During the previous seven years, she had slowly rebuilt her life after the devastating effects of her sister Sarah's death. The happiness of her 'delicious' childhood in rural Eyam and her adolescent and teen years in Lichfield had ended abruptly when little Sarah died. Now, contented again, she divided her time between writing, the study of literature and her needlework, each of which pleasurable activities she combined with time spent with her blue dressing-room coterie.

According to Richard Lovell Edgeworth, Seward was then 'in the height of youth and beauty'. A striking and vivacious figure with a melodious voice, she was tall, beautiful, plump, with spectacular red-gold hair and lustrous eyes of exactly the same shade. In his memoirs, Edgeworth recounts in surprisingly sharp detail an anecdote concerning his first meeting with her at Erasmus Darwin's house which reveals her sociability, intelligence and wit. Seward did not know that Edgeworth was married, and as they were seated together at the dinner table, they flirted over a discussion of a romantic passage from one of Seward's favourites, Prior's *Henry and Emma*. Edgeworth remembered that they talked of the scene where the heroine cleanses her lover's wounds with her tears, dries them with her long hair and binds them with strips torn from her clothes. At that moment, Edgeworth lavishly complimented Seward's own 'beautiful tresses'. To her astonishment, the watchful Mary Darwin immediately jumped up to propose a toast to 'Mrs. Edgeworth's health'. Seward was not at all embarrassed by the ensuing laughter. 'Miss Seward's surprise was manifest', affirmed Edgeworth. 'But the mirth this unexpected discovery made fell but lightly upon its objects, for Miss Seward, with perfect good humor, turned the laugh in her favor.'[12]

When alone, Seward corresponded with friends, writing and receiving around seven long letters each week, some extending to ten or more pages. She also practiced her music under John Saville's tutelage and wrote poetry with the support of Erasmus Darwin. In her published poetry edition, it is clear that she had continued to compose poetry despite her father's disapproval, as she classified specific poems that she had written between the ages of seventeen and twenty-three as 'juvenile'. She was twenty-three when she and Saville fell in love, and this was

---

[12]   Edgeworth, *Memoirs of Richard Lovell Edgeworth*, vol. I, p. 167.

the year of her metaphorical coming of age. Her posthumous poetry edition shows that she was prolific during the 1770s, with the collection of poems addressed to Honora, a sequence of gracefully simple songs and ballads (some of which were written for Saville to perform), several works addressed to friends, and poems and sonnets relating to the events of this period. Most remarkable, however, is a series of fifteen love poems whose source was 'not entirely imaginary' but was a collection of love letters between 'a lady of birth, rank, beauty and talents, the daughter of wealthy parents, and a gentleman, much her inferior in family and station, without fortune, and her equal only in intellect, merit and affection'.[13] The collection of epistolary poems, entitled *Love Elegies and Epistles*, was written between the protagonists 'Evander' and 'Emillia', and they mirror her early relationship with Saville.

At the start of the decade, life in Lichfield was busy, and there were extended visits to friends and regular trips to London. There was consolation for Sarah's death in Honora, who also provided a channel for Seward's intellect. She treated Honora as a cherished little sister but also as a pupil, even though she attended a local day school and her aptitude was more for mathematics and things mechanical than literature. Predictably, when considering Sarah's fate, Seward's major concern was always for Honora's health, which had been problematic as she was consumptive and frail. But they shared a sisterly kinship, united by the love of books and music and their close circle of friends.

The intimate relationship that Seward and Saville had privately shared for the previous four years was secure as long as it remained a secret. They had decided between themselves that as marriage was not open to them, they would settle for a companionate relationship and value the time they were able to spend together.[14] When Mary Powys revealed that people were gossiping about them, they were concerned about what they might have to confront:

> The first terror [on hearing about the gossip] that mingled a *constant* dread with the sense of our happiness, was the information [Mary Powys] gave me in the year 1770, that the breath of Censure threaten'd to blast our tranquillity. – Yet I fondly hop'd it might not have *power* to wound us – however, the blended fear had too surely 'clogg'd the dance of joy' in my spirits, and perhaps I never after knew what it was to be *quite* happy.[15]

Although they agreed on mutual loyalty and decided that together they would endure public condemnation from the 'rash young' and the 'ill-nature'd old' alike, Seward was fearful for her future.[16] Certainly she felt no shame and she did not

---

[13]   Seward, 'Love Elegies and Epistles', *Poetical Works*, vol. I, p. 25.

[14]   Divorce was by Act of Parliament and expensive. Saville's only option was to separate from Mary and continue to support her.

[15]   JBM, MS 38/10, Seward, 'Letter to Mary Powys' (11 December 1781).

[16]   Cambridge UL, MS DAR 227. 3: 24, Seward, 'Letter to Erasmus Darwin' (16 March 1772).

consider that it was her duty to stop seeing Saville. 'Fate left us Friendship', she wrote to Dorothy Sykes, 'allow'd us to converse for hours ev'ry day. Resign'd to our Destiny, we pleaded only for *that*.'[17] She assumed that her reputation would remain intact as long as she had the support and understanding of parents and friends.

Before the murmurs of scandal took hold, Seward's letters to Mary Powys were filled with enthusiastic, mostly cheerful chatter and gossip. There is a complacent edge to her thoughts; any problems were easy to surmount. A painful gum abscess, which Erasmus Darwin told her would lead to the loss of teeth unless she immediately consulted a dentist, meant a hastily-arranged trip to London with Honora's relative, Captain Sneyd, as her escort. There were consolations. She looked to London for an intoxicating blend of music and theatre, a diversion from the routine of Lichfield. She loved the bustle of life in the capital and particularly the round of operas, oratorios and theatre productions. The winter season was her favourite, and it was always a thrill for her to witness the performances of David Garrick, the leading actor and producer of the day, whose Lichfield relatives were good friends of the Seward family. Far more fashionable than a theatre performance was a glamorous night spent beneath the glittering chandeliers of the London opera, where protocol insisted that a lady's splendid evening dress, fine jewels and grand appearance were as important to her status as was being accommodated in the best seats in the house.

If she had to visit London outside the season, Seward explained to Mary, the experience was disappointing, with 'no oratorios & when Garrick does not act'.[18] She commemorates the winter season in her poem of 1779, 'Amusements of Winter', which pays homage to the dazzling production of theatrical and musical events. The scenes on stage, 'that glitter azure and that glitter gold', are matched by the scenes of rivalry in the audience between the fine ladies, resplendent in their full-plumed headdresses. In her poem, she describes tragedy and comedy but is clearly most delighted with opera. Summoning Euphrosyne, the third Grace who personifies merriment, she links music with love and joy, transposing Gray's mournful curfew knell to a pleasant world filled with friends and books, talk and music.

> So fly November's monsters o'er the lea,
> And leave the world to Music – Love – and THEE.[19]

---

[17]   JBM, MS 35/2, Seward, 'Letter to Dorothy Sykes' (27 July 1773).

[18]   JBM, MS 38/1, Seward, 'Letter to Mary Powys' (23 April 1770).

[19]   Seward, 'Amusements of Winter', *Poetical Works*, vol. II, p. 25. Seward pays homage to Gray's opening lines from 'Elegy' and the ploughman who 'homeward plods his weary way, / And leaves the world to darkness and to me.' (Thomas Gray, 'Elegy Written in a Country Churchyard', *The Poems of Thomas Gray, William Collins and Oliver Goldsmith*, ed. by Roger Lonsdale (London: Longmans, 1969), p. 117).

The circle of blue dressing room friends now included John André and the 'dear Quartetto' of Thomas Day, Richard Lovell Edgeworth, Erasmus Darwin and John Saville. Darwin's first wife, Seward's friend Mary (Howard), had died from a long-term illness in 1770 in a haze of pain-relieving alcohol and opium, like Johnson's wife Tetty.[20] Now in his late thirties, Darwin had embarked on an affair with his son's nursemaid, eighteen-year-old Mary Parker, who subsequently gave birth to two daughters. Edgeworth was on an extended visit to Day, and Saville lived locally, escaping from his wife to join the congenial group whenever possible.

A regular feature of the letters to Dorothy Sykes and Mary Powys is Seward's pleasure in Honora Sneyd's happiness. Throughout the correspondence, the story of Honora's engagement, marriage, illness and death unfolds in detail that is not available from other sources. Seward laughingly paints a picture of the popular nineteen-year-old, surrounded by all her beaux. Both Thomas Day and 'the lively, the sentimental, the entertaining, the accomplished, the learned, the scientific, the gallant, the celebrated' (but the married) Edgeworth were fascinated by the beautiful and intelligent young woman.[21] Seward's letters to her two friends, together with her correspondence from Day during his time in France in 1771, confirm him to be a more attractive and humorously ironic figure than the dour, controlling pessimist depicted in her *Memoirs* of Darwin. The letters to Powys and Sykes were contemporaneous with Seward and Day's close friendship. As the *Memoirs* were written in retrospect and the story of Day intended to provoke, if not scandalise, it is reasonable to assume that Seward exaggerated his 'misanthropic gloom and proud contempt of common-life society' to embellish her biography.[22]

Early in the 1770s, Seward liked and admired Thomas Day, referring to him as the only man quite worthy of Honora, 'except one', which was a reference to John André, who appeared to be fonder of Honora than she was of him at this time.[23] A London counting house clerk, André was a family friend and a regular visitor to the Palace as a member of Seward's inner circle. He and Honora wanted to marry, but were dissuaded by both families as he had very little money. Too restless to remain an accountant, he joined the army, fighting in America and becoming involved in secret missions for General Clinton and Benedict Arnold. He was captured and then tried by court-martial to be hanged as a spy at Tappan in 1780, a few months after Honora's own death. Seward and 'Cher Jean', as his friends called him, were very close and were publicly affectionate, so much so that Edgeworth, on first meeting them, presumed them to be more than friends. In his memoirs, Edgeworth writes of the visit to the Bishop's Palace when he first met them:

---

[20] King-Hele, *Erasmus Darwin*, p. 90; Christopher Hibbert, *The Personal History of Samuel Johnson* (London: Pimlico, 1998), p. 85.

[21] JBM, MS 38/1, Seward, 'Letter to Mary Powys' (23 April 1770).

[22] Seward, *Memoirs of Dr Darwin*, p. 13.

[23] JBM, MS 38/2, Seward, 'Letter to Mary Powys' (c. 1771).

[F]rom the great attention which Miss Seward paid to him, and from the constant admiration which Mr. André bestowed on her, I thought, that, though there was considerable disproportion in their ages [André was 8 years Seward's junior], there might exist some courtship between them. Miss Seward, however, undeceived me.[24]

Seward clearly placed André in a brotherly role and, following his death, she let loose her anger in a poem, 'Monody on Major André', in which the narrator accuses General Washington of being the 'cool, determined murderer of the brave' and curses him:

And when thy heart appall'd, and vanquish'd pride
Shall vainly ask the mercy they deny'd,
With horror shalt thou meet the fate thou gave,
Nor pity gild the darkness of thy grave![25]

The poem, which challenges the futility of war and illustrates personal grief, was hugely successful and helped construct Seward's reputation as a national poet. When her forceful complaints against Washington were brought to his attention, he decided to absolve himself by sending his envoy to Lichfield at the end of the war to meet privately with Seward and to show her the letters and documents which explained his blamelessness in the affair. With the sincere conviction in her poem overturned, Seward was filled with 'contrition for the rash injustice of [her] censure' although obviously pleased with the impact her poem made.[26]

It is André's own words, taken from his letters to Seward which were published together with her commemorative poem, that describe Seward's coterie and summarise his relationship with her, Honora and the other friends:

The happy social circle, Julia [Seward], Honora, Miss S[impso]n, Miss B[?]n, her brother, Mr S[avill]e, Mr R[obinso]n, &c. are now, perhaps, enlivening your dressing-room, the dear blue region, as Honora calls it, with the same sensible observation, the tasteful criticism, or the elegant song; [...] dreading the iron-tongue of the nine o'clock bell, which disperses the beings, whom friendship

[24] Richard Lovell Edgeworth and Maria Edgeworth, *Memoirs of Richard Lovell Edgeworth, Esq. Begun by Himself and Concluded by his Daughter, Maria Edgeworth*, 2 vols (London: Hunter, 1820), vol. I, p. 243. Edgeworth also claimed that Seward had been the 'rival' of Erasmus Darwin's first wife, Polly, although there is no evidence for this and Seward was merely thirteen years old when Darwin married (p. 161).

[25] Seward, 'Monody on Major André', *Poetical Works*, vol. II, p. 85.

[26] Seward, *Letters*, vol. V, pp. 143–44. Seward wrote a letter to Sarah Ponsonby describing how Washington's envoy brought her the papers which explained the circumstances of André's court martial, giving details of how Washington had made attempts to save his life. It appears that the subject was first raised by Ponsonby, and Seward was at pains to correct Ponsonby's mistaken assumption that Washington sent a letter, by explaining in meticulous detail the contents of the documents 'as faithfully as I can recall them, at such a distance of time' (p. 144).

and kindred virtues had drawn together. [...] My imagination attaches itself to all, even the inanimate objects which surround Honora and her Julia; [...] that have beheld their graces and virtues expand and ripen; [...] my dear Honora's, from their infant bud.[27]

Edgeworth also gives a detailed account of his time in Lichfield in his memoirs. Leaving his sickly, bad-tempered wife at home in Ireland, he made a prolonged visit to Day's house at Stow Hill. Most days, the popular young men visited the Bishop's Palace, sometimes with Sabrina, who was the foundling ward Day was 'training' to be his wife. Obviously besotted from the first with Honora, the twenty-six-year-old Edgeworth wrote about her in his memoirs, and his most interesting comments concern comparisons with Seward, who 'shone so brightly, that all objects within her sphere were dimmed by her lustre'.[28] Thomas Day was equally fascinated by Honora, yet, as an ascetic, he found her too sophisticated, too worldly. She danced too well, her dress and manners were too fashionable, and he complained that her arms were not round or white enough for him.

By 1771 Day had discarded the feisty, impossible to 'train' Sabrina, and he now set about the task of convincing Honora of the merits of his own eccentric and controlling strictures on marriage, wanting to prove to her that a life of seclusion and intellectual pursuits away from the *beau monde* would be ideal for her. He underestimated Honora's firm principles on independence and equality, which were influenced by Seward's opinions, and her 'clear, dispassionate view of the rights of women'.[29] His long, rambling marriage proposal was rejected by Honora with a remarkable statement of her desire for self-determination in marriage. Edgeworth wrote admiringly:

> Miss Honora Sneyd would not admit the unqualified control of a husband over all her actions; she did not feel, that seclusion from society was indispensably necessary to preserve female virtue, or to secure domestic happiness. Upon terms of reasonable equality, she supposed, that mutual confidence might best subsist; she said, that, as Mr. Day had decidedly declared his determination to live in perfect seclusion from what is usually called the world, it was fit she should decidedly declare, that she would not change her present mode of life, with which she had no reason to be dissatisfied, for any dark and untried system, that could be proposed to her.[30]

Honora's assertive response instigated a reversal of stereotype as Day became quite faint on her refusal and had to be bled by Erasmus Darwin. But within a few weeks he had fallen for the fifth Sneyd daughter, pretty, lively Elizabeth, who had been brought up with her cousin, Mary Powys, at the Abbey in Shrewsbury.

---

[27] John André, 'Letter to Anna Seward' (1 November 1769), reproduced in *Poetical Works*, vol. II, pp. 89–104 (p. 102).

[28] Edgeworth, *Memoirs of Richard Lovell Edgeworth*, vol. I, pp. 241–42.

[29] Edgeworth, *Memoirs*, vol. I, p. 250.

[30] Edgeworth, *Memoirs*, vol. I, p. 250.

Day was attracted to Elizabeth largely by her *inability* to dance well and her seemingly compliant nature. Presumably he also found her arms attractive. Like her sister Honora, Elizabeth decided against committing herself to a man with such controlling impulses as Day, and she persuaded him to go to France to learn fashionable gentlemanly behaviour. The ensuing episode that Seward describes, based on Day's letters from Lyons, illustrates what fashion considered appropriate training for young men. Poor Day put himself in the hands of dancing teachers and fencing masters and endured the agony of two hours each day in a set of constricting frames designed to straighten his back and point his feet. He practiced bowing, dancing and walking with a fashionable military gait. In a humorous but touching letter to Seward, he implores her to explain to him 'what a Gentleman should be'. He continues:

> If I live to return to the Land of Fogs and Sea-coal again, you shall see me an attendant. I will define him to you so exactly that he shall seem to live and breathe before you. [...] let him know his own Accomplishes and merits and be very vain of them. Let him have from nature Insolence, Frivolity, Unfeelingness; from Education, the Politeness of the world which is Affectation, the Gallantry of the world which is Hypocrisy; from his dancing master Grimace; from his travels Impertinence, and from his Taylor fine Cloathes upon credit. [...] What progress I have made in straining forward to this sublime point of Perfection, I have too much modesty to determine.[31]

Following trends was not for Day, and his old habits were deep-seated. Refusing to become the fashionable gentleman, he returned home a figure of ridicule in his fancy new clothes. He was turned down by Elizabeth and resumed his old way of life, eventually meeting and marrying Esther Milnes. It was Edgeworth, in fact, who married both Sneyd sisters – first Honora on his first wife's death in 1773 and then Elizabeth, just a few weeks after Honora's death in 1780.

'We were a smart cavalcade', wrote Seward, describing the wedding party. Her letters of this period provide enlightening details about the relationship between Edgeworth and Honora, and her own feelings about the marriage, beginning with their wedding day. The guests arrived at the cathedral, and at nine o'clock Thomas Seward performed the ceremony under the vaulted canopies of the magnificent Lady Chapel. Seward was Honora's bridesmaid. Honora's father, Edward, had initially disapproved of the groom. Seward claimed they were 'too different to like each other', yet he eventually relented and 'gave away' his daughter with good grace.[32] The wedding breakfast was at the Sneyds' house, and at noon the couple

---

[31] Lichfield RO, Seward Family MSS, D262/1/6, Thomas Day, 'Letter to Anna Seward from Lyons, France' (10 December 1771).

[32] JBM, MS 35/3, Seward, 'Letter to Dorothy Sykes' (27 July 1773 [not November 1773]). As a wedding present, Edward Sneyd offered Honora £1,000 and promised to leave her the same amount in his will. Edgeworth made her a settlement of a £400 annuity, should she survive him, with a further £600 until her children should receive their own fortunes. His income, wrote Seward, was a substantial £1,500 per annum.

climbed into Edgeworth's phaeton and left. Seward's delight in the wedding and in Honora's absolute happiness in her choice of partner was marred only by the thought of the couple's imminent departure for Ireland. 'They are made for each other', she wrote to Mary Powys, 'but alas, seas divide her from my fond arms – thus fade my promis'd joys, thus wither all my blight'd pleasures [...] She is happy and I bless Heaven that she is, but she is *absent*, and I must *mourn*.'[33]

Honora once more revealed her assertive nature by stepping outside the boundaries of duty and insisting on marrying the man of her choice, although her father disliked him intensely. The judgemental Lichfield neighbours responded by openly siding with Edward Sneyd. Seward hints at Sneyd's cruelty to Honora without giving any firm details. As a child, she had been brought up to endure 'cold severity' with 'fortitude and resignation', and at last she had the opportunity to fight back.[34] The Lichfield gossips expressed their opinions on what they saw as Honora's aberrant behaviour, and, judging her to be morally ambivalent, they predicted unhappiness for the young newly-weds: '[They] spare her not for presuming to judge for herself and for being too wise to sacrifice her felicity to her Father, and to Mr Groves' (an interfering family friend). Seward was supportive in the face of almost universal condemnation. With an empathic understanding of the situation, she praised Honora's determination to make her own decisions, and she commended her courage in standing up to her father and coping with the 'World's idle prejudices'. She equated Honora's dilemmas with her own. 'Fortune has placed her many a shot above their impotent malice', she told Mary Powys.[35]

Seward also told Mary Powys and Dorothy Sykes about the correspondence she shared with Honora after the wedding. Within a week, she was alarmed to receive a letter from her to say that she had been very ill, worn out by the wedding preparations and the fatigues of the journey to Ireland, but that her new husband was taking great care of her.[36] Honora wrote again a few weeks later to reassure Seward that her health had improved but that her new estate was marshy and bleak, a disturbing thought because of her fragile constitution. The following year, Honora wrote to announce the first of her two pregnancies, and Seward continued to worry about her health, advising her to move from Edgeworthtown to Dublin to get proper pre-natal care.[37] Honora's immune system would have been weakened by her chronic tuberculosis, and as pregnancies and labour were often difficult, there were high mortality rates for mothers and babies. By now, Seward was beginning to show doubts about Edgeworth's ability to look after Honora, as he

---

[33] JBM, MS 35/3, Seward, 'Letter to Dorothy Sykes' (27 July 1773 [not November 1773]).

[34] JBM, MS 38/10, Seward, 'Letter to Mary Powys' (11 December 1781).

[35] JBM, MS 38/5, Seward, 'Letter to Mary Powys' (c.1773).

[36] JBM, MS 35/3, Seward, 'Letter to Dorothy Sykes' (27 July 1773 [not November 1773]).

[37] JBM, MS 35/20, Seward, 'Letter to Dorothy Sykes' (c. 1774).

spent a good deal of his time travelling. She wrote, somewhat enigmatically, to Mary Powys that his 'baseness' had been 'unveiled' to her.[38]

Ultimately, Seward apportioned much of the blame for Honora's death to Edgeworth. In 1779, he visited Lichfield alone and arranged to call on Seward specifically to show her a new portrait of Honora by John Smart. By now, Honora was very ill with tuberculosis and Edgeworth intended to take her to the Bristol spa with the hope of alleviating some of her symptoms. Seward knew her foster-sister was beyond treatment and was furious that he had left it so late: 'If he had taken her last year, she would have been saved.' She was also angry with Edgeworth's flippancy when he teased her by hiding the portrait from her until she had to beg him to see it. The painting was not a good likeness, much to Seward's disappointment, 'for when she is no more, I might perhaps have purchas'd a copy'.[39]

As well as giving news of Honora, Seward wrote to her two friends about John Saville's enduring state of despondency over his unhappy marriage – 'Il Penseroso', who welcomes 'divinest Melancholy', sighing and singing poignant songs to the group of blue dressing room friends.[40] Although the richest source for details about Mary and John Saville's marriage is found in Seward's angry letter to Erasmus Darwin, she specifically revealed her own despair about the situation to Dorothy Sykes, her judgemental friend who lived with husband Joseph, son Richard and daughter Marianne at Westella, Hull, which was then in Yorkshire. Another son, also named Joseph, had died at the age of nineteen, and Seward wrote one of her many elegies to his memory.[41] Originally from Derbyshire, the wealthy Sykes family had been friends since Seward's childhood, when she was a regular visitor to their mansion. She continued to visit the family in Yorkshire throughout the 1770s, sometimes staying for several months at a time.

John Saville had married Mary, a beautiful, uneducated, bad-tempered, controlling woman, when he was very young, and they had two daughters. According to Saville, Mary was unreasonably jealous of all his friends, particularly Seward, and tried to prevent him from seeing them. When this invariably failed she resorted to spreading abusive gossip, publicly accusing him of mistreating her and their daughters. Her allegations were shocking, considering Saville was a gentle, exceptionally devout man. On one occasion, she complained that he had fallen to his knees and prayed to God to curse her. On another, she told friends that he beat her regularly. Not content with spreading rumours about her husband's infidelity and Seward's immorality, she threatened to expose them by writing to Thomas Seward. When an anonymous letter duly arrived, a 'vile, incendiary, artful, nameless paper', Mary, who was illiterate, denied sending it. Seward and Saville both believed that she had dictated it to one of her friends, Erasmus Darwin's

---

[38]   JBM, MS 38/5, Seward, 'Letter to Mary Powys' (c.1773).

[39]   JBM, MS 35/18, Seward, 'Letter to Dorothy Sykes' (c.1779).

[40]   In Milton's poem 'Il Penseroso', the narrator welcomes 'divinest Melancholy'.

[41]   Seward, 'Elegy on the Death of Mr Joseph Sykes at the Age of Nineteen', *Poetical Works*, vol. II, p. 5.

brother-in-law, Charles Howard, who was an alcoholic.[42] Seward argued that she was not to blame for the disintegration of the marriage:

> Mrs Saville *deserv'd* to lose [her husband's] esteem and love, long before *my* friendship, that *disgraceful* circumstance existed but I know the censures people cast upon *him*, and meant for *me*.[43]

When Saville was appointed as Seward's music teacher in 1766, he poured out his misery to her and she sympathised: '[T]he more I saw of Mr Saville, the more I heard of his sentiments, the more he rose in my esteem.'[44] As they indulged in his sadness together, his melancholic disposition became appealing to Seward's notion of sensibility. 'My taste demands some shaded features of the mind, some penseroso tints in the manners', she wrote.[45] Both Seward and Saville were steeped in the values of sensibility drawn from their favourite reading materials. Without a classical education, Seward tended to emphasise her knowledge of the English classics, and this naturally drew her towards Shakespeare, Spencer, Milton and Pope as her models, with Richardson and Rousseau, Goethe, McPherson's *Ossian* and Percy's *Reliques* in their train. In 1777, she took pleasure in devising a teaching programme for Marianne Sykes, basing it on reading the English classics.

Seward's contemporary, the poet and religious writer Hannah More, recommended reading material that was concerned with improving morals and upholding Christianity, and she suggested reading Johnson and Addison for this purpose. Seward was less concerned with the religious aspects of her reading material and more with the emotional. The importance of sensibility is evident in the juvenile letters, where she is preoccupied with recording the attributes of refined emotion and compassion. In the Powys and Sykes letters, however, she tends to portray Saville's susceptibility, rather than her own. The series of letters to Mary Powys begins in a similar way to her juvenile letters, with a reference to the significance of friendship and the 'involuntary impulse' of an empathic relationship, loving someone the better for their experience of the 'sensations of pain and pleasure kindred to one's own'.[46] This aside, there is little self-conscious reference to sensibility. Saville's own response to sensibility was in his inveterate sadness. This was not in the same class of episodic melancholia suffered by James Boswell, which descended on him in attacks of inexplicable gloom. Nor was it the kind of bleak, intolerable depression experienced regularly by Samuel Johnson. It was not even what Dr George Cheyne fashionably labelled the 'English malady', the rank-specific neurological disorder brought about by 'assaults on the nervous

---

[42] See King-Hele, *Erasmus Darwin: A Life of Unequalled Achievement*, p. 32.

[43] Cambridge UL, MS DAR 227. 3: 24, Seward, 'Letter to Erasmus Darwin' (16 March 1772).

[44] Cambridge UL, MS DAR 227. 3: 24, Seward, 'Letter to Erasmus Darwin' (16 March 1772).

[45] JBM, MS 35/15, Seward, 'Letter to Dorothy Sykes' (29 August 1777).

[46] JBM, MS 38/1, Seward, 'Letter to Mary Powys' (23 April 1770).

system produced by modern lifestyles, with their social emulation, copious eating and drinking, lounging, tight lacing, late hours and heady, competitive talk'.[47]

John Saville was genuinely miserable about being tied to a vicious, insensitive wife he did not love and therefore unable to marry Seward. His malaise, however, was more likely to have been inflated into the bittersweet variety that was prevalent at the time, particularly so in Lichfield. Like Richardson's Clarissa, who sought her own 'private madhouse where nobody comes',[48] this was the introspective yet rational contemplation of a man of sensibility, a man of nature: the melancholia which manifested in Saville in sighs, tears and mournful songs. His study of the new scientific discipline of botany united him with both nature and rationality. His love of literature, poetry, landscape paintings and his specialist area of music, Handel oratorios, aligned him with sensibility. Seward told Helen Maria Williams that he was 'open' to the *Messiah*, and 'unites poetic taste, and the vivid emotion of a feeling heart, and of an high and kindling spirit, to a rich, extensive and powerful voice'.[49] With his humanitarian principles, he gave much of his earnings to the poor. With his 'affections', he wept openly on the death of a pet dog. With his nature-inspired awe, he thrilled the blue dressing room friends with a spontaneous, tearful song at the sudden end of a long and wearying drought.[50]

The major influence on the tendency for melancholia in Lichfield emanated from the writings of the Swiss philosopher Jean-Jacques Rousseau, who was in Staffordshire in 1766–67, shortly after the publication of *Emile*, his radical work on education and the civilising effects of nature. Seward greatly admired this as a literary work. She first read it in 1769, and although she believed most of it to be virtually impracticable, she admitted that some sections might prove useful in the education of children. During his stay in Staffordshire, Rousseau socialised with the members of the Lichfield literary circle, notably Seward's friends Sir Brooke Boothby of Ashbourne Hall and Erasmus Darwin. Thomas Seward belonged to the local literary society, which met regularly for lectures, debates and discussions and which circulated books that could be borrowed by the members for a limited period of time. There is nothing in Seward's writings to indicate that she was invited to the gatherings or that she met Rousseau, although she does confirm that she regularly borrowed the books on the society's circuit. Many of the literary-minded young men of Lichfield became Rousseau's devout followers. When Boothby went to Paris ten years later, the now-exiled philosopher secretly gave him his autobiography to bring back, translate and publish. Rousseau died in 1778 and Boothby published the book in Lichfield just two years later.

---

[47]   Porter, *Enlightenment*, p. 282.

[48]   Richardson, *Clarissa*, p. 895.

[49]   Seward, 'Letter to Miss Helen Williams' (25 August 1785), *Letters*, vol. I, p. 76.

[50]   Seward 'Letter to Rev. R. Fellowes', *Letters*, vol. VI, pp. 101–6. Seward wrote to Robert Fellowes after Saville's death, describing his funeral and giving information about his character.

An imaginative portrait of Sir Brooke Boothby by Joseph Wright of Derby brings together all the elements which encompass the notion of the melancholia of sensibility to which Saville was so susceptible.[51] Portraits of aristocrats such as Boothby usually displayed the signifiers of their wealth and possessions: their property, their family, their horses and dogs. Wright's portraiture rarely deviated from this imagery. In Boothby's portrait, though, the wealthy aristocrat is dressed in plain, dark, informal clothing that harmonises with his natural environment. At one with nature and, most unusually for a gentleman's portrait, casually reclining on a river bank, Boothby is surrounded by the shady, wooded scenery of Derbyshire. Chin resting on hand, he gazes out of the gloom at the viewer in a contemplative reverie, a closed copy of Rousseau's work in his hand. Around his legs and feet and on the bank on which he reclines are entwined the herbs and plants typically associated with melancholy and its remedies, including sweet violet, dew cup and valerian. In the far background, yet central to the portrait, Wright evokes a contrasting scene of sublime landscape with a distant golden, glowing lake and mountain tableau.

In portraiture, the man of sensibility's emotional response to sights and situations was emphasised by an intensive gaze and by a move away from the depiction of the luxurious, often effeminate costume of the wealthy to plainer colours and dress, as in the Boothby portrait. By way of contrast, John Smart's 1770 miniature portrait of John Saville shows him wearing a formal powdered and curled wig, yet his plain shirt, buttoned jacket and intensive, heavy-lidded gaze link him to this genre. In addition to contemporary portraiture, a further connection between pantheism, love and sadness emerges from the contemporary literature and poetry to which Saville was drawn. The forerunners were Seward's favourites, *Julie*, which Rousseau had published in 1761, a few years before his visit to Staffordshire, and Richardson's *Clarissa*, of 1747–48. These were followed by Goethe's *The Sorrows of Young Werther* in 1774, the seminal novel of the confessional genre. This was one of Seward's long-standing favourites, and Saville, too, came to an empathic identification with the deep sensitivity, tears and sighs of the Ossian-reading, lovesick protagonist.

The portrait of Saville was, of course, one which held immeasurable significance to Seward, enough so for her to give it a carefully-planned female line of descent and to leave instructions on its care in her will. It is now in private ownership. After Saville's death at the age of sixty-seven, Seward sketched out a complimentary word portrait of him in his prime. He had a remarkably youthful appearance, she wrote. His hair was raven-black and luxuriant, and when it turned grey, he concealed its lack of colour with hair powder. He was a handsome man of average height and build, and his limbs had the most 'perfect shapeliness' to the very end of his life. Fundamental to the image outlined by Seward is Saville's mouth, which the Smart portrait depicts with full, shapely lips, and his voice, particularly his musical talent. His speaking and reading voice was clear and strong

---

[51]   *Brooke Boothby*, by Joseph Wright of Derby (1781), Tate Gallery, London.

and his singing tone mellow, with a most exceptional range from bass to tenor to contra-tenor. 'Ah! that you could hear as I have heard, "My Sheep I've neglected I've lost my sheep hook"', Seward told Walter Scott in 1805. 'But the lips, that so sweetly, and so emphatically, expressed the charming air, to which Arne set those beautiful words, are closed in eternal silence.'[52]

At this time, nearly everyone had some form of tooth decay. Seward was particularly proud of her own teeth, which were still healthily 'free from decay or discolour' well into her later life.[53] Erasmus Darwin lost all his teeth at an early age, and the consequent exposure of his gums and tongue when speaking had a repellent, ageing effect. Seward drew attention to this in her memoirs of Darwin by issuing a forceful disclaimer of his attributed habit of walking along with his tongue hanging out of his mouth. This, declared his detractors, gave him an appearance of 'idiot-seeming indelicacy'. If she was unconvinced by this depiction, she was confident enough to describe Darwin's eccentric appearance and faults in fine detail. Her illustration of his prematurely-aged, smallpox-scarred features, his portly body with heavy limbs, his habitually gloomy expression, his acute stammer, combined with his sarcastic scepticism and his concealed emotions, counterbalances her description of her perfect man: Saville.[54]

Adding to his charismatic appearance, John Saville's teeth and gums were exceptionally fine, she wrote, with no suggestion at all of decay, loss, imperfection or even of discolouration. He sang in public for most of his life and organised and conducted grand musical events and smaller private musical soirées. At one time, Seward considered writing Saville's biography, but he dissuaded her, as he wanted no attention at all outside his professional role. He refused to give his permission, reminding her of the 'unworthy reflections' she had been subjected to over their relationship.[55] In spite of Seward's depiction of a charming and handsome man, Saville had a poor self-image. Seward thought his diffidence to be 'the point of insanity in [his] disposition'. Eventually, the effects of age, his ill health and an undisclosed 'affliction' made him feel unattractive and ignorant. 'Few are so well informed, or have so much natural genius', she asserted, 'yet with tears in his eyes, and with the most pathetic earnestness, he is continually protesting that it is a disgrace to me to have so stupid, so unaccomplished a friend.'[56] When an intermittent neurological disease, which first started in 1792 and caused dizziness and faintness, made it difficult for him to travel, he cut down on many of his singing engagements but not his choral work at the cathedral. Smart painted his portrait in 1770, at the time when Saville and Seward were blissfully happy in

[52]   NLS, MSS, 3875, fols 58–60, Seward, 'Letter to Walter Scott' (9 March 1805).

[53]   Huntington Library, MSS JE 756–80, Seward, 'Letter to Edward Jerningham' (24 June 1800).

[54]   Seward, *Memoirs*, pp. 1–4.

[55]   Seward, 'Letter to Mrs Blore' (17 May 1804), *Letters*, vol. VI, p. 175.

[56]   Seward, 'Letter to Thomas Sedgewick Whalley' (22 March 1782), in Hill Wickham, *Journals and Correspondence of Thomas Sedgewick Whalley*, vol. I, p. 354.

their clandestine love. To Seward, he was the handsome, tragic hero, trapped in a loveless marriage with an evil wife, yet prepared to sacrifice his career and reputation for love. She was prepared to do the same.

In May 1773, Seward wrote to tell Dorothy Sykes that the gossips and mischief-makers who had tried to ruin her reputation had finally succeeded. Her parents became oppressive and she blamed them for the 'stain upon her character' by believing Erasmus Darwin's accusations of adultery. Once more, her father threatened her with 'worldly disadvantage', no little threat, as this would entail living a life of poverty, beholden to relatives or the kindness of friends. She now resisted any pretence of daughterly duty, insisting that she would not give in to their demands. She showed her contempt with the words: 'no creatures submit contentedly to their equals, much less to their inferiors'.[57] In her defence to Dorothy, she quoted the entire essay on parental callousness that Samuel Johnson had published in the *Rambler*: 'Dangerous and detestable are the cruelties often exercised in private families'.[58] Johnson believed that parents had no rights to 'control the inclinations of their daughters' in marriage matters. He often wondered why young women married at all, perceiving them to have much more freedom and attention when single, eventually concluding that their motive was 'the mechanical reason'; it was what young women did.[59] The cultural taboo of disobeying parental authority would hardly seem to have been a feasible option for her, as her father controlled her financial future and Saville had no money. Yet her decisions were conclusive; she would fight to retain her friendship with him. It was not possible to marry him, and as she refused to consider marrying without love, she would remain single.

In an expression of despair and disgust at the fate of 'spinsters' and their eventual metamorphosis into 'old maids', with their punishment supposedly continuing into the afterlife, as 'ape-leaders in hell', she railed against the conventions that kept unmarried women on the periphery of civilisation with a nebulous role in life, tied to their fathers, entirely financially dependent and at the mercy of traditional notions of parental duty:

> An unmarried woman from 25 until fifty, is often obliged to earn her daily bread by the most abject submissions to people, perhaps her inferiors in understanding, because they gave her a being which they render wretched. The disposal of her time, the choice of her friends, the dearest affections of her soul are wrested from her by caprice, or wrong judgement, the joy of her youth is turned into a mourning.[60]

Her unpublished sermon written for the Lichfield charitable ladies which encourages all women to find fulfillment through employment clearly indicates

---

[57]   JBM, MS 35/1, Seward, 'Letter to Dorothy Sykes' (May 1779).

[58]   Boswell, *Life of Johnson*, vol. III, p. 377.

[59]   Boswell, *Life of Johnson*, vol. II, p. 471.

[60]   JBM, MS 35/1, Seward, 'Letter to Dorothy Sykes' (May 1779).

her views on the value of women's contribution to society, regardless of their wealth or their marital status.[61]

At this time, Seward gave much thought to the nature of relationships and was most sympathetic to those around her whose love was unreciprocated and those who either chose or were forced to accept a celibate life. In her letters to Mary Powys, she speculated on the *feme sole* and the bachelor, on the origins of their single state, on their misogamy or their celibacy within marriage. A mutual friend, Mrs Wolseley, for example, had a 'warm imagination' but was 'disappointed in the joys of love'and had suddenly converted to Methodism. Now she directed all her energy towards spirituality. Seward believed that this was because her husband no longer wanted a physical relationship with her and that she had substituted religious fervour for sexual passion. Mrs Wolseley now had to 'set her heart upon raptures which her husband has not given her [and] she resolves to have divine ecstasies since *lawfully* she cannot have *human* ones.'[62]

This attitude was not uncommon. Traditionally, the church endorsed a husband's superiority over his wife and a father's authority over his daughters. At the start of the century, Mary Astell's *Reflections on Marriage* advise submission as the only possible alternative to a husband's authority, stating:

> What can the poor Woman do? the Husband is too wise to be Advis'd, too good to be Reform'd. She must follow all his Paces, and tread in all his unreasonable Steps, or there is no Peace, no Quiet for her, she must obey with the greatest exactness. 'Tis in vain to expect any manner of Compliance on his side, and the more she complies, the more she may.[63]

Later, the influential Anglican essayist and poet Hester Mulso Chapone strongly advised women trapped in unhappy marriages to turn to spirituality for alternative consolation: 'The comforts and helps of religion, with a firm resolution not to be driven out of the path of duty, can alone support you under such sorrow.'[64]

In her letters to Dorothy Sykes, Seward speculated about her father's curate at Eyam, Peter Cunningham, who had the manners of a gentleman, 'if not the powdered hair'. She believed that he had also turned to the church when disappointed in love, like Mrs Wolseley. Despite his long, dishevelled hair, his affected nasal delivery, his profound deafness that made Seward wish he would use an ear-trumpet, and his extreme short-sightedness for which he wore spectacles, he was exceptionally popular with the young women and with the widows of

---

[61]   NLS, Sir Walter Scott MSS, 880, fols 174–81. 'A Sermon written for the charitable Female Society at Lichfield about the year 1784 and frequently preached on its anniversary by one of the Clergymen at that Cathedral' (1784).

[62]   JBM, MS 38/1, Seward, 'Letter to Mary Powys' (23 April 1770).

[63]   Mary Astell, *Some Reflections on Marriage Occasioned by the Duke and Duchess of Mazarine's Case; Which is Also Considered* (London: John Nutt, 1700), p. 28.

[64]   Hester Mulso Chapone, 'Letter to a New-Married Lady', in *The Works of Mrs Chapone*, 4 vols (London: John Murray, 1807), vol. IV, p. 142.

the parish. Yet it was his choice to remain unmarried. Mary Powys was also set on remaining single for reasons which are unclear. On more than one occasion Seward urged her to consider changing her mind, as she believed that her friend would only find fulfillment with a husband. Disapproving of Mary's empty 'polite' circle, where 'folly and senseless etiquette' ruled, Seward ideally wanted to see her happily married.[65] Seward's advice to her friend to marry for mutual love and settle in the country, away from the shallow rituals of polite society, was most probably a projection of her own desires.[66]

Unsurprisingly, Thomas and Elizabeth Seward did not attempt to choose Anna's marriage partner as they had Sarah's, on the understanding that Anna would never be persuaded to enter an arranged marriage. She was not prepared to become a victim of the marketplace, yet the notion of withholding her inheritance if she married against their wishes was a constant threat which was sanctioned by the force of the church's authority. As far as marriage was concerned, the death of Sarah worked in her favour. It is not unreasonable to conclude that Thomas and Elizabeth wanted their remaining daughter to stay at home and care for them in their old age. She did live at the Palace for the rest of her life, but her letters clearly indicate that when her parents became ill, they were each nursed by old and trusted servants.[67]

'Spinster' and then 'old maid'– Seward had made her choice. She continued to see and to speak with John Saville whenever the occasion arose, and this forced a delicate negotiation between her reputation and her virtue. As she insisted that their relationship was innocent and thus her virtue was unaffected, there was no reason to forego Saville's friendship. But the stigma of her damaged reputation haunted her for years to come. As late as 1777, she was still flinging poison pen letters from London onto the fire. By far the worst part was being denied Saville's company. Defiant as always, she swept off to church each day. The morning service was the one event which her parents could not under any circumstances forbid her from attending. Each morning, she sought out Saville in the hope of a brief, stealthy word with him to find out the state of his health and, more importantly, that of his melancholy spirits. She describes her cheerless situation to Dorothy: 'This is all that remains to me of those happy days of friendship and confidence when the partaken pleasures of books, music & improving conversation wing'd the hours.'[68]

There were additional problems for John Saville. His livelihood as vicar-choral with the church was at risk. The old dean of the cathedral had decided to take action, and he sent for Saville to offer to continue his income if he moved away

---

[65]   JBM, MS 38/11, Seward, 'Letter to Mary Powys' (17 August 1782).

[66]   JBM, MS 38/4, Seward, 'Letter to Mary Powys' (c.1772).

[67]   Seward is generally presumed to have cared for her parents at the expense of her writing. The Powys and Sykes letters clearly indicate that although Seward was concerned for her parents' health and welfare, they were cared for by servants and maids.

[68]   JBM, MS 35/2, Seward, 'Letter to Dorothy Sykes' (27 July 1773).

from the area. Unable to contemplate life without Seward, Saville sent back word of his absolute refusal to listen to the proposal, telling Seward later that he would only be willing to leave Lichfield if it would make things more tolerable for her. But, he said, if he did move away, 'it would cost him his life', and Seward, too, could imagine nothing worse than losing sight of him completely.[69] In her practical way, she suggested that as the dean was extremely old and his decisions were only applicable during the course of his term at the cathedral, Saville was right to stand up to him. Time would work in his favour. Words of encouragement also came from Honora, who believed that the pair should defy parental and church authority.

There was little support from Dorothy Sykes. She urged Seward to consider her duty and end the relationship, suggesting that she should give up all hope of happiness and settle for vicarious pleasure in other people's joy. She added that her reward for being compliant would be in Heaven. The outspoken Dorothy blamed Seward's influence for her son Richard's recent 'undutiful behavior'. Richard openly supported Seward's rebellious obstinacy and had consequently become estranged from his parents. Seward wholeheartedly disagreed with Dorothy's notion of duty. She had lost her faith in an intervening, providential God, and she was now in a confused state, believing that she was destined for misery. She began to question the nature of the afterlife:

> I can never be persuaded that it is my duty to renounce the sight of [Saville] and those little transient conversations we sometimes have or that there wou'd be any virtue in doing it therefore I cou'd never expect the reward you mention of Heaven for bringing so much and such insupportable torture upon myself, ev'n if I believed that Providence made all worthy people happy here which that it does not […] I lov'd Saville for his virtues. He is entangled in a connection with the vilest of Women and the most brutally despicable. He cannot be my Husband but no law on earth on heaven forbids that he shou'd be my friend or debars us the liberty of conversing together while that conversation is innocent. The world has no right to suppose it otherwise.[70]

This was not the first time that Seward negotiated religious discourse with a challenge to the authority of the Church of England tenets and, consequently, to the control exerted over her by the Church's representative, her father. In the early 1770s she became fascinated by the religious beliefs of her close friend, the beautiful Quaker Mary (Molly) Knowles, who was born in nearby Rugeley, Staffordshire. Molly was well known for her needlepainting, using her skill at sewing to embroider finely-detailed pictures from famous paintings onto worsted.[71] She was particularly famed for a needlepainting of George III, which was a skilful

---

[69]   JBM, MS 35/1, Seward, 'Letter to Dorothy Sykes' (May 1773).

[70]   JBM, MS 35/1, Seward, 'Letter to Dorothy Sykes' (May 1773).

[71]   The term *needlepainting* originated in the seventeenth century, when it was used to describe the realistic designs of flowers and saints worked in smooth silks on vestments in French convents. Margaret Swain, *Embroidered Georgian Pictures*, Shire Albums: 307, I, Title II, Series 746.440941 (Haverfordwest: Shire Publications, 1994).

copy of his portrait by Zoffany. She also embroidered a remarkably intricate self-portrait in which she depicts herself at her frame, working at the needlepainting of the King.[72] Despite Molly being an eloquent rhetorician, a skilled writer, an accomplished garden designer and a campaigner against slavery, she was, and still is, best known for her needlepaintings. In the 1770s, she lived in London with her husband, the physician Dr Thomas Knowles, who was a member of the Committee of Six, the organisation set up by Quakers to oppose the slave trade.

In 1771, the 'pretty Quaker' and a companion known only as the 'Traveller' had visited the Bishop's Palace while Thomas Seward was in Eyam, and he was impelled to write, in his tiny, badly-punctuated copperplate, a long, pedantic outburst against the 'horrid Nonsense' of most religions other than his own, but particularly against Quakerism.[73] From Thomas's words, it is evident that Seward was greatly attracted to the work and way of life of the Quakers and that her natural curiosity led her to investigate matters of piety and spirituality outside her father's sphere. What appealed to her about dissenting religion was the prominent role taken by women. She enjoyed the sensation of her own sermons being preached, although the congregation had no knowledge of their female authorship. Thomas intended to remain the model for his daughter's Christian beliefs and was sufficiently irritated to question her wisdom:

> What therefore must be done by you whose Knowledge is of so very small extent both in sacred and profane History? Would you give up your whole Religion? And hazard your Salvation? Or would you apply to those who are more conversant in the Scriptures than yourself for better Information? – You do indeed sometimes apply to me; but it rarely seems as if you wish'd to have the Objections clear'd. You urge them with eagerness, and seem unwilling to be convinced.[74]

In his letter, Thomas claimed that as he and his daughter became far too heated in their theological arguments to ever reach a satisfactory conclusion, he was obliged to set out his opinions in writing. He appealed to her sense of duty, with just a suspicion of the fear of relinquishing control over her: '[B]elieve my dear Girl that when we endeavour to keep you steadfast in the Faith You were educated in, we are so far from endeavouring to *enslave* You, as You in your warmth told us we did.'[75]

---

[72] *George III*, by Mary Knowles (1771), Victoria and Albert Museum; *Needlework self-portrait*, by Mary Knowles (1779), HRM The Queen's Collection, Buckingham Palace.

[73] Lichfield RO, Seward Family MSS, D262/1/5, Thomas Seward, 'Letter to Nancy' (12 November 1771).

[74] Lichfield RO, Seward Family MSS, D262/1/5, Thomas Seward, 'Letter to Nancy' (12 November 1771).

[75] Lichfield RO, Seward Family MSS, D262/1/5, Thomas Seward, 'Letter to Nancy' (12 November 1771).

Molly Knowles was a powerful woman and a role model of the kind that Seward liked best. She describes Knowles' self-assurance and rhetorical command in a letter dated 1785 to her other strong role model, Anne Mompesson. Knowles put forward a persuasive, reasoned defence on behalf of a young Quaker friend, Jenny Harry, who had been distressed to the point of tears by an irately forthright Samuel Johnson.[76] The wealthy eighteen-year-old heiress, daughter of an East India planter, was at school in London when she converted to Quakerism, much to the concern of her father, who threatened to disinherit her. Knowles was instrumental to the conversion and supported her young friend's remarkable decision to turn down her inheritance of one hundred thousand pounds for the sake of her faith. As a friend of Jenny's guardian, Samuel Johnson was fond of her but was infuriated following her conversion. Jenny Harry chose to make her own decision about her religion, and there are parallels with this and Seward's battle with her father for her own freedom of spiritual expression. Although Knowles calmly faced up to Samuel Johnson's angry reasoning on Jenny's behalf, Seward raged back at her father, accusing him of attempting to force her into the dependency she despised.

The claustrophobic pressure from Thomas and Elizabeth was unrelenting. They persisted in attempting to manipulate what Seward did, what she thought, who she saw, who she was. As she struggled to gain a measure of self-determination and make sense of her new situation, she was forced to acknowledge that in matters of finance she was utterly dependent on them. Theirs was the ultimate monetary control, yet she was able to pull away from her father's doctrines and formulate her own philosophy. 'One likes to trace one's ideas and feelings to their *source*',[77] she confirmed to Mary Powys. Her predisposition to independent thought, her belief in expanding the mind when young, finds expression in an early poem in the manner of Spenser, 'Knowledge'. The poem has a similar approach to the anecdote of Harriet, whose sense of worth centred on her looks, not her capacity for learning. In 'Knowledge', she writes:

> Youth is life's spring, the seed-time, when the mind
> Fosters each new idea planted there;
> If we neglect to sow the grain refined,
> No future pains can raise a harvest fair;
> And memory, warm and soft in early year
> As yielding wax, disused, grows cold and hard,[78]

It was not just Quakers that Thomas Seward detested. Like many Anglicans, Anna Seward had been force-fed the belief that Roman Catholics were 'bigoted, superstitious, gloomy, tyrannic and absurd'. Yet a rare foray into literature in her correspondence with Mary Powys shows a tolerant approach in her theological opinions, and although she was not completely free of social prejudices, she was

---

[76] Jane Harry, the natural daughter of Thomas Hibbert.

[77] JBM, MS 38/6, Seward, 'Letter to Mary Powys' (27 February 1777).

[78] Seward, 'Knowledge', *Poetical Works*, vol. I, p. 10.

far more distanced from her father's own understandable limitations. She told Mary that she had read Pope Clement's *Letters* and that through them, much to her own surprise and pleasure, she had gained a fresh insight into human nature. She had also pushed her received prejudices aside to reveal a new perspective on Catholicism by exploring the religion from a literary viewpoint. Pope Clement was the Roman student of the Apostles, St Peter and St Paul, who was exiled in Crimea and eventually martyred. His letters, like St Paul's, were read as inspired scripture by the early church, and he was adopted as 'Ukraine's Pope'.[79]

She was quite fascinated by Clement's writings, finding in them examples of determination and wisdom. 'With what delight must one peruse his ev'ry sentiment', she wrote, gratified to have discovered a model for natural integrity that was greater than 'one has reason to expect from the frailty of our species'[80] and certainly superior to the 'enslavement' of the spiritual values imposed by her father. In Seward's writing, there is a notable absence of description of Thomas's spiritual headquarters, the cathedral, and scant details of the services and events there which she must have attended regularly. She could see its extraordinary three spires, the 'Ladies of the Vale', from the windows of the Bishop's Palace, yet she dissociated herself from what might have proved a wealthy source of poetic material.

The crisis of faith and exploration of theology was part of Seward's rebellion against the enforced structure of her life. But she had to come to terms with far more than being perceived as a scorned and pathetic 'spinster' on the road to loneliness and dependency as an 'old maid'. She also had to endure the implication of being considered an immoral, 'fallen' woman. There was also the battle against the prejudice surrounding what Walter Scott called 'that dreadful phaenomenon, a learned lady'.[81] Without the controlling influence of a man, the image of an intellectual woman was often perceived as too assertive. If Samuel Johnson believed Elizabeth Carter to be the rounded woman because she was able to make a pudding as well as translate Epictetus, he was in the minority. Molière's *femmes savantes* disrupted the household with their scientific studies:

> No science is too profound for [women]. [...] They know about the movements of the moon, the North Star, Venus, Saturn and Mars [...] but they don't know how my dinner, which I need, is coming along.[82]

James Miller's 1730 play, *The Humours of Oxford*, contrasts the figure of an elderly female scholar, Lady Science, with that of the male housekeeper to emphasise the

---

[79] Alexander Roman, 'Anchored in Christ: A Celebration of Ukraine's Pope', *Ukrainian Orthodoxy.* http://www.unicorne.org/orthodoxy/janfeb/stclement.htm.

[80] JBM, MS 38/7, Anna Seward, 'Letter to Mary Powys' (c.1777).

[81] Scott, 'Biographical Preface', *Poetical Works*, vol. I, p. vii.

[82] Molière [Jean Baptiste Poquelin], *Les Femmes Savantes* (Boston: D.C. Heath, 1896), Act II, Scene 7, p. 36.

supposed absurdity of the reversal of the traditional role. Miller's play satirises scholarly Oxford and the character Gainlove states:

> Why, People of either Sex, Madam, are generally imposed on, when they concern themselves with what is properly the Business of the other. The Dressing-Room, not the Study, is the Lady's Province – and a Woman makes as ridiculous a Figure, poring over Globes, or thro' a Telescope, as a Man would with a Pair of Preservers mending Lace.[83]

Lady Science agrees: 'I'll convert my Air-Pump into a Water-Pump, send all my Serpent's Teeth, Mummy's-Bones, and monstrous Births, to the Oxford's Museum; for the Entertainment of other as ridiculous Fools as my self.'[84]

To maintain control of their traditional intellectual activities, men's response was often to direct women back to their own traditional domain, reminding them that they were 'more suited to hold a needle than a pen'.[85] Seward, of course, manoeuvred both.

---

[83]   James Miller, *The Humours of Oxford: A Comedy* (1730), Act V, Scene 1, p. 79. http://lion.chadwyck.co.uk.

[84]   James Miller, *The Humours of Oxford*, p. 79.

[85]   Classen, *The Colour of Angels. Cosmology, Gender and the Aesthetic Imagination*, pp. 86–88.

Chapter 4
Lost Years:
The Powys and Sykes Letters

Far from wanting to be seen as domesticated, Seward was nevertheless proud of her sewing expertise, and her youthful self-construction included the portrayal of her proficiency with both pen and needle. In later life, the professional image she created for herself incorporated the notion of domesticity in order to divert attention from negative connotations of her single status, her relationship with Saville and her appropriation of male literary fields. In reality she provides no details at all of undertaking actual household tasks apart from her sewing. Scott's unambiguous reference to her compulsory 'ornamental' needlework gives the impression of a futile pastime of the idle rich.[1] But this was not useless employment; Seward's 'work' was infinitely practical and satisfying.

To a certain extent, she complied with the gendered conventions of needlework by pursuing a feminine occupation but combining it with an activity of masculine intellect. This was through simultaneous needlework and literary study. 'We are resuming our reading, and Working Parties', she wrote to Emma in 1764, indicating a gratifying but atypical blend of the two activities, as there are few references in literature to needlework as a sociable group activity for women, or to blending it with intellectual pursuits.[2] She mentions similar recreational activities in her juvenile letters, describing social situations involving sewing, such as a card party at the Bishop's Palace: 'You know the Lichfield young women do not play at cards. Six or seven of us were loitering at the windows and round the card tables, – expectation too busy with us for us to be busy with our needles.'[3] Later, in 1767, she describes a family holiday in the countryside where the mornings were spent 'at work', with the group of women sewing industriously while one of the party read aloud.[4]

As much as needlework was perceived to be entirely within the female domain, skill in embroidery endowed a woman with social status, and the ability to sew well was a useful practicality, if not a necessity. In a letter to Benjamin Pratt dated March 1804, Seward wrote tellingly that if she had to support herself financially, she would prefer to be a seamstress rather than a writer: 'If, from scarcity of money, my situation was *dependant*, I would seek to obtain my bread by my needle, at which I should prefer toiling 14 hours a day, rather than throw myself on the precarious

---

[1]   Scott, 'Biographical Preface', *Poetical Works*, vol. I, p. vii.

[2]   NLS, Sir Walter Scott MSS, 879, fol. 60 (August 1764).

[3]   Scott, 'Biographical Preface', *Poetical Works*, vol. I, p. cxvi.

[4]   Scott, 'Biographical Preface', *Poetical Works*, vol. I, p. cxc.

taste of the Public for *literary* composition.'[5] When she blended her traditional female 'work' and her male scholarship, she presented an intriguing dichotomy in the self-expression of her status. She conformed to the stereotype of the upper-class woman with her inherent talent for fine, creative embroidery, what Moll Cobb called her 'catgut genius', yet even this had a functional aspect. The catgut lace was more than an imaginative invention of 'ornamental' embroidery; it also had its practical uses: she wore it. Her laces assume an additional importance by their inclusion in her will. Like Richardson's Clarissa, who frames her embroidery and bequeaths it to her friends in her own will, Seward left her 'best laces, whether they be on gowns or handkerchiefs, or lie unmade up in my drawers' to Elizabeth Smith, who was John and Mary Saville's daughter.[6]

Elizabeth 'Eliza' Smith, who had been left a young widow on the early death of her spendthrift husband, was a nervous but gifted professional singer, trained by her father. As Eliza grew, Seward took a great pride in her singing talent, encouraging her progress from a timid young woman in local performances to a singer of national repute, like her father. Eliza's achievements are celebrated in the poem 'To Mrs Smith, Daughter of Mr Saville, on her Singing in Public, January 1789', which compares her voice to a forest brook heard at midnight:

> And would'st thou a resembling music hear
> And learn how meet thy notes the general ear,
> Come to the wild wood, and the glen with me,
> When leafy June has curtain'd every tree;
> There, in the still noon of the lunar night,
> Shall sounds congenial thrill thee with delight,
> When, his beneath long grass, a liquid tune
> The bubbling runnel warbles to the moon.[7]

Eliza lived with her father and she travelled with Seward and Saville on holidays and on visits to friends. She sometimes resented Seward's maternal concern for her, thinking that she meddled in areas that did not concern her. There was a short estrangement between them when Seward told her off for her extravagance. She explained to her friend, the poet Thomas Whalley, how her own indifference to fashion was at variance with Eliza's expensive habits:

> Six weeks since [Eliza] was offended at my observing that, since the fashions change so perpetually, I wondered she should choose to purchase a new black beaver hat, the second she has bought within the last year, and a new bonnet of expense, both at the same time, on her return from the Continent. Upon my adding, 'Indeed, my dear, I should have thought myself extravagant in purchasing

---

5   Lichfield RO, Seward Family MSS, D262/1/16, Seward, 'Letter to Benjamin Pratt' (March 1784).

6   Lichfield RO, Seward Family MSS, D262/1/35, p. 1.

7   Seward, 'To Mrs Smith, Daughter of Mr Saville, on her Singing in Public, January 1789', *Poetical Works*, vol. II, pp. 350–51.

two such hats at once,' she rose with a countenance of scorn, saying as she left the room, 'I am not at all afraid of being thought extravagant for that.' From that time she has never entered my doors.[8]

The fraught situation was not helped by Saville's indulgence. He thought Seward was harsh, accusing her of jealousy. He complained that she was 'disposed to look with the eye of unjust prejudice upon all [Eliza's] conduct'.[9] The rift was eventually healed and, in the traditional symbolism of a female skill passed from mother to daughter, the bequest of laces emphasises Seward's maternal feelings for Elizabeth.

It was usually the work of female servants, and there were many at the Bishop's Palace, to perform plain sewing duties. Despite this and regardless of the many shops which sold ready-made clothes and fashion accessories to an increasingly consumerist female market, Seward sewed her own dresses and she made items for friends. At one time, she made a set of 'ruffles' and a work-bag for Dorothy Sykes, and on another occasion she sent her a dress pattern, saying she had just completed a dress for herself in coloured worsted. She also embroidered an elaborate waistcoat for a Lichfield friend, Charles Buckeridge, to wear at the assemblies. Creative needlework was an infinitely more suitable occupation than creative writing for a young woman of Seward's status, and, as she occupied the tedious hours in the absence of the friends who had deserted her over her relationship with Saville, she still sought a satisfactory identity for herself. Her solution was to shift her needlework into an intellectual arena in the 1770s with one practical project and another which offers an insight into her own perception of her skill.

As a charitable exercise, she made a set of net letter-cases with an original poem sealed inside each one. Four of these were donated to the Lichfield Charitable Repository to raise money for their various causes. Each letter-case had its individual designation and a relevant poem. The first is addressed to a young married lady, and its purpose is to preserve 'each tender animated line' from an absent husband; the second is to a young unmarried lady, a 'silken cage' for 'thy future swain's fond letters'; the third is to 'the lady, whether single or married, who shall charitably purchase this trifle'; and the fourth is to the lady who 'may purchase this envelope, and who may not be a celebrated beauty'. A fifth letter-case was for the Dowager Lady Blakiston, an old friend.[10] The letter-cases exemplify the dexterous skill with which Seward negotiated 'housewifely art' within the sphere of intellect. In this instance, her 'work' was a synthesis of needlework, charity work, letters and poems.

Whereas Clarissa's framed embroidery is a decorative and lasting memento, Seward's bequeathed laces had a transitory value. They were intended to be

---

[8] Seward, 'Letter to Thomas Sedgewick Whalley' (12 January 1792), in Wickham, *Letters and Correspondence of Thomas Sedgewick Whalley, DD*, pp. 68–69.

[9] Seward, 'Letter to Thomas Sedgewick Whalley', p. 68.

[10] Seward, 'Inscriptions, sealed up and inclosed in net letter-cases, presented to the Charitable Repository at Lichfield', *Poetical Works*, vol. III, pp. 109–13.

usefully applied, to be worn. If her needlework was not a recording for posterity, her embroidery within her poetry certainly was. In the sequence of epistolary poems that make up her juvenile work, *Love Elegies and Epistles*, one of the two elegies written from Emillia to Evander is entitled 'Elegy. Emillia Embroidering – And Jealous'. Seward presents embroidery as the signifier of sensibility. It is the narrator's natural sensitivity to the appeal of 'grace and beauty' which enables her 'obedient needle' to create artificial flowers. She points to this potent sensibility as the cause of her over-sensitive attraction to 'Evander's charming form' and to her subsequent jealousy of Lydia, a rival for his love. The narrator portrays herself surrounded by a group of friends who admire the intricate handiwork of her embroidery. She confesses that her skilful stitches emanate from the source of a 'treacherous sense' and that the idea of her reaction to nature, to the 'brilliant glow' of the flowers that her work mimics, relates to her 'delusive joy'. Her mimic flowers represent the illusory nature of physical attraction:

> My partial friends, ye praise the mimic flowers,
> Which from my hand, in gay creation, rise;
> But, ah! this little talent's flatter'd powers
> No pleasing gleam of self-applause supplies.
>
> Vainly ye descant on the golden light,
> Vainly the soft and blended shades ye praise;
> Observe my florets swell upon the sight,
> And curve, and float from their entwining sprays.
>
> Fatal to me has proved this native sense
> Of grace and beauty, that their brilliant glow
> Taught my obedient needle to dispense,
> And lead their wavy lines in easy flow.
>
> But for that treacherous sense, with calm survey,
> These eyes EVANDER's charming form had met,
> Then had my peaceful night, my jocund day,
> Escaped delusive joy, and long regret.[11]

The delicate interlacing of flower buds that drift free from their glimmering landscape background evokes the deep emotion of sensibility through more than the sense of sight, but also through smell and touch, which represent feminine sensibility, as opposed to masculine reason. The trope of release is inspired by Emillia's 'obedient' needle, which conforms equally to the passive feminine stereotype and to the sense of heady freedom that she bestows on the objects of her imagination, the flowers, as they appear to escape their confines. Sensibility moves ambiguously towards sensuality in the description of 'my florets', which 'swell',

---

[11]   Seward, 'Elegy: Emillia Embroidering – And Jealous' from 'Love Elegies and Epistles', *Poetical Works*, vol. I, pp. 31–32.

'curve' and 'float' free of their 'entwining sprays', adding a physical dimension to an otherwise aesthetic perception. By uniting her writing and needlework talents in this way, Seward did not comply with conventional standards but adapted them to suit her own needs. There is certainly no genuine impression of the shrinking passivity that the cult of sensibility demanded from women.

From 1774 onwards, the letters to Dorothy Sykes and Mary Powys change in tone, becoming more mature. There is a greater attention to detail and punctuation, and there is now a slight formality to them, despite Seward's constant apologies for carelessness due to the pressures of so much writing. Elizabeth Seward was sickening quite badly from a whole series of disorders and was nursed devotedly by Seward's old servant, Molly Clarke, who became Elizabeth's indispensable 'right hand'.[12] Dorothy Sykes continued to urge Seward to forget about Saville and Seward continued to refuse, although she was becoming increasingly isolated. Her book-loving coterie had deserted her, and some of her oldest friends, Isabella Coltman for one, were openly and publicly cruel to her. In 1772, Seward had commemorated Isabella in a poem in which she indicates that her friend was an intellectual and that she '[shuns] the haunts of pride and envious strife'.[13] Isabella's rejection was painful and the implications of isolation were becoming tedious. Seward wrote to Dorothy Sykes that she looked forward to an invitation to her home, Westella, where she could once more enjoy the reading parties that she missed so much. Her father Thomas was continually confrontational and single-minded, always irritable when his opinions were challenged. 'When his sentiments are oppos'd, his way is to fall in a passion, and abuse the book or person who expresses contrary ideas',[14] she complained to Dorothy, aligning him with the kind of men who make use of invective when their own argument is weak.

By the end of December 1775, the situation had altered a little; she was now seeing Saville quite openly again and her relationship with her mother had improved. Saville had contracted a serious eye condition with a painful inflammation, and, most alarmingly, an opaque film was spreading downwards and clouding his vision. Concerned for his sight, Seward wrote to Molly Knowles in London to ask if her physician husband knew of a suitable eye surgeon, or 'occulist'. The 'great Sharpe' was recommended, and Saville left Lichfield to stay at the Knowles' house in the capital while he had his treatment. Samuel Sharpe was the famous surgeon at Guy's Hospital who treated George Frederick Handel's blindness. His remedy or surgery must have worked well for Saville, as there are no further references to his vision. Writing with a great deal of affection and pride, Seward told Mary Powys that Saville's singing was becoming enormously popular throughout the country. As his reputation spread, she was convinced that a restrained, temperate lifestyle had made his voice improve with age. He had been offered five guineas a

---

[12] JBM, MS 35/4, Seward, 'Letter to Dorothy Sykes' (10 January 1774).

[13] Seward, 'To Mrs Coltman of Hull', *Poetical Works*, vol. I, pp. 108–9.

[14] JBM, MS 35/5, Seward, 'Letter to Dorothy Sykes' (12 January 1774).

night for a series of performances, but like his daughter, Elizabeth, he was modest and worried about the enormity of the task.

Away from Lichfield, not all the unmarried men Seward met were overly concerned about the rumours of immorality that surrounded her. Following a quarrel with Saville in 1777, there was a breakdown in whatever communication was open to them and this caused serious misunderstandings. For a short while, she believed that he no longer loved her. She concealed the argument from her friends and family for as long as she could, as she knew that both Dorothy Sykes and her mother would relish this new situation. Dorothy found out, however, and joined Elizabeth Seward in making plans for her future, having first complained that Seward had not confided in her. Seward responded, 'That I did not mention to *you* the quarrel between Mr S. and myself, by no means arose from want of confidence but from the same reason that keeps my silence on the subject from my Mother – I know she wishes the connection broke off, I know also that you have the same wish & are kind enough to interest yourself warmly in my destiny.'[15]

Despite Seward's attempts to keep her personal life private, when the news of the quarrel leaked out, the matchmaking began. At Eyam that summer, a friend called Mr Vernon rode over regularly from his home in Buxton with the sole purpose of seeing her. A widower with three children, he made his feelings towards her obvious, but although he was wealthy and educated she found him unattractive, thin and awkward, and 'he wears a *wig*!'.[16] She dismissed any attempts by her Eyam friends to match her with Peter Cunningham, her father's curate, her excuse being that there was 'no beauty in his eyes'.[17] At the Sykeses' mansion in Yorkshire, she listlessly ignored the attentions of a wealthy family friend, known only as Mr W— from Hull. Despite the Sykeses' best attempts at matchmaking, the couple were not realistically compatible; he was much older and they had no common interests. Clearly responsive to the negative undercurrents that eddied around her reputation, she remarked that it would have only been possible to encourage his advances if they had been closer in age, if she had been his 'type' of woman and, most significantly, if her conduct 'had never been censor'd'.[18] Seward and Saville resolved their misunderstanding a little while later.

Health is a recurrent theme throughout the Powys and Sykes correspondence. Aside from her mother's and Saville's health, Seward's own health was becoming a cause for anxiety. She developed a violent cough, always a concern when respiratory diseases were widespread and so very many young people died of tuberculosis, pneumonia or bronchitis. To complicate matters, an influenza epidemic was sweeping through Lichfield 'like a plague', leaving many deaths in its wake.[19] The 'moat' of running water surrounding Erasmus Darwin's house had

---

15   JBM, MS 35/16, Seward, 'Letter to Dorothy Sykes' (5 September 1777).
16   JBM, MS 35/15, Seward, 'Letter to Dorothy Sykes' (29 August 1777).
17   JBM, MS 35/15, Seward, 'Letter to Dorothy Sykes' (29 August 1777).
18   JBM, MS 35/16, Seward, 'Letter to Dorothy Sykes' (5 September 1777).
19   JBM, MS 35/8, Seward, 'Letter to Dorothy Sykes' (10 December 1775).

long since dried up and, as Lichfield had no other renewable water source and was surrounded by marshy fields, the sanitary conditions were not the best and diseases tended to spread rapidly. By 1776, Seward's health began to reflect her depressed mental state. Darwin treated her for unexplained violent stomach pains which, as she explained to Dorothy Sykes, were not due to the 'stone',[20] but to a 'strong concretion of the bile' that caused vomiting followed by the 'exquisite torture' of constant queasiness and dry retching.[21] Her skin darkened and she lost her appetite and felt depressed, lethargic and utterly demoralised by Lichfield life.

Throughout this series of illnesses, Seward did not lose any of her excess weight; her figure remained dropsically stout. 'I shall never lose my flesh till my little sisters feed upon it', she confided, morbidly quoting a gruesome poem by David Mallet, '"The hungry worm my sister is".'[22] Until she was thirteen years old, Seward was slim – 'light as a wood-nymph' – and healthily energetic with an 'Eveish desire' for countryside pursuits.[23] But a month's stay at the country seat of Sir George Coldbrand, which coincided with the onset of puberty, generated a tendency for plumpness which remained with her throughout her life.[24]

In a letter to Mrs Cotton dated 23 March 1787, Seward describes the events leading to her dramatic change in shape. Despite her age, her parents were concerned about her apparent sexual maturity. Lady Coldbrand, much to Thomas Seward's concern, evidently held expectations for her puny, effeminate, 'shadow of a shade' nineteen-year-old son or his younger brother, insinuating that both her sons would prove to be men of 'gallantry and intrigue' during Seward's visit. When they arrived at the Palace to collect Seward, her father was relieved to see no possible threat from the young men, and he mocked their feeble appearance: 'What have we here? These Coldbrands the giants! These same mighty men! [...] In the name of chastity let the girl go. If she can be in danger from such heroes, she must be infinitely too seducible to escape by any possible restraints parental prudence can impose.' During the course of the long, hot August Seward, who was accustomed to the simplest of food, was fed 'like a porket' and deprived of all exercise of the body and mind. Food was plentiful and existence was slothful:

> [...] with chocolate, drank in bed at eight; a nap till ten; tea and hot-rolls at eleven; pease soup at one; a luxurious dinner at four; and an hot and splendid supper at midnight – the day-light intervals filled up with slow airings in the old coach, along the dusty roads, for it was in the heats of a blazing summer; and with lying on a couch, picking honesty from madam's flower-pots, without any danger of molestation from her puny sons.

---

[20]   The term for a bladder infection.

[21]   JBM, MS 35/9, Seward, 'Letter to Dorothy Sykes' (1 June 1776).

[22]   JBM, MS 35/9, Seward, 'Letter to Dorothy Sykes' (1 June 1776). David Mallet's poem, 'Margaret's Ghost' was published in Thomas Percy's *Reliques of Ancient English Poetry*, 2nd edn (London: J. Dodsley, 1767).

[23]   Seward, 'Letter to Mrs Cotton', (23 March 1787), *Letters*, I, 268.

[24]   'Letter to Mrs Cotton', 23 March 1787, *Letters*, vol. I, pp. 265–70.

This excursion into the realms of the idle rich taught Seward that the interface between mind and body relied on the 'charms of nature', and the varied amusements from 'city resources', for its health. Isolated from her usual, vigorous pastimes, with no walking or riding, no reading or socialising, and where even needlework was frowned on as 'vulgar', Seward found herself mentally and physically flabby. She was able to counteract the former, but not the latter.

The quantity of food and drink served by one's host was an indicator of wealth, although there was an awareness of the link between diet and health. Samuel Johnson wrote a *Rambler* essay against 'gulosity', but James Boswell placed this in perspective with a description of his voracious appetite, writing '[Johnson] was not a *temperate* man either in eating or drinking'.[25] But then neither was Boswell. There was more than an expression of wealth in food consumption; there were also complex implications of self-image and behavioural characteristics. Dr George Cheyne, the fashionable Bath physician, suggested a vegetarian diet with abstinence from all liquor apart from 'only a pint of wine a day'.[26] His own severe obesity problems (at one time, he weighed over thirty-two stone) led to his study of the connection between spirituality and corporeality. Linking weight loss with religious and secular fasting, Cheyne adapted Pythagoreanism, and many of his patients and followers were seen to be taking the diet to extremes by half-starving themselves. Particularly in the case of women, there appears to be an element of control in his systems. Women did control their weight by diet, and sometimes by self-starvation, in order to wear the stylish *petite* and dainty, boned, laced and corseted clothes which fashion demanded. Frances Burney hints at anorexia nervosa and bulimia nervosa in her writings; in *The Witlings*, young women are depicted as dieting to excess, and there is the more disturbing trait of bingeing in *The Woman-hater*.[27] Burney was tiny and picked at her food, in public at least. Even Clarissa Harlowe, whose creator Samuel Richardson was a follower of George Cheyne, attempts to exert control over her life through semi-starvation.[28]

A little closer to home, Erasmus Darwin took a great interest in food and drink. His only recorded drinking session resulted in a fully-clothed swim in the river Trent and a garbled address to the people of Nottingham market whilst standing on top of a tub. He recommended that his patients follow his own diet of milk, cream, fruit, vegetables, meat, butter and sugar. When the prison reformer John Howard visited Seward at Lichfield, she was fascinated that he was both a teetotaller and a vegetarian, which she felt added to his charisma and 'super-human Virtue'.[29] She rarely mentions food and its effects in her letters, other than temperance and

---

[25]   Boswell, *Life of Johnson*, vol. VI, pp. 468–69.

[26]   Lisa Picard, *Dr Johnson's London: Life in London, 1740–1770* (London: Weidenfeld & Nicolson, 2000), p. 161.

[27]   Claire Harman, *Fanny Burney: A Biography* (New York: Alfred A. Knopf, 2001), p. 71.

[28]   Richardson, *Clarissa*, pp. 1053–54.

[29]   JBM, MS 38/12, Seward, 'Letter to Mary Powys' (c. 1782).

moderation, although she refers to her weight with regret. The cause of her excess weight lay in her health. Certainly in later life, she was plagued by the lymph disorder dropsy. Eating disorders in adolescent girls, breaking cultural rules and codes of conduct, are now associated with family identity crises, and it is feasible that despite her denials, Seward over-ate as a psychosomatically-induced revolt against her stifled and controlled adolescence.

At times during the 1770s, Seward was so drained with life in Lichfield that she wanted to move to London, saying she needed just a small amount of money to survive on and to pay for theatre and opera visits. Yet, she wrote, she would miss Lichfield's fresh air: 'I shou'd sadly regret the freshness and sweetness of rural gales in Summer', which she associated with good health.[30] Her various ailments did not leave her confined to the house, and she thought physical pain was preferable to inner turmoil, the 'foreboding sickness of *heart*'.[31] Even a spell in Eyam was no help, because the continual round of breakfast, dinner and evening parties always took precedence above sewing and books. There was some consolation in visiting the wealthier families in the area, who provided delicious exotic fruits, such as pineapples and bananas, and lit their rooms with an extravagance of wax candles.[32]

Seward's state of health had never been particularly good, as she had suffered from painful chronic rheumatism from youth. A serious knee injury sustained in an accident at twenty-six became a constant source of agony, and while she concealed the disability most of the time, she was left with a permanent weakness that caused her leg to give way occasionally. Other illnesses troubled Seward, including high blood pressure, with frequent and alarming nose haemorrhages, and dropsy. At one time she had whitlows on her fingers and toes, which caused her nails to fall out but did not prevent her from writing. Following an accident where she fell against the fireplace and injured her breast, she developed an extreme horror of breast cancer, which even the reassurance of top medical specialists could not dismiss. Although the pioneering research by surgeons such as John Hunter and his brother William, whose lectures Erasmus Darwin attended, identified age, heredity and climate as the major causes of breast cancer, her fear of a cancer-causing blow had its foundations in the death of Hester Thrale Piozzi's mother, Hester Maria Salusbury, whose own breast cancer was attributed to an accidental blow. Seward knew about this and about mastectomy operations. The pain, haemorrhaging and risk of infection involved in this type of procedure were fearful to all women.[33] The pain from Seward's accident was with her for several years, and she found a measure of relief for this and for her rheumatism in the comforting spring waters and baths of Bristol, Buxton and Matlock and the less-welcomed sea bathing in the chilly waters of the Yorkshire resort of Scarborough, a cure recommended by

---

[30] JBM, MS 38/6, Seward, 'Letter to Mary Powys' (27 February 1777).
[31] JBM, MS 38/6, Seward, 'Letter to Mary Powys' (27 February 1777).
[32] JBM, MS 35/15, Seward, 'Letter to Dorothy Sykes' (29 August 1777).
[33] Seward, 'Letter to Mrs Price' (1 September 1796), *Letters*, vol. IV, pp. 243–47.

Erasmus Darwin. As a wealthy woman, she was fortunate that she could afford to travel for treatments and to pay for advice and care from the best doctors, and, of course, one of the most renowned and innovatively successful in the Midlands was Darwin himself.

Seward's lethargy rallied a little when she became involved in the education of Marianne, the eleven-year-old daughter of Joseph and Dorothy Sykes. Dorothy had written to say that she was looking for a tutor for Marianne, and Seward was concerned that the child would pick up a Yorkshire accent from a local teacher. She persuaded her friends to consider sending her to a reputable boarding school instead. 'A polished manner of speaking is important to young Women', she wrote.[34] She recommended a boarding school, run by Mrs Lattufier, which Honora had attended as a day pupil for two years and which had now moved to Derby. Children at boarding school generally slept two to a bed, but Mrs Lattufier could accommodate Marianne with the luxury of a bed to herself for a fee of twenty-five guineas per annum.

The following June, despite being weakened by a violent, recurrent illness which caused vomiting and a constant fever, Seward wrote to reassure an anxious Joseph Sykes that his daughter would be safe at the Lattufier boarding school. Writing that she knew all the staff there, she spoke of their good qualities.[35] Marianne had become a little favourite during Seward's visits to the Sykeses at Westella, and Joseph had asked her to 'cultivate their daughter's talents'.[36] It was agreed that Marianne would spend a few weeks at the Palace in preparation for school. There were parallels with Seward's previous pupil Honora, who had been a willing student of literary lessons, and she filled her empty days in excited preparations for the child's education. It was rewarding for her to have purpose in her life at last:

> I have the *inclination* to impart instruction on this dear Girl. To that end I have enter'd upon a strict plan of studies with her, which employs us from nine in the morning to five in the afternoon. The task is pleasing, for she is gentle, and of quick comprehension – she recalls to my feelings the delightful hours of Honora's opening youth.[37]

Seward arranged for music lessons from the cathedral organist, Mr Brown, while teaching Marianne reading and a little needlework herself. She decided that a cultural education for her temporary ward was necessary and took her to her mother's parties and on visits to aristocratic friends, such as Lady Smith. For a brief moment, she was in her element. Keeping her 'sweet pupil's' anxious parents informed of their daughter's progress, and insisting that they bear in mind what kind of woman they wanted her to become, she assured them that she would follow

---

34   JBM, MS 35/7, Seward, 'Letter to Dorothy Sykes' (c. 1775).
35   JBM, MS 35/9, Seward, 'Letter to Dorothy Sykes' (1 June 1776).
36   JBM, MS 38/7, Seward, 'Letter to Mary Powys' (c. 1777).
37   JBM, MS 38/7, Seward, 'Letter to Mary Powys' (c. 1777).

their wishes in every respect.[38] After a few days, Seward's enthusiasm soured when she discovered that Marianne had nothing in common with Honora and rather than work hard at her books and sewing, she had a tendency to laziness. She willingly relinquished her charge, writing to Dorothy to explain the boarding school system in remarkable detail. She told her friend to contact the school's governess, requesting that Marianne be allowed to have tea for breakfast and to ensure that she was given mittens to wear in cold weather. Most importantly, she must have her own keys for her locker, said Seward, so that the 'little Harpies cannot steal her cake and toys'.[39] Later, when Marianne was a teacher by profession and had established two charity schools, Seward spoke with tremendous pride of 'my pupil'.[40]

The leaden hours of the latter part of the 1770s gave Seward the time to indulge in reminiscence. A fascinating letter to Mary Powys, dated 1781 and written during the early days of Seward's career as a published writer, looks back on the cheerless times of the previous few years. By now, Elizabeth Seward, Honora Edgeworth and John André were all dead. Thomas Seward was slowly descending into senility following a stroke. The letter is written in response to Mary's congratulations on Seward's successful publications and the new literary acclaim pouring in from all quarters. The letter is partially censored. It is just possible to read some of the text beneath the unknown censor's thick, black scribbled lines. Seward regrets the passing of happier times and explains that she would rather relinquish all her honours to live the life she had once lived. She believed that she was now paying the price of happiness which, she claims, alternates with sorrow: 'Perhaps few have tasted the delights as *liberally* as myself.'[41]

Her estrangement from Honora is not fully explained in the letter, although Seward puts the blame on Edward Sneyd. The two met regularly and wrote for several years, and then something happened to end their close friendship: 'I saw her no longer, she no longer lov'd me.' In this letter, Seward also writes of her 'long friendship' with Saville, how she 'softens his discontent' and he comforts her on the loss of Honora. Throughout her life, she said, she put little value on literary fame. Of all her Lichfield friends, there was now only Saville left to share the accolades with her. She wrote that the tributes were meaningless to her. Her memories of her life before this time were more precious to her than all the honours she had ever received, or might receive in the future.[42]

After Honora left Lichfield for Ireland, Seward began to place a greater significance on reminiscence and on the consolation to be found in the remembrance of an idyllic past. She felt these nostalgic memories could only be shared with her friends who had been there with her. Mary Powys was one of the few loyal friends left who could share the reminiscences. The memory of the past was a comforting

---

[38]   JBM, MS 35/12, Seward, 'Letter to Dorothy Sykes' (4 January 1777).

[39]   JBM, MS 35/12, Seward, 'Letter to Dorothy Sykes' (4 January 1777).

[40]   Seward, 'Letter to Mrs Short' (29 July 1793), *Letters*, vol. III, p. 287.

[41]   JBM, MS 38/10, Seward, 'Letter to Mary Powys' (11 December 1781).

[42]   JBM, MS 38/10, Seward, 'Letter to Mary Powys' (11 December 1781).

force, Seward claimed, one that 'softens the pangs of deprivation', and this theme reverberates through her poetry of the time.[43] She was drawn to reflection on the bittersweet notion of transience very much in the style of Goethe. Her writings of this time echo Werther's contemplations that the font of man's contentment becomes the source of his misery, as he mourned for his earlier years when he optimistically believed in the eternal energy of nature:

> [O]nly the recollection of those times gives me any pleasure. Even the effort of recalling those inexpressible feelings and uttering them once more uplifts my soul, and then leaves me doubly aware of the fearfulness of the condition I am now in.[44]

Like Charlotte Smith's similar tribute, Seward's literary homage to Werther's sorrows is to be found in a collection of sonnets.[45] There is also a poem entitled 'Written in the Blank Page of the Sorrows of Werter' [*sic*].[46] Taking the opportunity to speak out against the novel's detractors, she puts forward a defence against its perceived moral ambiguity in an extensive footnote. She is bent on opposing the critics who believed the character should have been portrayed as wicked because of his 'criminal' indiscretion. 'There has been much ridiculous cant about the fancied immorality of these interesting volumes', she maintains. 'Werter, by giving way to his affection for an engaged woman, though without the least design to seduce her, renders his own existence insupportable.'[47] As engagement was covered by moral and legal obligation, and as Seward believed the narrative to be based on actual events, she criticises the notion of indulging in a 'hopeless passion'. Yet, she also makes a forceful acknowledgement of Goethe's depiction of human frailty, with which she surely identified, taking into consideration her own experiences of this time.

She concludes that there could be no possible inducement to copy the conduct of the characters. What she is saying here is that Goethe's novel actually transmits a moral warning rather than inciting moral turpitude. Her own poem appeals to the reader's sense of compassion for 'the wretched victim', and, in line with her fixation on transience and reminiscence, she wants to capture and immortalise Werther's happier past in the reader's imagination:

---

[43]   JBM, MS 38/10, Seward, 'Letter to Mary Powys' (11 December 1781).

[44]   Johann Wolfgang von Goethe, *The Sorrows of Young Werther*, trans. by Michael Hulse (London: Penguin Books, 1989), p. 66.

[45]   Charlotte Smith wrote five sonnets which were 'supposed to have been written by Werther' (Curran, *The Poems of Charlotte Smith*, pp. 26–29).

[46]   Seward, 'Written in the Blank Page of the Sorrows of Werter', *Poetical Works*, vol. II, pp. 130–32.

[47]   Seward, 'Written in the Blank Page of the Sorrows of Werter', *Poetical Works*, vol. II, p. 130.

Still, as thou weep'st their unresisted powers,
The virtues of the lost-one's happier hours
Shall oe'r his fatal errors gently rise,
Live in thy heart, and consecrate thy sighs![48]

Her use of 'consecrate' gives a spiritual value to the idea of remembrance, whether her own thoughts of times and people past or the shared memory of her own, and Goethe's, readership. She challenges the notion of Providence once more in her reference to Werther's 'fatal errors', his suicide, an action condemned by many contemporaries as a mortal sin with no hope of forgiveness. The intrinsic worth of his virtues, she intimates, more than compensates for his human failings.

Seward's tribute continues with her series of three sonnets written in the character of Werther in which she expands on the sentiments and images taken from one of the protagonist's letters to Wilhelm. In Goethe's narrative, Werther is drawn to a moonlight-flooded valley. As he stands watching the raging torrents, his thought is to end his sorrows by leaping into the abyss, but an overwhelming sense that his time has not yet come stops him. In the first of her Werther sonnets, Seward describes the floods as metaphorical 'tides of misery and disgrace'. In the second, the narrator imagines, longs for, death in the torrent and contemplates what spells keep him rooted to the spot. The final sonnet invokes the soothing effect of memory on the narrator's tortured soul:

Yet O! lest my remorseless fate decree
That all I love, with life's extinguish'd rays
Sink from my soul, to sooth this agony,
To balm that life, whose loss may forfeit thee,
Come dear Remembrance of Departed Days.[49]

In her four poems and the footnotes, Seward showers compassion on the actions of an obsessed, suicidal character and urges her readers to act similarly. Whatever her own relationship to the Werther story, she achieves more than the self-reflection of personal sorrow. She endorses the expression of humanitarian values and sensibility.

Seward's letters to the two close friends of this time, particularly those to Mary Powys, who was fond of both Saville and Honora, are filled with shared memories, and in her will she left Mary an 'unfavourable, and most imperfect' miniature portrait of Honora which had been sketched by John André at Buxton in 1769. She knew Mary would treasure the portrait because of her 'true and inextinguishable love of the Original'.[50] These thoughts are in keeping with Seward's poetry of the time. Previously, for example in her juvenile work, the optimistic 'Ode to

---

[48]   Seward, 'Written in the Blank Page of the Sorrows of Werter', *Poetical Works*, vol. II, pp. 130–32.

[49]   Seward, 'Sonnets LXXXVIII; LXXXIX; XC', *Poetical Works*, vol. III, pp. 209–11.

[50]   Lichfield RO, Seward Family MSS, D262/1/35, p. 2.

Content', which she wrote before the problems started, she apostrophised the abstract categories, 'Pleasure', 'Fancy', 'Truth', and 'Love', and specifically 'Content', pleading for its influence to shine on Honora, for:

> More does she prize one halcyon plume of thine
> Than all that decks Ambition's jewel'd brow.[51]

These characterisations serve to emphasise her youthful close familiarity with the pleasant, comfortable aspects of existence, with no real consideration for transience. Conversely, her ideas directly after Honora's departure and Saville's enforced estrangement are drawn from a melancholy reflection on her previous happiness and its usurpation by bleak loneliness. She now juxtaposes the two conditions with a response more sensory than that of the aesthetic sonnets. In her poem 'Time Past', an elegy on the 'thrill'd remembrance of the vanish'd hours', written in 1773, she echoes *Werther* with her exquisitely painful yet soothing recollections of the vanished 'blest years'.[52] At this particularly isolated period of her life she asks the question, where are 'Affection, Friendship, Sympathy' now? She recalls the lost pleasure of shutting out the cold of the 'bare, bleak fields' of winter to bask in the sensory warmth of the fire's glow, in the welcome presence of her friends.[53]

Following her pattern of creating a poem from a foundation of epistolary prose, she dejectedly repeats the sentiments that she first expressed in far happier times in a letter to Emma, where she describes a cold February evening when her parents had gone out to a card party. As her sister Sarah came downstairs with their work-bags and Honora fetched a book to read aloud, she illustrated the scene: 'the curtains are dropt, and the chill white world shut out. The candles shine chearily, and the fire burns bright in the clean hearth. Little Honora draws her chair to the table as I write, [...] Honora looks at me, her eyes sparkling with intellectual avidity, – The young mind must not be deprived of its evening nutriment.'[54] The poem transforms the material factor of the hearth in the letter into the spiritual value of the warmth of companionship:

> Yes, for the joys that trivial joys excel,
> My loved HONORA, did we hail the gloom
> Of dim November's eve; – and, as it fell,
> And the bright fire shone cheerful round the room,
> Dropt the warm curtains with no tardy hand;
> And felt our spirits and our hearts expand;
> Listening their steps, who still, where're they come,
> Make the keen stars, that glaze the settled snows,
> More than the sun invoked when he first tints the rose.[55]

51   Seward, 'Ode to Content', *Poetical Works*, vol. I, pp. 74–75.
52   Seward, 'Time Past', *Poetical Works*, vol. I, pp. 87–88.
53   Seward, 'Time Past', *Poetical Works*, vol. I, p. 88.
54   Seward, 'Literary Correspondence', *Poetical Works*, vol. I, pp. lxxxiv–lxxxv.
55   Seward, 'Time Past', *Poetical Works*, vol. I, pp. 87–88.

The reference to 'their' approaching steps indicates that although the room has become the small, warm space isolated from the cold of the outside elements, it is also the symbolic edifice of friendship, protected from all negative external influences. The occupational domain of the work box and the work book is replaced by the conceptive domain of 'spirits' and of 'hearts'.

Some of the imagery here is 'borrowed' from a letter from John André dated October 1769, four years before Seward wrote her poem, in which he presents the blazing hearth as emblematic of friendship. André was in London and missing the warm camaraderie and the 'clean hearth' of the blue dressing room. 'What would I not give to enlarge that circle', he writes, picturing the group of friends gathered round the fireplace:

> You seem combined together against the inclemency of the weather, the hurry, bustle, ceremony, censoriousness, and envy of the world. The purity, the warmth, the kindly influence of fire, to all for whom it is kindled, is a good emblem of the friendship of such amiable minds as Julia's and her Honora's – Since I cannot be there in reality, pray imagine me with you; admit me to your *conversationes*; – Think how I wish for the blessing of enjoying them! – and be persuaded that I take part in all your pleasures, in the dear hope, that ere it be very long, your blazing hearth will burn again for me.[56]

It is one of the cycle of the poems dedicated to Honora that best accentuates Seward's vision of fleeting life and the lure of reminiscence. The 'Elegy Written at the Sea-Side, and Addressed to Miss Honora Sneyd' compares life's transience with the enduring nature of love, literature and the grave. The narrator juxtaposes the transient image of Honora's name written on the sand and washed away by the waves with the permanence of a memorial carved onto a tombstone, the verse a lasting monument to love:

> But Time's stern tide, with cold Oblivion's wave,
> Shall soon dissolve each fair, each fading charm;
> E'en Nature's self, so powerful, cannot save
> Her own rich gifts from this overwhelming harm.
>
> Love and the Muse can boast superior power,
> Indelible the letters they shall frame;
> They yield to no inevitable hour,
> But will on lasting tablets write thy name.[57]

---

[56] John André, 'Letter to Anna Seward' (19 October 1769), *Poetical Works*, vol. II, pp. 95–100.

[57] Seward, 'Elegy Written at the Sea-side and Addressed to Miss Honora Sneyd, *Poetical Works*, vol. I, p. 82.

Again, there are echoes of *Werther* and his scepticism of the notion of nature's eternal energy, and of Gray's 'Elegy' with his 'inevitable hour'.[58] The overarching theme of the transience of life and the enduring quality of 'Love and the Muse' is one that Seward and Mary Powys willingly shared.

With the disappointing failure of her teaching project, Seward now had to make a supreme attempt to compensate for the absence of Saville and Honora from her life. Writing helped. 'I took up my pen', she confirmed, 'because I had no other way of beguiling the tedious time.'[59] She collaborated on an epic poem with Erasmus Darwin and Francis Mundy, a wealthy landowner, magistrate and would-be poet who lived at the elegant Markeaton House, near Derby. For a short period of time the poem *Needwood Forest* (1776) became exceptionally famous. Mundy was credited with bringing fox-hunting to the area, and his poem reflects the love of the chase, which Seward claimed was of absolutely no interest to her. She and Darwin wrote large sections of the poem for Mundy. 'I dress'd the Furies, [Darwin] gave them their music', she informed Mary Powys. 'The description of the Witches, all but the last couplet, and that of *Murder,* are *mine*', she affirmed, adding that she also wrote the description of Lichfield, as seen from the forest.[60]

Neither of the two collaborators sought an acknowledgement for their contribution to the poem, and they have remained unacknowledged. Darwin published a response to Mundy's poem, *The Swilcar Oak*, in 1776 and this has become closely associated with the original.[61] Exactly twenty years after Seward's revelations to Mary Powys about Mundy's poem, she sent a letter to Lady Eleanor Butler which included a short critique of 'a favourite poem of mine', *Needwood Forest*. In the letter she asks mischievously how Lady Eleanor likes 'the dark pictures of witchcraft and murder? Is not that of the latter, starting at the sight of his bloody hands, beneath the sudden gleam of the shrouded moon, original and impressive?'[62]

Seward first met the poet and novelist Anna Rogers Stokes, who lived in the village of Dronfield, in 1778. Rogers Stokes had sent one of her poems to Matthew Boulton, the Birmingham engineer, who was a member of Erasmus Darwin's Lunar circle. Boulton passed the poem to Darwin, who, 'polish'd, japan'd, and handed up the verses', but not before he had shown them to Seward, who asked to meet their author.[63] The two began an enduring friendship, meeting when they were able and

---

[58]   Thomas Gray, 'Elegy Written in a Country Churchyard', in *The Poems of Thomas Gray, William Collins, Oliver Goldsmith*, ed. by Roger Lonsdale (London: Longmans, 1969), p. 124.

[59]   JBM, MS 35/16, Seward, 'Letter to Dorothy Sykes' (5 September 1777).

[60]   JBM, MS 38/6, Seward, 'Letter to Mary Powys' (27 February 1777).

[61]   King-Hele, *Erasmus Darwin*, p. 132.

[62]   Seward, 'Letter to Lady Eleanor Butler' (28 February 1796), *Letters*, vol. IV, p. 169.

[63]   Erasmus Darwin, 'Letter to Matthew Boulton' (11 January 1778), in Desmond King-Hele, *The Letters of Erasmus Darwin* (Cambridge: Cambridge University Press, 1981), p. 217.

writing poetry together for their own amusement, although Rogers Stokes stopped writing for publication when she married physician and botanist Jonathan Stokes. While Rogers Stokes was writing, Seward saw her as a friend and a friendly rival: '[T]he palm will be shifted from my brow to yours, and *vice-versa*, as the taste of the reader shall lean to the delicate or the strong, the sombre or the beautiful.'[64] On one occasion, they took a pedestrian translation of an Arabian Ode by Dr Russel, and each wrote her own poetic version in a form of good-natured literary duel. Russel's lines,

> The stars succeed one another
> In the blue firmament;
> The fire of love is in my bosom,
> Which all the waters in the sea cannot quench.[65]

are interpreted by Rogers Stokes in a gently assonant identification with insomnia and sorrow:

> In vain, my body on the couch is laid,
> In vain, gay poppies round my tent entwine,
> These sleepless eyes still ask my lovely maid,
> In vain they ask – no gleam of hope is mine;
> Thou radiant moon, ye stars that glitter bright,
> Not all your rays can cheer a lover's night.[66]

The hypnotic repetition, 'in vain', and the passive, 'is laid', suggest an enervated vulnerability rather than restlessness. The 'body' is presented as weak and helpless, reflecting the situation of the narrator, and the poppies and night sky emphasise the still heat of summer. Seward's version, in which she intended to include 'the expansion of metaphor, an introduction of collateral circumstances, and a sort of moral application of them to the situation of the complainant',[67] is forceful, restive and anxious:

> Wide o'er the drowsy world incumbent night,
> Sullen and drear, his sable wing has spread;
> The waning moon, with interrupted light,
> Gleams cold and misty on my fever'd bed.
> Cold as she is, to her my breaking heart
> Shall pour its waste of woes, its unavailing smart.

---

[64] Seward, 'Letter to Court Dewes, Esq.' (9 March 1788), *Letters*, vol. II, pp. 61–67.

[65] Dr Williamson (other name Rev. Dr Russel) 'Dr Russel's literal Translation of an Arabian Ode' in Lord Henry Home Kames, *Six Sketches on the History of Man, containing, the progress of men as individuals and with an appendix, concerning the propagation of animals and their offspring*, 2 vols (Philadelphia: R. Bell and R. Aitken, 1776).

[66] Anna Rogers Stokes, 'Poetic Paraphrase', in Seward, 'Letter to Court Dewes, Esq.' (9 March 1788), *Letters*, vol. II, p. 65.

[67] Seward, 'Letter to Court Dewes, Esq.' (9 March 1788), *Letters*, vol. II, pp. 63–64.

Thro' the long hours, – alas how long the hours!
My restless limbs no grateful langours know;
Griev'd tho' I am, yet grief's assuaging showers
From burning eye-balls still refuse to flow;
Love's jealous fires, kindled by Aza's frown,
Not the vast, watery world, with all its waves, can drown.[68]

In contrast to the warmth of Rogers Stokes's bright moonlight, Seward's verse begins with an allusion to death, 'his sable wing', and her wintry, decrescent moon is 'cold and misty', presenting a sense of loss as its cycle ends. Nature's icy harshness contrasts with the heat of the 'fever'd' body, and 'burning' eyes that are incapable of tears, with further allusions to inner passion, in 'fires' which are 'kindled', imparting a physicality and energy to the imagery. Whatever interpretation Seward anticipated for the poems, her own is the 'strong' and 'sombre' and Rogers Stokes's is the 'delicate and beautiful'.

It was most probably Rogers Stokes's influence that led Seward to enter the annual writing competition at Bath-Easton, as the young Derbyshire poet had herself won it a few years earlier and had then seen her poems successfully published in the *Poetical Amusements at a Villa near Bath*, in 1776.[69] Here was an opportunity for Seward to move on, and to prove her self-worth. She entered her poem 'Charity' and took the first prize. In an act of public assertion of her new status as poet, she proudly wore her winner's myrtle wreath in her cap at the Cecilian concert at Lichfield cathedral.

---

[68]   Seward, 'Letter to Court Dewes, Esq.' (9 March 1788), *Letters*, vol. II, p. 64.

[69]   Lady Anne Miller, *Poetical Amusements at a Villa Near Bath*, 2nd edn, 4 vols (London: Edward and Charles Dilly, 1776).

Chapter 5
'Born to write':
1780–1809

When Anna Seward wore her winner's myrtles in public, it was an open declaration of her new status as a poet. It was what she thought she deserved. '[I]t was almost inevitable that the world would know, that I was "born to write, converse, and live in the ease of pecuniary independence",' she confirmed.[1] By staking her right to intellectual vision, she was also claiming her independence, and she was met with a series of events at the start of the decade which enabled her to begin the process of constructing her 'fame', her literary reputation.

The year 1780 marked a transitional moment in Seward's life as the previous wretched decade culminated in a tragic time of sickness and death. Honora Sneyd died on 30 April, and Seward's mother, Elizabeth, on 4 July. John André too died that year, hanged as a spy in America, and Thomas Seward had the first of a series of debilitating strokes that weakened both his body and his mind. The accumulating anguish caused by these events seemed to inspire more determination than ever in Seward. Allowing nothing and no one to halt her progress, at the age of thirty-seven she finally cut free from the previous dismal decade's traumas, which she had laid bare in the tear-stained letters to Dorothy Sykes and Mary Powys. She disentangled herself from the intrusive influence of her literary friends in Lichfield. Recording her progress through correspondence to friends, which she reproduced daily in her autobiographical letter books, she now prepared herself for the role of a successful published author in her own right. She was soon to become the 'Lichfield Swan'.

The catalyst for Seward's first steps towards a self-constructed public persona had an intriguing source. On 7 September 1780, Erasmus Darwin sent Seward a love letter together with a poem.[2] The letter was addressed to her cosseted little pet cat, 'Po Felina', from his large white Persian, 'Snow'. The following day Seward replied on behalf of her cat with her own much longer letter and a poem. In her biography of Darwin, which was the only site of publication for the 'Cat Letters', she describes the ostensibly frivolous exchange as a 'whimsically gay effusion' with a 'ludicrous' subject matter that she had hesitated to publish in the memoirs.[3] Yet, she eventually conceded to the demands of her friends who persuaded her that there was a direct relevance to the letters. Although her concern was that the

---

[1] Seward, 'Letter to Thomas Sedgewick Whalley' (16 January 1799), in Wickham, *Journals and Correspondence of Thomas Sedgewick Whalley*, vol. II, p. 113. Seward (mis)quotes Alexander Pope: 'born to write, converse and live with ease', from Epistle VII, 'To Dr Arbuthnot'.

[2] Seward, *Memoirs*, pp. 96–105.

[3] Seward, *Memoirs*, p. 96.

compositions might have appeared to be 'below the dignity which a biographic sketch of deceased Eminence ought perhaps to preserve',[4] she wanted to portray the private Darwin through his personal life, wit and creativity, more so than the familiar dignified public persona.

The reviewers confirmed Seward's initial fears: 'Our gratification is too often dashed by the frivolity of the information which is conveyed [in the memoirs]. The reader may look in vain for any thing which merits the name of just biographical narrative', groused one of the more influential literary reviewers, who continued to find fault with what he scathingly called the 'tea-table talk of Lichfield'.[5] The exchange of the 'Cat Letters', however, is more than an excursion into whimsy. It is also more than a portrait of Darwin's ingenuity and poetic ability. Under the cover of light-hearted dialogue, Seward clearly reaches a self-realisation and declares her new self-sufficiency. Even as the exchange emphasises the authors' shared literary ventures at a time when each was considering writing for publication, the contents of the letters and poems disclose the tensions present in their literary and personal relationships, particularly so with Seward's letter.

Seward reached her point of transition with the success that followed the publication of the 'Elegy on Captain Cook' in 1780. No longer the dispirited, directionless young woman of the previous decade who, at the expense of a constructive role, had resisted attempts from family, neighbours and convention to mould her into a controllable shape, she was now conscious of what her work was to be. Fuelled by the awareness of her new public standing, she set out to construct a fresh persona through her letter books. She wanted to demonstrate her knowledge of current affairs, politics, the arts, as well as literature. Her new position in literary society constituted an authority that is enacted through her correspondence and presented with autobiographical formality. The 'Cat Letters' construct a bridge between the internally focalised dialogue of the Powys and Sykes letters and the self-conscious narrative of the published letters. Seward's 'Cat' letter, in particular, reveals her restive desire for literary and personal independence.

The letters were written at the time when Darwin was absorbed with sensuousness, which he explored in his writings, and when he was fixated with sensuality, which he sought to discover in his life following the end of his long-term relationship with Mary Parker. Darwin had already met and fallen in love with his future wife, beautiful and clever Elizabeth 'Eliza' Pole, who was still married to the fearsome Colonel Edward Sacheveral Pole. Thirty years Eliza's senior, the Derbyshire Colonel was a fierce, battle-scarred ex-soldier who had engaged in eleven battles and been badly wounded by gunfire, 'the ball going in at his left eye and coming out at the back of his head'.[6] The couple had married in 1769 when Eliza discovered she was pregnant. Darwin was their physician, travelling to

---

[4]   Seward, *Memoirs*, p. 96.

[5]   'Miss Seward's *Memoirs of Dr Darwin*', *Edinburgh Review* (1804), IV, 230–41 (p. 234).

[6]   King-Hele, *Erasmus Darwin*, pp. 126–27.

their home at Radburn Hall near Derby to treat the wealthy couple and their three children. Between 1775 and the Colonel's death at the end of November 1780, Darwin had written several love poems for Eliza, which his family suppressed after his death, although Seward placed one in her Darwin memoirs. In addition to these, he had composed an unsubtle series of saucy riddles for her. An example of his sexual innuendo can be seen in the following:

> Far in the North, where Winter keeps his reign,
> Ladies! I rose like Venus from the Main;
> To aid your charms I rose, and still my care
> Is to adorn, and to support the Fair.
> Nor love nor hate I know, nor care nor sin,
> Yet hold a heart, that pants and beats within.
> Eliza now my folding arms are pressed
> Round your fine waist, and clasp your snowy breast.[7]

The solution to the riddle is 'whalebone stays'. Following Colonel Pole's death, his young widow, Eliza, who had been left a jointure of six hundred pounds a year with her young son inheriting the estate, rejected her mass of followers: 'young fox-hunting esquires, dashing militaries, and pedantic gownsmen',[8] and married Darwin, who moved his family from Lichfield to live with her at the Derbyshire estate, thus cutting his literary ties with Seward. Before this, the forty-nine-year-old Darwin was actively seeking a sexual partner, and he briefly turned his attention towards Seward. His coded 'Cat Letter' is full of complex imagery, as is Seward's reply.

Fearsome Snow, the 'rough and hardy, bold and free' cat narrator, opens his letter with a declaration of love to aloof Po Felina. He has secretly spied on her as she washed her 'beautiful round face, and elegantly brindled ears, with [her] velvet paws, and whisking about, with graceful sinuosity, [her] meandering tail', and as she dipped her white whiskers in 'delicious cream'. Complaining that he has been smitten by the arrow of 'that treacherous hedgehog, Cupid', he urges Po Felina to sing him a song of tribute. If sung, the mock-heroic song would confirm her consent to his address and it carefully avoids any mention of whether it is a respectable address.[9]

Darwin's cat narrator boasts of his advantages of birth, his fine lineage derived from Persian kings, his education and beauty. He displays his machismo by killing an 'enormous Norway rat', tearing off its head and offering to lay this at the feet of the object of his love.[10] The response is complex. Po Felina, an indulged little pet that Seward trained to live peaceably with an assortment of tame birds: a canary, a lark, a robin and a dove, stresses her moral stance. Seward determines her journey

---

[7]   University College, London Library, The Pearson Papers, MS 577, p. 85.

[8]   Seward, *Memoirs*, p. 107.

[9]   Seward, *Memoirs*, pp. 97–99.

[10]   Seward, *Memoirs*, p. 98.

towards her future career through the subtext of her reply letter, setting out her proposal for independence. While Po Felina can appreciate Snow's bravery, his fierceness is repulsive to her, and she declines his suit: 'my heart died within me at the idea of so preposterous a union!'.[11]

The cats assume the characteristics of their respective owners. Certainly the innuendo present in Darwin's letter from the fierce rat-catcher, Snow, points towards the suggestion of some form of relationship with Seward, although not necessarily marriage: 'You know not, dear Miss Pussey Po, the value of the address you neglect.' His songs reverberate through the 'winding lanes and dirty alleys', and his companions are a band of 'catgut and catcall'.[12] Refined Po Felina, who inhabits the genteel lawns of the Dean's Walk, and looks down over Lichfield from high up on the roof tiles above the Palace, puts forward her unequivocal rejection, translating the advance as an offer of marriage: 'Marry you, Mr Snow, I am afraid I cannot; since, though the laws of our community might not oppose our connection, yet those of principle, of delicacy, of duty to my mistress, do very powerfully oppose it.'[13] A more open acknowledgement of the true focus of Snow's attention is confirmed in her accompanying verse. With the simple device of moving from soft consonants to hard, she gives emphasis to the words 'dire disgrace', 'deeply brand' and 'stigma fix':

> O, should a cat of Darwin's prove
> Foe to pity, foe to love!
> Cat, that listens day by day,
> To mercy's mild and honied lay,
> Too surely would the dire disgrace
> More deeply brand our future race,
> The stigma fix, where'er they range,
> That cats can ne'er their nature change.[14]

The implication of procreation, of the deeply branded 'future race', suggests the notion of illegitimacy. Further, the idea of a cat's inability to change its nature suggests illegitimacy's obviously unwelcome consequences.

The letters' thematic concerns mirror wider issues within the literary relationship, as the cat narrators offer differing perspectives on the gendered values of education and its privileges. Darwin's narrator perceives a key distinction between the writers: 'I am not destitute of all advantages of birth, education.' Snow acknowledges Seward's status as a poet and Darwin's as a scientist: 'you sleep hourly on the lap of the favourite of the muses, and are patted by those fingers which hold the pen of science'.[15] Countering the reference to education,

---

[11]   Seward, *Memoirs*, p. 103.
[12]   Seward, *Memoirs*, p. 99.
[13]   Seward, *Memoirs*, p. 103.
[14]   Seward, *Memoirs*, p. 104.
[15]   Seward, *Memoirs*, p. 98.

Po Felina concedes that 'the happiness of a refined education was mine; yet dear Mr Snow my advantages in that respect were not equal to what yours might have been'.[16] Although bold enough to challenge Darwin on theories of science and nature in her review of his major work *The Botanic Garden*, Seward makes poetry her own definitive 'territory' in the 'Cat Letters'.[17] In opposition to the physicality and multi-sensory perceptions of Snow, whose paws are bloody, stained with the gore of the Norway rat, Seward's cat narrator is more concerned with the aesthetic senses. She describes her own province by offering a poetic description of the ethereal moonlit scene in the Dean's Walk and the view towards Stowe Valley and beyond.

Acknowledging Darwin's encouragement and his contribution to her literary vocation ('I had acquired a taste for scenic beauty and poetic imagery, by listening to ingenious observations upon their nature from the lips of my own lord'), the narrator is, however, adamant in her desire for self-determination.[18] Seward employs the analogy of one of her bugbears, pollarded trees. Unlike the trees which are deliberately restricted in growth, 'tortured into trim and detestable regularity' by the hand of 'Dulness', her own poetic trees have a metaphoric freedom to develop into the 'thousand various and beautiful forms' of their own, or certainly of nature's, choosing.[19] The world beyond Lichfield, lit by the refracted light of moonbeams, is thrown 'into perspective' when viewed through the frame of the 'liberated boughs'. Rather than compliantly repeating Snow's song, Po Felina insists on writing her own words. Her response is self-assured, assertive: 'As to presiding at your concert, if you extremely wish it, I may perhaps grant your request; but then you must allow me to sing a song of *my own* composition.'[20]

The poets' diverging attitudes on sexual identity and moral issues are emphasised in Po Felina's reaction to Snow's brutal violence, as she remonstrates with his display of physicality and the nature of his politics, a 'fierceness' which is at odds with his 'benevolence and philosophy'. The notions of brutality and sexuality merge as she counteracts Snow's hereditary violence. In response to his claim to a warrior glory inherited from his warlike Persian ancestors, she responds, 'while you give unbounded indulgence to your carnivorous desires, I have so far subdued mine'.[21] This assertion is designed to overturn the idea of 'fair game' due to her relationship with Saville (a relationship which, judging by his revelations to Thomas

---

[16]   Seward, *Memoirs*, p. 100.

[17]   In Seward's critique, she notes that Darwin attributes the improvement of artificial magnets to an old friend of his, John Mitchell, as though they had not been effective before this (*Memoirs*, p.158). She also mentions that Darwin describes miniature Darba grass as 'tall' (pp. 214–15) and criticises his lack of knowledge about the techniques used by the paper flower artist, Mary Delaney, and provides a full account of her methods (pp. 229–30).

[18]   Seward, *Memoirs*, p. 101.

[19]   Seward, *Memoirs*, p. 101.

[20]   Seward, *Memoirs*, p. 103.

[21]   Seward, *Memoirs*, p. 100.

and Elizabeth Seward at the dinner party, Darwin believed to be sexual) and to her damaged reputation. Ironically, Po Felina gives warlike Snow a matriarchal lineage here, carefully displacing his own claims of direct extraction from Alexander the Great to that of the conqueror's 'large white female cat'. Even then she places vast distances between them: 'thy grandmother, in the ten thousandth and ninety-ninth ascent'.[22] In reality, Seward had an interesting perspective on Darwin's masculinity at this time. She wrote with unconcealed amusement to Lady Marianne Carnegie on how his love for Eliza Pole had transformed him from masculine scientist to feminised 'distaff handler':

> The poetic philosopher [...] transfers the amusement of his leisure hours, from the study of botany and mechanics, and the composition of odes, and heroic verses, to fabricating riddles and charards! Thus employed, his mind is somewhat in the same predicament with Hercules's body, when he sat among the women, and handled the distaff.[23]

Darwin's 'Cat Letter' came at just the right moment for Anna Seward. Whatever his intentions, his letter evidently brought out a sense of self-realisation in her. She had already published her poem 'Elegy on Captain Cook', which she had clearly written in collaboration with Darwin, and she had received instant acclaim.[24] Other successful publications swiftly followed as she added to her store of poetry composed during the previous anxious years. If the 'Cat Letters' seemed too trivial to be included in her main body of work, they had enough substance to be incorporated into the Darwin memoirs. She was now buoyant, confident. The 'Cat Letters' provided her with a timely opportunity to analyse her literary and personal life and to present her conclusions through a blend of poetry and eloquent prose. Her literary collaborations with Darwin were not now necessary to her future success; she was self-reliant, she could 'sing a song of [her] own composition'. She did not need a husband or lover; she had Saville, whom she now called 'Giovanni'; she had control of her 'carnivorous desires'; she had a purposeful existence. If indeed the 'Cat Letters' have more depth than is at first apparent, and Seward does subtly accentuate the fact that the correspondence is in the *name* of their respective cats, then she effectively uses them to cut free from the disappointments and anxieties of the previous decade in order to set out her self-assured terms for the future.

There had been other poetic collaborations with Erasmus Darwin before Seward's move from private coterie to public arena. In 1777, Darwin had purchased a secluded and overgrown tract of land on the fringes of Lichfield.

---

[22] Seward, *Memoirs*, p. 102.

[23] Seward, 'Letter to Lady Marianne Carnegie' (21 March 1785), *Letters*, vol. I, pp. 33–4. The connotations of the imagery used by Seward to describe Darwin's changed activities suggest that his work had become less than masculine. The archaic meaning of 'distaff' is 'a woman's work and concerns'.

[24] Seward, 'Elegy on Captain Cook', *Poetical Works*, vol. II, pp. 33–46.

Seward describes how the 'wild and umbrageous' valley was cultivated by the doctor in an experiment to unite the study of botanic science with the beauty of sublime landscape.[25] Darwin, who was passionate about the new science of botany, completely redesigned and landscaped the valley, adding small lakes, planting trees and flowers, and nurturing specimens of rare plants. A particularly captivating feature was a natural waterfall in the centre of the valley. Proud of his beautiful, scientific retreat, Darwin turned to poetry to express his sense of achievement. He dedicated an inscription to the 'Naiad of the Fountain', with the title 'Speech of a Water Nymph':

> If the meek flower of bashful dye,
> Attract not thy incurious eye;
> If the soft, murmuring rill to rest
> Encharm not thy tumultuous breast,
> Go, where Ambition lures the vain,
> Or avarice barters peace for gain![26]

Seward recounts how she first paid a solitary visit to the valley and rested on a charming little flowery bank. With Darwin's inscription on her mind, she took out her notebook and expanded his verse into a five-stanza poem. When he read it, Darwin was so impressed that he sent it to the *Gentleman's Magazine* for publication without Seward's knowledge or permission, but not before had he altered the last few lines. The poem was a catalyst to Darwin's creative energy as he envisaged it as an exordium leading into a greater work: a poetic exploration of the Linnaean System of botanical classification which he had been contemplating writing for some time.[27] Much to Seward's anger, he went on to claim her poem as his own.[28] Even Walter Scott commented on Darwin's plagiarism, writing that the action 'must remain a considerable stain upon the character of the poet of Flora'.[29] Darwin decided that the epic was to be written in heroic couplets and, without losing its sexual content or terminology, it would use an inverted form of Ovidian *Metamorphoses* to portray the interaction between personified flowers. 'I will

---

[25] Seward, *Memoirs*, pp. 71–74.

[26] Erasmus Darwin, 'Speech of a Water Nymph', in Seward, *Memoirs*, p. 127.

[27] The Linnaean System was a series of botanic, encyclopaedic works by the Swedish naturalist, Carl von Linné, who was known as Linnaeus or Linneus. Darwin collaborated on a translation of his works with the botanist William Jackson and with Sir Brooke Boothby, who had built his own huge conservatory, stocked with rare and precious plants and with a zoo of wild animals, at his country seat of Ashbourne Hall in Derbyshire. The translation was published in 1783 as *A System of Vegetables*, translated from the thirteenth edition of the *Systema Vegetabilium* of Linneus by a Botanic Society at Lichfield, 2 vols (Lichfield: J. Jackson, for Leigh and Sotheby, London, 1783).

[28] Seward included her original version in the posthumous poetry edition with a note explaining their authorship and origin ('Verses Written in Dr Darwin's Botanic Garden', *Poetical Works*, vol. II, pp. 1–4).

[29] Scott, 'Biographical Preface', *Poetical Works*, vol. I, p. xxi.

write the notes, which must be scientific', Darwin offered, 'and you shall write the verse.'[30] Seward declined, reasoning that a poem with so much apparent sexual content would not be accepted from a woman. Also, at this stage, she believed that the epic form was more suited to Darwin's writing style than her own.

This is not to say that Seward was prudish. She clarified her opinion on the propriety of the subject matter in her response to a letter from her friend, Mrs Childers, who had complained of licentiousness and 'shades of moral imperfection' in the published work. Where Darwin had displayed his 'floral ladies' and their multiple husbands as enjoying 'connubial affection', this was the general rule of nature, argued Seward, and therefore perfectly inoffensive. His vegetable nymphs and swains, who exchanged the most modest of kisses and caresses, might easily pass for brother and sister. She completely dismissed the notion of indecency, believing that young women would have to be extremely over-sensitive to be offended by the poem. She joked that they 'must have a temperament so unfortunately combustible as to render it unsafe to trust them with the writings of our best poets, wherever love is the theme'. In her robust defence of the morality of Darwin's epic, she teases her friend for her prudish objections: 'the mind must remain unmoved by the marriage of a truffle with a gnome'.[31]

Darwin's original reticence to publish poetry exclusively under his own name corresponded with a fear of losing his professional standing. Seward persuaded him that as the poem's subject and notes related to pathology, his reputation was not likely to suffer. In the light of his claim to the authorship of Seward's five-stanza poem it is probable that, if there had been collaboration, Darwin would have taken the major credit. Continuing alone, however, he wrote the immensely successful *The Botanic Garden*, an epic in two parts: *The Economy of Vegetation* and *The Loves of the Plants*. Curiously, he published the second part before the first, placing Seward's slightly altered verse as the unacknowledged exordium.

Seward read the proofs at each stage of writing. It would be impossible to estimate the extent of any revisions Darwin may have made from Seward's suggestions, although she does clearly indicate in her Darwin memoirs that he certainly emended some sections at her recommendation. In *The Loves of the Plants*, for example, Darwin makes moralistic observations on 'Ninon de L'Enclos', and Seward challenges the 'personal and mental injustice' of his judgemental opinions.[32] On the first count, his representation of Madam Lenclos is of a 'wrinkled, grey, and paralytic' woman. Seward cites the courtesan's biographers, who clearly demonstrated that their subject had a charm and beauty 'considerable enough to procure her young lovers at the age of eighty'. Second, and more importantly,

---

[30]   Erasmus Darwin, quoted in Seward, *Memoirs*, pp. 130–31.

[31]   Seward, 'Letter to Mrs Childers' (30 March 1804), *Letters*, vol. VI, pp. 40–50.

[32]   Anne Lenclos (1616–1706), known as Ninon de Lenclos, was a French courtesan. She had two illegitimate sons but abandoned them, expressing no maternal feelings for them. One son, who became Lord Jersey, unknowingly fell in love with her and committed suicide when told that she was his mother.

Darwin had implied that Lenclos had encouraged her own son's advances with incestuous 'harlot smiles'. Seward angrily insisted that this, at least, be removed and replaced with 'fatal smiles'. 'Dr Darwin was influenced by the author of this memoir to rescue the form of Ninon from the unreal decrepitude he had imputed to it and her principles from such an unnatural excess of depravity,' she confirmed.[33]

What most outraged Seward here was the inequality of standards of virtue and morality, a subject made vivid by her personal experience in the previous decade, and she was unwilling to let Darwin's false allegations rest on the memory of Lenclos. She discusses her views at length in her criticism of his treatment of female morality:

> 'Generally speaking, the least fault of an unchaste woman is her unchastity.'
> Considering this remark as an axiom, the reason probably is, that chastity being the point of honour, as well as of virtue in women, its violation has a strong tendency to engraft deceit and malignity upon the secret consciousness of self-abasement; a consciousness more fatal to the existence of other good qualities than voluptuousness itself; a consciousness too likely to produce hatred and envy towards people of spotless reputation, together with a desire to reduce others to their own unfortunate level. The great Moralist of the Old Testament says, 'There is no wickedness like the wickedness of a woman;' not because the weaker sex are more naturally depraved, but from the improbability that a fallen female should ever, even upon the sincerest repentance, regain the esteem and confidence of society, while it pardons a male libertine the instant he seems disposed to forsake his vice, and too often during its full career.[34]

Given Darwin's earlier interpretation of Seward's morals, his condemnatory judgement of her relationship with John Saville, his own publicly conducted affair with Mary Parker, his illegitimate children, and his open pursuit of the married Eliza Pole, Seward had every right to use the biography as a means to respond to the hypocrisy of gendered manners.[35] She also firmly reclaimed the verse that Darwin had taken for his exordium, offering the full story of how she came to write it.

If a poetic cooperation on *The Botanic Garden* was not to be, her next literary collaboration was to bring fame to Seward. Her 'Elegy on Captain Cook' was printed by Dodsley and sold at the price of one shilling and sixpence per copy. It was reviewed as a new book in the *Monthly Review* of June 1780 and achieved

---

[33]   Seward, *Memoirs*, pp. 208–10.

[34]   Seward, *Memoirs*, pp. 210–11.

[35]   Darwin fathered fourteen children: five by his first wife, Mary, seven by his second wife, Eliza, and two illegitimately by Mary Parker. It is generally written that he brought up his illegitimate children, Mary and Susanna Parker, alongside the ones who were legitimate; thus the implication is that he treated all his children equally. Mary and Susanna worked in private households as assistant teachers or governesses. Eventually, he bought them their own school in Ashbourne. Despite his eight-year relationship with Mary Parker, he did not consider marriage with her.

immediate success, receiving praise from all quarters, including a flattering tribute from Samuel Johnson. James Boswell records that, following some admiring comments which Seward made to Johnson on Madame du Boccage's *The Columbiade*, Johnson countered, 'Madam, there is not in it anything equal to your description of the sea round the North Pole, in your Ode on the death of Captain Cook.'[36] Seward was so surprised by Johnson's generous comments that she blushed scarlet, curtsied and swiftly changed the subject. After her death, rumours circulated that the poem had been entirely rewritten by Darwin before publication. Most of the evidence for this emanated from that unreliable source, Richard Lovell Edgeworth, who wrote that to his certain knowledge, 'most of the passages, which have been selected in the various reviews of that work, were written by Dr Darwin'.[37]

The same theory is reiterated by Darwin's biographer, Desmond King-Hele. Centring his own evidence on an analysis of poetic style, King-Hele asserts that his 'own assessment supports Edgeworth' and insists that the physician, Darwin, was the co-author and 'perhaps the main author' of the work.[38] It has to be recognised, however, that though the Lichfield coterie worked and reworked each others' texts, the writer who declared authorship of a specific piece of literature was generally the originator and the major author, as with Mundy and his poem, *Needwood Forest*, for example, which was subject to anonymous additions from Seward and Darwin.[39] Before Seward made the transition from writing with the private coterie to publishing in the public literary sphere, from the amateur poet who worked in partnership with other poets to the independent writer who became one of the most popular female writers of the 1780s and 1790s, she wrote in conjunction with Darwin and her friend Anna Rogers Stokes amongst others. The extent of their intertextual relationship is revealed in Darwin's letter of 1778 to Matthew Boulton about Rogers Stokes' poetry:

> Dear Boulton, I have polish'd, japan'd, and handed up, the verses of Miss Rogers, which you sent me. This, I think the greatest compliment I could pay to the lady: since if I had not thought the contour fine, and several of the figures graceful and vivid, I would not have taken the labour to have touch'd them over again, have preserved the keeping, and put on the varnish. Miss Seward sais [*sic*] they are the most beautiful lines she ever saw, and longs to be acquainted with the lady-author; and I beg leave to say, that if the fair Poetess should not be displeased with the liberty I have taken with her poem, and at any time wishes my criticism on any of her future productions, I shall be happy with her correspondence.[40]

---

[36]   Samuel Johnson, quoted in Boswell, *Life of Johnson*, vol. IV, p. 331.

[37]   Richard Lovell Edgeworth, quoted in Ashmun, *The Singing Swan*, p. 75.

[38]   King-Hele, *Erasmus Darwin*, p. 165.

[39]   A letter from Seward dated 1799 and addressed to Mundy contains a critique of a sonnet written by Mundy which he had clearly sent to Seward for her comments. NLS, MS 2255, Seward, 'Letter to F. N. C. Mundy' (25 May 1799).

[40]   Erasmus Darwin, 'Letter to Matthew Boulton' (11 January 1778), in King-Hele, *The Letters of Erasmus Darwin*, p. 82.

It is possible, however, that it was Anna Seward alone who succeeded in composing the timely poem that made such a vital impression on the public consciousness.

Most of Seward's writings were now intended for the public domain. As she began to keep letter book copies of her correspondence for future publication, her writing style shifted to a new formality which had not been in evidence in the unpublished Powys and Sykes letters. Now the letter contents were literary, there were few personal observations, and her style had become elaborate, almost poetic. The published letters' editor, Archibald Constable, was not impressed by the ornate style, writing in his *Advertisement* to the volumes that although Seward displayed an 'independent and vigorous mind', her prose was not as 'fortunate' as her poetry:

> [I]t is to be feared, that even in these familiar epistles, several affectations of style, arising mostly from too free an use of poetic imagery, may tend to somewhat obscure their real merit. But when this peculiarity is got over, the reader, it is presumed, cannot fail to be struck with the many intellectual and moral excellencies which they display.[41]

In offering this, Constable was not making allowance for his own and others' censorship of the fascinating anecdotes, personal sketches and political comments that would have maintained equilibrium with the remaining literary debate. There is no doubt, however, that Seward retouched the letters as she copied them into the letter books, to give them a finer literary gloss.

Where Walter Scott and Archibald Constable despaired of Seward's 'peculiarity of taste' in her ornate writing, it was widely read in its time in parallel with Darwin's and Hayley's poems. Alexander Dyce, in his *Specimens of British Poetesses* of 1827, confirms how quickly popular taste moved on:

> That the poems of Anna Seward, which are now forgotten, should have excited much contemporary admiration, need not surprize us, if we consider that they were published at a period when Hayley's 'Triumphs of Temper' was esteemed a work of first-rate ability. [...] She was endowed with considerable genius [...] but her taste was far from good and her numerous productions (a few excepted) are disfigured by florid ornament and elaborate magnificence.[42]

By the start of the nineteenth century, the reading public had lost interest in the elaborate poetry that Seward thought enduring. It was very much of its time, and Scott and Constable's assessment was from an early nineteenth-century perspective. When it was first published, there were other notable writers who found it perfectly acceptable, even deserving of generous and public praise. In August 1782, Seward left her sickly father at home in the care of his trusted servant and set out for Eartham, near Chichester, to visit the poet William Hayley and his wife, Eliza. Her

---

41   Archibald Constable, *Letters of Anna Seward*, vol. I, p. vii.

42   Alexander Dyce, *Specimens of British Poetesses, selected and chronologically arranged by Alexander Dyce* (London, T. Rodd, 1827), p. 285.

initial apprehension for Thomas Seward's health – she was troubled by thoughts that he might die during her absence – was alleviated by Hayley, who persuaded her not to worry. While she was at Eartham that summer, she was introduced to an intellectual and artistic circle. During the course of the extended visit, Hayley commissioned his friend, the artist George Romney, to paint Seward's portrait.[43] On its completion, the painting was loaned to her for a month, and later Romney painted a duplicate copy for Seward, which she gave to her father to hang in the dining room of the Bishop's Palace. Seward's friend, the writer William Bagshaw Stevens of Repton, found the portrait a little too flattering. He wrote in his journal that he saw it on a visit and pointed out that it was 'somewhat handsomer than the original'. He could not deny Seward's beauty, however, and confirmed that Romney had succeeded in recreating the striking effect of her red-hazel eyes.[44]

William Hayley admired Seward's writing style and the symbolic content of poems such as the 'Elegy on Captain Cook' and its successor, 'Monody on Major André', works with an address to patriotism and a contribution to the restoration of a national culture.[45] Exceptionally popular with the public, if not with all of the critics, Hayley achieved his greatest success with his poem, *The Triumphs of Temper* (1781), at the time Seward was also becoming widely read. He had published his work, *Essay on Epic Poetry*, in 1782 with the intention of persuading the literary community to return to the epic, the 'grandest of poetic forms', as part of the revival of national culture. Seward and Hayley were drawn close by their literary ideals.

The lack of a classical education did not prevent Seward from adopting some neoclassical values of Augustan rhetoric, which she combined with her strong expression of sensibility. What suited her aspirations was the neoclassical theory that long and careful study of the great classical writers was essential to the production of fine poetry, and that all writing of worth was a continuation of tradition.[46] She had to adapt the principles to conform to her own limitations. Her programme of self-education had long been sustained by her Lichfield coterie of Rousseau's friend Sir Brooke Boothby, Francis Nöel Clarke Mundy, Thomas Day and Edgeworth when they were in the neighbourhood, John André, Anna Rogers Stokes and, of course, Erasmus Darwin. It included the study of the 'best' English poets and the 'best' Greek and Latin translations, recommended by her father. There was no sense of scholarly deprivation, as she firmly believed that her own studies were specialised in ways that the typical university curriculum could

---

[43]   *Miss Anna Seward*, by George Romney (1782), The Fleming Gallery, University of Vermont.

[44]   William Bagshaw Stevens, *The Journal of the Rev. William Bagshaw Stevens*, ed. by Georgina Galbraith (February 1793), p. 66.

[45]   Seward ordered sixty copies of the 'Monody' to give away to friends. The poem was selling for 'three half-crowns' [seven shillings and sixpence]. Johnson BM, MS 38/13, Seward, 'Letter to T. S. Whalley' (c. 1784).

[46]   Seward, quoted in Walter Scott, 'Biographical Preface', *Poetical Works*, vol. I, p. xiii.

not equal. 'A masculine education cannot spare from professional study, and the necessary acquisition of languages', she explained to Scott, 'the time and attention which I have bestowed on the compositions of my countrymen.'[47]

Walter Scott conceded that some of Seward's poetry was exceptional when, that is, she was able to forget the '"tiara and glittering zone" of the priestess of Apollo'. His favourite work was one of her simple, unadorned songs entitled 'To thy rocks, stormy Lannow, adieu'.[48] The values of the poetry of her literary landscape stressed a formal balance and harmony learned from the English classics: Shakespeare, Milton, Dryden, Prior, and Pope. She admired the works of contemporary writers such as William Wordsworth, but preferred to read her favourites, the poets 'who have charmed successive generations'.[49] Although she certainly did not evaluate the writings of her contemporaries by the same criteria she set for herself, she was exacting in her judgement. 'Poetry is like personal Beauty', she told Scott, 'the homeliest and roughest language cannot conceal or disguise the first, any more than can the coarsest apparel the second.'[50]

There was no real arrogance in her treatment of the work of the self-taught 'peasant poets' like her friend William Newton, who was known as the 'Minstrel of the Peak', or Robert Burns, neither of whom had received a classical education. She particularly liked Ann Yearsley's and Thomas Chatterton's poems. She confessed to Thomas Park that Chatterton's work was such an inspiration to her that she had inadvertently plagiarised one of his elegies.[51] If she did not use simple expression herself, she did not necessarily condemn it in others. In poetry, it was the way in which language and form created the image, appealed to the intellect, charmed the sensibility, instructed, delighted, that was all-important to her:

> Mean colloquial phrase, in numbers inharmonious, verse that gives no picture to the Reader's eye, no light to his understanding, no magnet to his affections, is, as composition, as little worth the Reader's praise, as coarse forms and features, clad in beggarly raiment, are worth his attention.[52]

In the case of Seward's much-debated analysis of Charlotte Smith's sonnets, her disapproval was centred on her plagiarism and her sonnets' lack of 'original ideas and poetical imagery'.[53] William Hayley, who was Charlotte Smith's friend, charged Seward with vanity-fuelled jealousy in her criticism of the sonnets. Her immediate response was that she preferred to express her honest literary opinion,

---

[47]   Seward, *Poetical Works*, vol. I, p. xiii.

[48]   Scott, 'Biographical Preface', *Poetical Works*, vol. I, p. xxvii.

[49]   NLS, MSS, 3875, fol. 51, Seward, 'Letter to Walter Scott' (25 June 1806).

[50]   Seward, 'Letter to Walter Scott' (29 April 1802), *Letters*, vol. VI, p. 14.

[51]   Seward, 'Letter to Thomas Park' (30 January 1800), *Letters*, vol. V, p. 271.

[52]   NLS, MSS, 3874, fols 140–44, Seward, 'Letter to Walter Scott' (25 April 1802).

[53]   In a letter to the Rev. Berwick dated 6 October 1788, Seward lists a selection of plagiarised phrases, together with the original quotations (Anna Seward, 'Letter to Rev. — Berwick', 6 October 1788, *Letters*, vol. II, pp. 161–66).

rather than false approval through respect for a sister-writer.[54] In another instance of criticism, Dr Anderson sent her some of Anne Bannerman's poems, requesting that she review them in the literary press. This time, Seward approved of the form but found the mix of 'borrowed' imagery incongruous, and she could not bring herself to praise them. She told Walter Scott that she was in a dilemma, as she should be grateful to Bannerman for sending her the 'terrible tales', but could not commit herself to the 'grossest flattering' of a dishonest review.[55]

There were very many other detractors, aside from Scott and Constable, who disliked Seward's approach to writing. When the Queen's Attorney-General, George Hardinge, wrote to her criticising her style, she took up the challenge, sending him a spirited response to justify her neoclassical principles. 'You seem to think my writings infected by the affectation of using uncommon words', she contended, aligning her use of descriptive language and lavish epithets with the writings of Shakespeare, Pope and Milton. 'I hope not;' she continued, 'but I choose, and shall always choose the strongest which spontaneously occur, to express my idea, whether in prose or verse, if the idea is elevated; mindless whether they do, or do not form a part of the fashionable vocabulary of Lord Fillagree and Lady Pamtickle.'[56] Later, she told Mundy that, because of her traditional literary expression, she believed her work was 'not inevitably perishable'.[57]

In addition to poetic form, traditional subject matter was also of great importance to her. Mythology, such as the classical Ovidian tradition reinterpreted by Erasmus Darwin in *The Botanic Garden*, and the translation of folk material, such as Walter Scott's *Marmion*, fascinated her. The popular antiquarian movement which revived ancient history in verse was equally appealing, but only when translated from unsophisticated rhyme to fluent, articulate poetry. Where some antiquarians found simplicity in the form of *faux naïf* material, she found only austerity and crudeness. It did not matter to her that Thomas Chatterton's Rowley poems were forgeries; she believed that their literary worth outweighed their dubious authorship. It was the same with the much-disputed *Ossian* translations, which were purportedly taken from Erse manuscripts found in the Hebrides by James Macpherson and which were discredited as forgeries by Samuel Johnson amongst others. She did not care when they were actually written. 'There are, I believe, no Erse manuscripts', asserted Johnson, but it was the beauty of the poetry's intensity which bestowed the 'greater glory', countered Seward.[58]

In attempting to disentangle this literary knot, Seward decided that *Ossian* was not to be judged as a work of historical accuracy: its provenance was not a critical factor to its worth. The poem's value was as part of a transcendent body of

---

[54] Seward, 'Letter to William Hayley' (29 January 1789), *Letters*, vol. II, p. 223.
[55] NLS, MSS, 865, fols. 25–28, Seward, 'Letter to Walter Scott' (20 June 1803).
[56] Seward, 'Letter to George Hardinge' (20 December 1786), *Letters*, vol. I, p. 232.
[57] NLS, MS 2255, Seward, 'Letter to F. N. C. Mundy' (25 May 1799).
[58] Boswell, *Life of Johnson*, vol. II, pp. 309–10.

'works of sublimity', and the poet's value, as one of the few capable of sublime expression. She wrote to Scott:

> A propos of Ossian; we have never interchang'd our sentiments on the reality or pretence of the bold poetic sources. I shou'd like to know *your* opinion, tho' for myself, I do not very anxiously care whether it be wholly ancient, or it was *almost* entirely inspiration in the genius of the ostensible Translators. I am disposed to adopt the intermediate opinion. Dr Johnson's scornful assertations on the subject have no weight with me.[59]

Interestingly, Seward's observations on writing for posterity and on the subject of historical accuracy in literature throw light on her own juvenile record of life in Lichfield. Although not a truly accurate representation of her history, it witnesses the tricky negotiations with convention encountered by her and her circle of friends during the 1760s and informs us of what life was like for the women of the era.

Seward's own excursion into the realms of antiquarianism involved reconstructing the ancient history of Wales and reinterpreting a Runic legend. This was inspired by a visit to Wales in 1795. She had been ill for several weeks and needed to 'get away from the pen'. She set out with Saville for a nine-week excursion to visit her relatives, the Roberts, in Barmouth. Together, she and Saville travelled adventurously through the mountains of Wales, staying at lodging houses on the way. With Saville galloping alongside on his horse, Seward travelled in a hired chaise with 'bad horses', occasionally being forced to get out and scramble up the steep mountainside path when the horses found the terrain too difficult. Saville managed to find two decent horses and enlisted the help of local workmen to push the chaise across the precipitous hills to their destination.[60]

While staying with the Roberts, they were invited to take tea with the celebrated literary 'Ladies of Llangollen', Eleanor Butler and Sarah Ponsonby, at their 'fairy Palace' in Llangollen Vale. The visit extended to two days and Seward was enchanted with the myth-laden landscape and particularly with their Gothicised house, the 'little Temple consecrated to friendship & the Muses & adorned by the hands of the Graces'.[61] The 'Ladies' had eloped from Ireland and set up household in an atmospheric slate-roofed cottage which they had tailored to suit their own eccentric taste, replacing the windows with ornate, stained glass leaded lights and adding fantastic carved heads to the doorways. The grounds hold a precarious cliff top summer house known as 'Lady Eleanor's Bower', a miniature dairy on the lawns, and a garden shaped around a reconstruction of a mystic standing stone circle, complete with central altar stone. Close by, and sheltered by the towering hills, lies the romantic and picturesque ruin of Valle Crucis Abbey, where Seward's party picnicked.

---

[59]   NLS, MSS, 3875, fol. 186, Seward, 'Letter to Walter Scott' (25 June 1806).
[60]   JBM, MS 38/15, Seward, 'Letter to Mary Powys' (16 November 1795).
[61]   JBM, MS 38/15, Seward, 'Letter to Mary Powys' (16 November 1795).

Moved by the ruggedness of the mountainous terrain and the mythology which rested on the valley, Seward published *Llangollen vale* in 1796.[62] The title poem is dedicated to Lady Eleanor and Sarah Ponsonby and describes the historic tradition of Llangollen. Amongst the poems in the volume is a tribute to the history of the town of Wrexham and its inhabitants, 'Verses on Wrexham', a descriptive pastoral on High Lake, 'Hoyle Lake', and a Runic translation, 'Herva at the Tomb of Argantyr'. Interestingly, Seward counters the antiquarian character of her volume with her poem 'Eyam', together with a handful of sonnets. On publication, the volume met with mixed reviews, from the *Monthly Mirror's* generous tribute to the writer who 'ranks with the first of those accomplished females who do honour to the literature of the present age' with her 'art and genius happily combined', to the *English Review's* hostile observations: 'With her favourite, Pope, before her, we are surprised that she has rather chosen to imitate the obscurity, tinsel, and tortuosity of the Della Cruscan school, than the language of nature and genuine taste.'[63]

The lure of classical mythology held strong in Seward's imagination, ultimately materialising in a series of twenty-six Horatian odes, *Paraphrases and Imitations of Horace*, which she published together with her cycle of one hundred sonnets in 1799. Only loosely based on the originals, the odes had first appeared in the *Gentleman's Magazine* throughout the year 1786. When the editor first commissioned Seward to produce them as regular monthly contributions, she was presented with translations by a scholar, Court Dewes from Warwickshire, and the 'learned, but too fastidious' neighbour, Mr Groves (the interfering family friend who supported Edward Sneyd in his attempts to prevent the marriage of his daughter Honora to Richard Lovell Edgeworth). Both men had separately approached her with offers of help.[64] Their translations, revisions, corrections and subsequent praise alleviated the sting of the reviewers' scorn, the 'cavils of illiberal criticism' that followed publication.

Warnings about the folly of meddling with the classics came from various sources, such as William Vyse, one of Lichfield Cathedral's canons, who cautioned, 'Nancy, take the advice of an old friend, never again attempt translating Horace

---

[62]   Seward, *Llangollen vale, with other poems*, ed. by Jonathan Wordsworth (London: G. Sael, 1796; repr. 1994).

[63]   Jonathan Wordsworth, 'Introduction', *Llangollen vale* [n. page]. Seward would not have appreciated being aligned with the self-conscious emotional writings of the Della Cruscan school, as she refers to its instigator, Robert Merry, as 'a writer of considerable genius; but whom self-confidence, and total want of taste, perpetually betrays into bombast, obscurity, and inelegance. Then the Anna Matilda verses are evidently his composition [they were, in fact, written by Hannah Cowley]; and is it not very sickening to see an author creeping beneath a veil of gauze, and proclaiming under it, that he is the first poet the world has ever produced?' Anna Seward, 'Letter to Hester Thrale Piozzi' (13 February 1789), *Letters*, vol. II, p. 244).

[64]   Seward, 'Letter to Eliza Hayley' (11 January 1789), *Letters*, vol. II, p. 217.

since you do not know Latin.'[65] It was more than the lack of knowledge, however. There was also the gendered issue of the appropriation of the classics and what was deemed suitable for female writing. In her introduction to the odes in the posthumous poetry edition, Seward comments:

> Men of letters have often observed to me, that in paraphrasing Horace, my sex would be an unpardonable crime with every Pedant, whether within, or without the pale of professional criticism.[66]

It would not have helped that she subtly feminised her compositions. She let it be known that she churned them out in the mornings at her dressing table as her maid curled her hair.

In addition to the Horatian odes, Seward spent a number of years working on her epic, *Telemachus*. She claimed that her poem was a 'lavish paraphrase' of Fénelon's *Télémaque*, and although it was never completed, she appeared to be very proud of what she had written and she left the manuscript to Walter Scott to publish with her posthumous poetry. To the annoyance of her cousins, the Whites, Scott felt it was not publishable. Harry White complained vociferously that he and the other executors could not understand why *Telemachus* had been left out, and in defence of the poem, the lawyer Charles Simpson wrote to Scott on behalf of the executors and family to make a case for the epic's value. He reasoned that Seward was not the first to attempt the 'bold task' of paraphrasing and that her work deserved a re-reading:

> [...] but if it be well done there can be no reason against the publication of it – Several Eminent Divines have published very indifferent paraphrases on parts of the Scriptures which are much weaker than the original and which certainly ought not to have been published. As they show the Vanity and Inefficiency of the Authors.[67]

Scott would not be persuaded in its favour, and once more it was the 'unpardonable crime' of her sex that hindered publication. The main reason why Seward put the poem aside without attempting to publish it herself was that she anticipated a poor reception from the reviewers. Writing to Sophia Weston about *Peru*, an epic written by their mutual friend Helen Maria Williams, Seward explained why she was so wary of publication:

> ... if I should complete and publish that work, I should know that an inundation of immediate sarcasm, proceeding from the pens of countless unsuccessful poetasters, would flow through the reviews, magazines, and newspapers, on what

---

[65]   William Vyse, in Ashmun, *The Singing Swan*, p. 146.

[66]   Seward, 'Paraphrases and Imitations of Horace', *Poetical Works*, vol. III, p. 223.

[67]   NLS, MSS, 865, fols 143–44, Charles Simpson, 'Letter to Walter Scott' (1 October 1809).

they would term the presumption of attempting the composition of Fenelon. But that story is much better calculated for verse, than prose.[68]

Although Scott conceded that she was exceptionally knowledgeable on all aspects of the English classics and that she could put forward scholarly debate on the subject, he made a very public statement about the form of her poetry. In his posthumous 'Biographical Preface', he does not hold back his contempt for her complex style:

> Miss Seward was in practice trained and attached to that school of picturesque and florid description, of lofty metaphor and bold personification, of a diction which inversion and the use of compound epithets rendered as remote as possible from the tone of ordinary language, which was introduced, or at least rendered fashionable, by Darwin, but which was too remote from common life, and natural expression, to retain its popularity.[69]

Her letter to the landscape gardener Humphry Repton, who wanted Seward to help him write a comedy, gave her a further opportunity to explain her approach to writing and her standards. In a monologue about the art of letter writing, she confirms that neither her letters nor her verses were calculated to 'please the popular taste'.[70] Unfortunately her continuing comments on the matter have been edited from the letter. Arguing that Seward's taste in poetry was flawed as it favoured works produced by her own poet friends, Scott contended that this 'caused an occasional anomaly in her critical system'. As a former recipient of Seward's patronage, and he briefly refers to this in the 'Biographical Preface', his comments here are ungenerous as most of her literary friendships flowed from the source of an appreciation of writing skills.

Scott was more gracious in his private letters to her, thanking her for her support. In one unpublished letter, he acknowledges her influence, equating himself with a General, 'neither the bravest nor the most skilful soldier in the Army [who] runs away with all the profit and half the applause acquired by the prowess of those who fought under his banners'.[71] He was not above pushing forward the work of his own friends, as he was aware of Seward's powerful literary influence. In one instance, he sent a book of poetry which had been published in Scotland and requested that Seward should 'give the little volume that celebrity, among your literary friends, which you can so easily confer by your commendation'.[72] On her part, she believed she was honest in the expression of her critical opinions whether or not they were on friends' works: 'I cannot flatter and am sorry to mortify',[73] or on others' writings: 'My pen, let me tell you, never troubles itself to manufacture

---

[68] Seward, 'Letter to Miss Weston' (23 December 1786), *Letters*, vol. I, p. 237.
[69] Scott, 'Biographical Preface', *Poetical Works*, vol. I, p. xxv.
[70] Seward, 'Letter to Humphry Repton' (23 February 1786), *Letters*, vol. I, p. 126.
[71] NLS, MSS, 854, fols 24–25, Scott, 'Letter to Anna Seward' (30 November 1802).
[72] NLS, MSS, 854, fols 20–21, Scott, 'Letter to Anna Seward' (20 February 1807).
[73] NLS, MSS, 3875, fols 73–76, Seward, 'Letter to Walter Scott' (17 April 1805).

unmeaning compliments.'[74] As for sycophancy, she considered this to be a 'crime of which I never yet was guilty, I hope never to commit'.[75]

Despite her protestations, Seward admitted to taking enormous pleasure from both giving and receiving the extravagant 'luxury of encomium'. Yet, she always stressed, this was purely where it was deserved. Her comprehensive critiques of the manuscripts that Scott sent her, for example, were candid expressions of her thoughts and literary experience. Where she found fault with these, she sugared her words: 'You know, however, where that pretty shoe must inevitably pinch me.'[76] She only ventured once into paid criticism at the request of one of the editors of the *Critical Review*, her friend, the poet Robert Fellowes, in 1807. It was not an enjoyable experience and she had no love of reviewers. They hid away, she said, sheltering themselves from the effects of their reviews with the '*imposing plural we*'. She thought it was important for writers to understand that the 'we' was not a 'council-board', but 'one solitary Coxcomb in his hiding place deciding upon claims which he has neither the power nor the will to appreciate justly'.[77]

Although acknowledging that there was a certain amount of undeserved flattery aimed towards her own works, she claimed that it was her enemies who overstated her generous impulses, deliberately devaluing her sincerity to the level of obsequious flattery.[78] When writing about her literary relationship with Hayley, she complained of the critics' and of her enemies' taunting distortions of the truth:

> How erroneously do the undiscerning many judge of character! My enemies say, 'Miss Seward flatters.' That is the construction which their spleen and coldness of heart puts upon a warm desire to please and oblige those I think estimable; upon the vivid glow of that praise which my heart delights to pour, when it can sincerely pour it. Truth can never be flattery. Alas! To the utter incapacity of flattering, even those I esteem and admire, I have, through life, owed the loss of much favour that was, in itself, most desirable to my affections – but sincerity is the first duty of friendship; I should blush to commend, if I had not courage to confess my disapprobation.[79]

The critics certainly had plenty of material on which to sharpen their knives. When William Hayley encountered Seward's first published poems, he immediately

---

[74]   Seward, 'Letter to H. Repton' (23 February 1786), *Letters*, vol. I, p. 125.

[75]   NLS, MSS, 865, fols 25–28, Seward, 'Letter to Walter Scott' (20 June 1803).

[76]   NLS, MSS 865, fols 23–24, Seward, 'Letter to Walter Scott' (15 March 1808).

[77]   NLS, MSS, 865, fols 107–11, Seward, 'Letter to Walter Scott' (4 November 1807).

[78]   In her letter to Humphry Repton, Seward claims she was aware that William Hayley publicly praised her 'Odes' because of his high esteem for her. 'His partial regard for me may render his praise too vivid for their merit,' she wrote. Seward, 'Letter to Humphry Repton' (23 February 1786), *Letters*, vol. I, p. 125.

[79]   Seward, 'Letter to Court Dewes, Esq.' (30 March 1786), *Letters*, vol. I, pp. 147–48.

responded with a sentimental impromptu, 'To Miss Seward', which apostrophises Britain as a mother mourning for her two lost sons, James Cook and John André, and for whom the Muse of Elegy feels pity and hopes to sooth. As Anna Seward is chosen to be the one bestowed with the Muse's 'heavenly power', it is solely her 'pathetic lyre' that can bring 'blest relief'. Not only does she alleviate the suffering of the nation's 'loveliest daughters' but, importantly, she inspires her 'bravest sons' to seek glory:

> ... who, in their every vein
> Feel the strong pathos of the magic strain,
> Bless the enchanting lyre, by glory strung,
> Envying the dead, who are so sweetly sung.[80]

Hayley's publication helped confirm her new role as the personification of British identity. Most of Seward's major poems received similar encomiums from poets who were widely read during the 1780s and 1790s, but have now faded into obscurity: Francis Nöel Clarke Mundy, William Grove, William Bagshaw Stevens, the Welsh language poet David Samwell, Robert Fellowes and Henry Cary. Seward singled out these tributes to be attached to her posthumous poetry, but Scott exercised his editing rights by excluding all encomiums except for Hayley's.

With William Hayley's gratifying public response to Seward's poems as a supplement to the praise from that other epic-writer, Erasmus Darwin, Seward offered her own return encomium to the poem *The Triumphs of Temper* in 1781 in the form of 'Ode to Poetic Fancy'. There followed a remarkable sequence of poetry between the two writers – a sentimental, poetic correspondence not unlike the later one between the Della Cruscans, Hannah Cowley and Robert Merry. When Merry published his poem of 1788, 'Adieu and Recall to Love', under the name 'Della Crusca', Hannah Cowley replied under the identity of 'Anna Matilda'. The resemblance to the Hayley and Seward poetic correspondence prompted speculation by Hester Thrale Piozzi, amongst many others, that Seward was the mysterious 'Anna Matilda' and that the poems were hers. Seward was hurt by the comparison and responded to Thrale Piozzi's lack of imagination with a strong statement of denial, 'Not they indeed', as she only occasionally published poetry anonymously.[81] Seward's own mistaken conviction was that the poems emanated from a single source, as they were so alike in composition, and that Merry was the author of the entire correspondence.

The sentimental poetic correspondence of mutual admiration between Seward and Hayley was easily lampooned. Dr Mansel, the scholarly Bishop of Bristol, published his own mocking parody which appears to ridicule Seward's physical appearance:

---

[80]   William Hayley, 'To Miss Seward. Impromptu', *Poetical Works*, vol. I, pp. 66–67.

[81]   Seward, 'Letter to Mrs Piozzi, on the Publication of JOHNSON'S letters' (7 March 1788), *Letters*, vol. II, pp. 41–42.

Miss S:	Prince of Poets, England's Glory,
	Mr. Hayley, *that* is you!
Mr. H:	Ma'am, you carry all before you,
	Trust me, Lichfield Swan, you do.
Miss S:	In epic, elegy, or sonnet,
	Mr. Hayley, you're divine!
Mr. H:	Madam, take my word upon it,
	You yourself are – all the Nine![82]

Despite the derision, Seward, Hayley and Darwin enjoyed a status as the leaders in their field of the poetry of traditional values. This prompted William Hazlitt's observation in his *Lectures on the English Poets* in 1818, 'I myself have already outlived one generation of favourite poets, the Darwins, the Hayleys, the Sewards. Who reads them now?'[83]

By 1784, so many people were writing to Seward that she began to find it difficult to keep up with her daily correspondence. In her published letters, she modestly intimates that her writing time was limited by her household duties and by caring for her sick father. In her private letters, however, she reveals that there was a stream of visitors passing through Lichfield who intended to meet her, with or without letters of introduction. There were also letters from admiring readers. Eminent writers and scholars, scientists, theologians, new writers who wanted critiques of their work, and autograph hunters sent letters which arrived daily on the wagon or by the boats on the Navigation canals.

Her famous elegies prompted a constant flow of requests from people who asked her to write individual poems for a specific occasion or an event such as the death of a relative, or on a particular theme. Josiah Wedgwood asked her to compose a poem on the abolition of slavery, but she declined on the grounds that others had already done this.[84] It was the popular epitaph that was her least favourite, but most requested, form:

> People teaze me with applications to write epitaphs upon their favourite friends. Of frequent compliance, there would be no end, and I would wish never to attempt another. That path of composition is so narrow, and so beaten, that one cannot hope to gather in it one novel floret, especially where an uneventful life, and a consequently monotonous virtue preclude the possibility of appropriate praise.[85]

---

[82] Dr William Mansel, in Morchard Bishop, *Blake's Hayley: The Life, Works, and Friendships of William Hayley* (London: Victor Gollancz, 1951), p. 70.

[83] William Hazlitt, *Romantic Icons*, ed. by Robert Woof and Stephen Hebron (Kendal: The Wordsworth Trust, 1999), p. 16.

[84] Seward, 'Letter to J. Wedgewood, Esq.' (18 February 1788), *Letters*, vol. II, pp. 28–33.

[85] Seward, 'Letter to Mrs Stokes' (9 August 1786), *Letters*, vol. I, p. 168.

As well as letters from old friends such as Mary Powys, Dorothy Sykes, Anne Mompesson and Molly Knowles, there were new regular correspondents, and she made an effort to reply to them all. Now she was corresponding with Hayley and Whalley, Helen Maria Williams and the scholars Dr Percival and George Hardinge. Seward also added the name of James Boswell to the growing list of prominent friends. She had recently published her poetic novel, *Louisa*, which she believed to have 'little chance to be popular', because it expressed unfashionable values.[86] She also anticipated hostile critical reviews. Boswell claimed to have a high regard for the work, and he was actively endorsing it with the literary press. James Boswell may well have found *Louisa* fascinating enough to endorse, yet, after meeting Seward, it was clearly the poem's author that held more appeal. Once he had inveigled his way into her blue dressing room he attempted to seduce her, writing secret love letters, to which she responded, and visiting the Bishop's Palace whenever he was able.

The secret letters have never been published and tend to be discounted by Boswell's biographers. It is not difficult to understand why the forty-two-year-old philandering Scotsman was attracted to Seward. To all appearances she was a beautiful and intelligent, single, independent woman, and he would have appreciated the fact that she had a 'history'. It is more problematical to understand why Seward responded to the secret letters in the first place and, for this reason, they deserve a re-reading. James Boswell was not the sort of man who would normally appeal to Seward. He was not particularly attractive, he had a wife, he was a heavy drinker, he was permanently short of money, and there was a distinct lack of dignity in his submissive admiration for Samuel Johnson. However, he was renowned for being exceptionally good company, as indeed Seward was.

It is also the case that Seward recognised Boswell's literary standing and influence and that out of deference, or even from vague feelings of insecurity surrounding her new status, she did not want to rebuff him outright in case he joined forces with her 'enemies'. She had a tendency towards effusiveness which was often mistaken for deeper affection, as Richard Lovell Edgeworth discovered when he presumed that John André was her lover and later thought that she had wanted to marry Erasmus Darwin. At this stage of her career she nurtured the esteem of certain men of influence in the publishing industry, not just Hayley and Darwin, but writers and critics such as George Hardinge. A flurry of letters written during the years 1784 and 1785 to Hardinge, who made no secret of his disapproval of Seward's writing style, evidence a spirited, almost teasing defence of her own work and of Darwin's. She even sent Hardinge extracts from Darwin's unpublished manuscript for *The Botanic Garden* in order to conduct an epistolary duel over its merits. Boswell had his own motives for cultivating Seward; she had known Johnson since her childhood and so she was able to supply anecdotes for Boswell's biography. His journals, however, show that his overarching motive was sexual conquest. Seward's early interaction with James Boswell was conducted

---

86   Seward, 'Louisa: A Poetical Novel in Four Epistles', *Poetical Works*, vol. II, p. 221.

along similar lines to her relationship with Johnson – superficially polite, but with significant undercurrents of wariness.

One of the main criticisms of Seward after her death (and still more recently) was her outspoken disrespect for Johnson, whom she met on most days when he was in Lichfield. Her letters reveal her admiration for the great writer, yet she was angered by his lapses into boorishness, and by what she saw as his literary jealousy. The fact that she had Darwin in her coterie did not help the situation, as the two men had little time for each other. Seward's observations on Samuel Johnson are well documented, yet his comments on her no longer exist, and she had every reason to believe that there would have been comments. In a letter to Hester Thrale Piozzi to congratulate her on her publication of Johnson's correspondence, she suggests that hostile remarks concerning herself or her writing had been removed:

> Since I see so many Lichfield people mentioned in these letters, whose visits were not much more frequent than mine, and whose talents had no sort of claim to lettered attention, there can be no great vanity in believing that he would not pass me over in total silence. Therefore is it that I thank you for your suppressions. I must have been pained by the consciousness of going down to posterity with the envenomed arrows of Johnson's malevolence sticking about me;[87]

Yet, after Johnson's death, her actions amounted to a form of idolisation. She gave his servant, Francis Barber, three guineas for an old threadbare carpet from Johnson's house. Although the carpet was worth no more than a guinea, she claimed to have paid the extra amount as she felt sorry for Barber, who had been 'very imprudent' with his inheritance and now found himself in serious financial difficulties. She did not want a 'good bargain', she told Boswell, merely the pleasure of 'treading upon a surface so classical'.[88]

As Seward's relationship with Boswell ultimately soured over wrangles about the veracity of her Johnson anecdotes, he made little mention of her in his *Life of Johnson*. In his pursuit of her, he appeared to be unaware of, or to disregard, her relationship with Saville, even though his first stay at the Palace as the guest of Thomas Seward was of full four weeks' duration. Despite this, there was the secret exchange of letters. Boswell's letters offer little more than a romantic fling, and Seward's reveal a desire to be taken seriously as a writer.

James Boswell noted in his diary that he first encountered Seward's 'bright eyes' on 24 March 1776, when he and Johnson were invited for supper by Thomas Seward.[89] His visits to Lichfield were infrequent, and he always called at the Palace to pay his respects, once noting that Thomas was in bed with a cold, 'according to his valetudinarian custom'. Thomas insisted on receiving his unexpected guest and came downstairs looking ridiculous in his black gown and white flannel

---

[87]   Seward, 'Letter to Mrs Piozzi, on the Publication of JOHNSON'S letters' (7 March 1788), *Letters*, vol. II, p. 44.

[88]   YUB, Letters of Anna Seward, MS C 2474, fol. 770, Anna Seward, 'Letter to James Boswell' (16 October 1790).

[89]   Lustig and Pottle, *Boswell: The Applause of the Jury*, p. 206.

nightgown.[90] Seward occasionally came across Boswell on her visits to London, and in May 1784, he returned to Lichfield. During this time, he lavished praise on *Louisa* and, a few days later, wrote to Seward that he was spreading word of the novel's merit amongst his friends and that he intended to use his influence to 'have a few extracts of it inserted in the newspapers, with short sentences endeavouring to point out the particular excellencies'.[91] Boswell had begun his pursuit of Seward in earnest. With the letter, he enclosed a note marked 'read this alone', which leaves no doubt at all about his intentions. On the previous visit, Seward had told him that she went to bed 'in a flutter' after his effusive praise of *Louisa*. 'I have been in a flutter ever since', he responded in his secret note. 'I am in vain of having some share of Miss Seward's regard. I had a wild inclination to intreat you would meet me anywhere, but for one evening, so impatient was I.' He asks her to reply in secret, enclosing as a love token a lock of 'that charming auburn hair I admired so much that delicious morning I was last with you.' This was to be his talisman against all temptation, he declared.[92]

Boswell recorded his feelings of infatuation in a letter to his old university friend, William Temple:

> Though not now a *girl*, she is still beautiful. Her eyes are exquisite, her embonpoint delightful, her sensibility melting. Think of your friend (you know him well) reclined upon a sofa with her while she read to me some of the finest passages of her *Louisa*. How enchanting! Many moments of felicity have I enjoyed. Let me be thankful.[93]

This is not how Seward wanted to interpret the episode. Surprisingly, she replied to confirm that she was prepared to correspond in confidence. Placing a great emphasis on the notion of 'friendship', 'respect' and 'esteem', she claimed to be 'flatter'd, pleas'd, *charm'd*' by Boswell's friendship, but she understood his motives perfectly. She was more than 'abashed, mortified, disappointed, grieved' by his 'voluptuous inclinations', which she had noticed during their time spent alone. She told him she had been too upset to express her anger at the time.[94]

Boswell would have been well aware of the rumours and gossip about Seward's past from his dealings with the people who knew her history. The old spectre of her damaged reputation, combined with the frustration of her intellect becoming occluded by her sex, was at the forefront of a frantic outburst:

---

[90]   James Boswell, 'Letter to Samuel Johnson' (22 October 1779), *Boswell: Laird of Auchinleck, 1778–1782*, ed. by Joseph W. Reed and Frederick Pottle, pp. 145–46.

[91]   YUB, Letters of James Boswell, MS L 1144, fols 1278, 1279, Boswell, 'Letter to Anna Seward' (11 June 1784).

[92]   YUB, Letters of James Boswell, MS L 1143, fol. 1277, Boswell, 'Letter to Anna Seward' (18 May 1784).

[93]   Boswell, 'Letter to William Temple' (6 July 1784), *Boswell: The Applause of the Jury*, pp. 256–57.

[94]   YUB, Letters of Anna Seward, MS C 2468, fol. 766, Seward, 'Letter to James Boswell' (22 May 1784).

Has the frankness of an affectionate and grateful spirit, which feels nothing which it need fear to disclose, worn the *appearance* of *levity*? – or has the cruel misconstruction which my Enemies have put upon the fervor of my Friendships, inspired ideas in Mr B's mind injurious to the purity of my sentiments and to that oblivion of the enamour'd passions, in which *time* and the disappointments of my youth have plung'd them? *Never* more can *they* awaken to disturb my peace, and fill my bosom with unattainable wishes.[95]

She asks Boswell to ignore all the implications of her sex and to treat her with the 'amity of a Brother'. She appeals to him to remain in London and not to attempt to come back to see her in the 'lazy and uniform insipidity' of Lichfield when the pleasures of the *senses* were to be found in the capital. Finally, she refuses to send the lock of hair, as he had intimated that it would connote a pledge she was not prepared to fulfill.[96]

Boswell was not easily deterred. Once more, he sent a letter of praise for *Louisa*, now claiming to be so intimately connected with the work that he had moments of 'blushing modesty' when overhearing it admired in the *salons* of London. The secret note sent with this was recorded by Boswell as the second dispatch to his 'voluptuous Muse', in which he had carefully avoided expressing terms of 'exuberant rhapsody'.[97] Rather than offer an apology for his behaviour, Boswell wrote that he was hurt by Seward's distress. 'Be not alarmed', he persisted. 'I shall be entirely as you would have me'.[98] He next quoted Alexander Pope: 'Give all thou can'st and let me dream the rest.' His reference here is to Eloisa's allusion to Abelard's castration and her continuing desire for him through 'other joys':

> Come! with thy looks, thy words, relieve my woe;
> Those still at least are left thee to bestow.
> Still on that breast enamour'd let me lie,
> Still drink delicious poison from thy eye,
> Pant on thy lip, and to thy heart be prest;
> Give all thou can'st – and let me dream the rest.
> Ah no! instruct me other joys to prize,
> With other beauties charm my partial eyes,[99]

---

95   YUB, Letters of Anna Seward, MS C 2468, fol. 766, Seward, 'Letter to James Boswell' (22 May 1784).

96   YUB, Letters of Anna Seward, MS C 2468, fol. 766, Seward, 'Letter to James Boswell' (22 May 1784).

97   YUB, Letters of James Boswell, MS L 1144, fols 1278, 1279, Boswell, 'Letter to Anna Seward' (11 June 1784).

98   YUB, Letters of James Boswell, MS L 1144, fols 1278, 1279, Boswell, 'Letter to Anna Seward' (11 June 1784).

99   Alexander Pope, 'Eloisa to Abelard', in *The Twickenham Edition of the Poems of Alexander Pope*, general ed. John Butt, 3rd edn, 6 vols (London: Methuen & Co; New Haven: Yale University Press, 1962, repr. 1972), vol. II, *The Rape of the Lock and Other Poems*, ed. by Geoffrey Tillotson, pp. 329–30.

As Boswell was quoting from one of Seward's favourite poems, he was aware that she knew the reference well, and his sensuous nature translates into Eloisa's description of what is still a partially physical relationship. Although seemingly complicit in Seward's refusal to have her 'passions awakened', he still implied that he wanted sexual intimacy, rather than the 'brotherly' friendship she suggested. There is an underlying persistence in his request for the lock of hair 'on which my fancy roves', but this time he confirms that there will be no misunderstandings about its significance as a love token.[100]

Once again poised uncomfortably between the sensitive issue of the expression of female intellect and the connotations surrounding female reputation, Seward's immediate response was to revert to the asexual aestheticism she employed whenever threatened by male physicality, as in the case of Major John Wright's advances during the moonlit carriage ride in Derbyshire, and in Erasmus Darwin's 'Cat Letter' from Snow. In a defiant attempt to divert Boswell's attention from corporeal to spiritual preoccupations, she resurrects the analogy of the flowering lime trees in the Dean's Walk of her 'Cat Letter'. For the first time in her memory, the trees have not been pollarded into a regular, conventional, controllable shape. Now, they possess 'enfranchised boughs' which can 'bend to the summer gale'. She continues, 'Much added beauty results from this liberation.'[101] She thanks Boswell for his efforts to endorse *Louisa* and sends him a hastily drawn sketch she has made of the east view from the cathedral. Most of the remainder of her letter is taken up with the first draft of a retrospective poem dedicated to Honora, which was later published as 'Lichfield, an Elegy', with the date given as 1781.

With the letter was enclosed a note marked 'When you are at *leisure* and alone', which contained the requested lock of hair tied round with a pink ribbon and a definitive rejection in the form of a little poem:

> With spotless lilies, cull'd from Friendship's bowers,
> That hide no thorns beneath their snowy flowers,
> By Boswell's hand be this light lock enwove,
> But never with the dangerous Rose of Love![102]

The innocent vulnerability of the 'spotless lilies', the symbol in Christian art of chastity, is countered by the veiled warning of the 'dangerous Rose of Love', which invariably has concealed thorns. Seward did not make the secret letters public or give the name of the poem's recipient. In her poetry edition, it was altered to a slightly more formal verse entitled 'With a Lock of the Author's Hair to a Gentleman who Requested it':

---

[100] Boswell, 'Letter to William Temple' (6 July 1784), *Boswell: The Applause of the Jury, 1782–1785*, pp. 256–57.

[101] YUB, Letters of Anna Seward, MS C 2469, fol. 767, Seward, 'Letter to James Boswell' (22 May 1784).

[102] YUB, Letters of Anna Seward, MS C 2469, fol. 767, Seward, 'Letter to James Boswell' (22 May 1784).

Not with the bright, yet dangerous rose of love,
By Florio's hand, be this light lock enwove,
But with the lily, cull'd from Friendship's bowers,
That hides no thorns beneath its snowy flowers.[103]

Her ongoing, very public, literary quarrel with Boswell has been analysed in different biographical works. Without recourse to the secret letters, much of the nuanced undercurrent of their early relationship is sidestepped, yet this must necessarily reflect on their later battles where a different picture emerges. Boswell was initially delighted with the information and anecdotes about Samuel Johnson, which Seward had provided for his *Life* at the cost of a considerable amount of her valuable time. However, not all of the information was firsthand, but came from her mother's old sources, such as Moll Cobb, and Boswell rejected it out of hand. He also rejected anything which portrayed Johnson in a way that did not match his own representation. There followed the 'Benvolio' letters in the *Gentleman's Magazine*, which were clearly written by Seward and which challenge the lavish panegyrics which had been written on Johnson's death, particularly those by Boswell. The 'Benvolio' exchange was very different from the secret letters. In one instance, Seward cynically quotes an 'illustrious literary character', probably William Hayley, who had written a private letter criticising Boswell's *Tour*:

It is a most amusing history of a learned monster, written by his shew-man, who perpetually discovers a diverting apprehension that his beast will play the savage too furiously, and lacerate the company instead of entertaining them.[104]

Not all the 'Benvolio' letters were directed at Boswell's writings, however, and not all his replies were aimed directly at Seward, and the controversy was more often than not a delicate balance of intellectual reasoning than the 'invective' it is most usually credited to be. It was the form of literary jousting, the 'doublet and hose' battles, that Walter Scott admired in Seward and in which she took such great pleasure. The 'Benvolio' letters provoked a controversy and were followed with interest by the reading public, with a mixed response. She was certainly not ashamed of her letters, despite their anonymity, and eventually gave a public acknowledgement for them in the *Gentleman's Magazine*, admitting that she had informed Boswell and all her friends of her identity at the time she first began writing them. Unable to view Seward in terms other than of her sex, Boswell eventually dismissed the whole affair, stating, 'I was wearied with this female criticism.'[105]

Publishing her poetry eventually became a tedious chore. By 1796, after the publication of *Llangollen vale*, Seward had completely ended her poetic

---

[103] Seward, 'With a lock of the Author's hair to a gentleman who requested it', *Poetical Works*, vol. II, p. 138.

[104] Seward, 'Benvolio Letter', in Ashmun, *The Singing Swan*, p. 140.

[105] Boswell, quoted in Peter Martin, *A Life of James Boswell*, p. 405.

contributions to the literary journals and miscellanies, although she was still to publish the odes and sonnets, and 'fugitive' verse still frequently found its way into the press. She told Walter Scott that whenever the 'furore' of writing took hold of her, the problems of publication were always uppermost.[106] Having to negotiate copyrights and wrangle with publishers was problematic, and then facing the critical reviews was never a pleasant prospect. In the main, her poems were now addressed to friends, and she even began to associate letter writing with ill-health and pain. Following the publication of the odes and sonnets in 1799, she told Mary Powys that she had written more than was good for her health. With Saville's meticulous help, she had corrected the proof sheets and published the volumes, but then she had received an influx of letters from new correspondents, from 'men of Genius', which she felt obliged to respond to.[107] When John Saville died in August 1803, suffering a seizure while bending over to cut a corn, she not only lost her life companion, but also her proofreader and the one person who supported her through her intricate dealings with publishers and booksellers.

There was still one major work to come. Her old friend Erasmus Darwin had died at Breadsall Priory, the magnificent ancient mansion surrounded by parkland in Derbyshire, which he had inherited from his suicidal son in 1802. Disappointed that most of her work on the Johnson anecdotes had been rejected by Boswell, Seward had been further disillusioned when Hester Thrale Piozzi published her *Letters to and from the Late Samuel Johnson*, believing the portrayal to be too 'benign' due to the heavy editing, although she acknowledged that the correspondence was sensitive and some censorship was necessary.[108] One reason for Seward's disappointment with Johnson's portrayal was her personal involvement with the edition. When compiling the correspondence, Thrale Piozzi had requested Seward's help in tracking down Johnson's letters to Hill Boothby, written between 1755 and 1756, which were in the hands of the Boothby family.[109] Johnson's affectionate relationship with Hill Boothby is evident in the letters, which appear in Bruce Redford's 1992 edition.[110] Redford confirms that Hill Boothby and Samuel Johnson differed on theological issues, but she was the 'most probable candidate' to be Johnson's second wife.[111]

Describing Boothby as 'fair and learned', Seward had been eager for the private, intimate side of Johnson's character to be revealed by Thrale Piozzi, rather

---

[106] NLS, MSS, 3877, fols 33–36, Seward, 'Letter to Walter Scott' (28 April 1808).

[107] JBM, MS 38/17, Seward, 'Letter to Mary Powys' (23 June 1799).

[108] Seward, 'Letter to Mrs Piozzi, on the Publication of JOHNSON'S letters' (7 March 1788), *Letters*, vol. II, p. 39.

[109] In 1786, Seward told Anna Rogers Stokes that Johnson had a 'platonic passion' for Hill Boothby and that she held copies of some of his letters to her (Seward, *Letters*, vol. I, p. 171).

[110] *The Letters of Samuel Johnson, 1731–1772*, ed. by Bruce Redford, 5 vols (Oxford: Clarendon Press, 1992).

[111] *The Letters of Samuel Johnson*, vol. I, pp. 119–20.

than James Boswell, who had been promised the letters, in the same way that she herself was about to expose Erasmus Darwin's obsession with his second wife, Eliza Pole.[112] Following many time-consuming and delicate negotiations with her friend, the 'unmanageable' old Baronet, Boothby, she finally succeeded in acquiring transcripts of the letters for Thrale Piozzi. When Thrale Piozzi published her book, she told Seward that there had been a minimum amount of editing, but she omitted a substantial part of the correspondence, leaving approximately eighty-five letters unpublished.[113]

Seward would have liked to have published more on Johnson herself, but she knew that her bluntness would not have been appreciated. The *General Evening Post* published her character of him anonymously for fear of upsetting his stepdaughter, Lucy Porter, who 'would resent the fidelity of the portrait'.[114] The private design of her letter books as a life writing venture gave her the opportunity to write with eloquence about Johnson, to paint a word portrait, to critique (often with the highest praise) his writing with a confident authority, to share his anecdotes, to find fault with his treatment of others, to marvel at his powers of rhetoric. In this way she was able to express her own relationship with the revered, complex character. A rumour was circulating the literary circles that Thrale Piozzi published Johnson's letters merely as a vehicle for her own. At this, Seward responded:

> It appears to me, that the natural desire of letting the world know how highly she was esteemed by a person so distinguished, – how constantly, during so many years, she engaged his revering attention, was the master spring of that publication.[115]

When Erasmus Darwin died, Seward was once more asked to find anecdotes for a forthcoming biographical preface to his writings. Darwin's son Robert wrote to her, asking for stories of his father's life in Lichfield, and as she collected her anecdotes together, she came to realise that this time she had too much material to pass on to someone else. She decided to write the biography herself.

Outlining her plan to Walter Scott, she explained that she intended to write about Darwin's friends and to include an extensive analysis of the work she knew intimately, *The Botanic Garden*. In terms of biographical writing, her complete disregard for the received rules of form and content ensured a hostile critical reception. Charles Darwin's 1879 biography of his grandfather, *The Life of Erasmus Darwin*, reveals the extent of the turmoil that Seward's memoirs caused within his family. Charles Darwin treated the book as an outrageously scandalous distortion

[112] Seward, *Letters*, vol. II, pp. 348–49.

[113] Hester Thrale Piozzi, 'Letter to Lady Keith' (31 January 1810), *The Piozzi Letters: Correspondence of Hester Thrale Piozzi (formerly Mrs Thrale), 1784–1821*, ed. by Edward A. Bloom and Lillian D. Bloom, 4 vols (London and Toronto: Associated University Presses, 1991), vol. II, p. 264.

[114] Seward, 'Letter to Miss Weston' (23 March 1785), *Letters*, vol. I, pp. 35–36.

[115] Seward, 'Letter to Rev. — Berwick' (6 October 1788), *Letters*, vol. II, p. 165.

of the truth about Darwin's character and his relationship with his suicidal son. Describing it as an 'unfortunate event' to the good name of his grandfather, he complained that Seward was not qualified to write the biography as she knew nothing of science or medicine, a fact she pointed out in her introduction to the work. Adding that her writing style was sickeningly pretentious, Charles Darwin continued:

> The many friends and admirers of Dr Darwin were indignant at Miss Seward's book, and thought it showed much malice towards him. No such impression was left on my mind when lately re-reading it, but only that of scandalous negligence, together, perhaps, with a wish to excite attention to her book, by inserting any wild and injurious report about him. [...] It is natural to inquire why Miss Seward felt so much malice towards a man with whom she had lived on intimate terms during many years, and for whom she often expressed, and probably felt the highest admiration. The explanation appears to be that Dr Darwin rejected her love. Even before his first marriage there appears to have been some love-passages between them.[116]

He gathered his evidence from Edgeworth's vague comments about the 'little pique' between Seward and Polly Darwin at the dinner party, but also from rumours of documentary evidence (subsequently destroyed by Charles Darwin's father) which had been produced as a threat to Seward when she was told by the family to retract what she had written about Erasmus Darwin's relationship with his suicidal son. For the second edition of the memoirs, Seward withdrew some of her comments about Darwin's cold-hearted response to his son's death. Charles Darwin could see no further than a stereotypical scorned woman: 'disappointed affection, with some desire for revenge, render intelligible her whole course of conduct'.[117] Extraordinarily, he concludes that his grandfather's plagiarism of Seward's *Botanic Garden* verse was a case of 'high-way robbery, or the exaction of blackmail', but that Erasmus Darwin thought it 'fair play', as he had helped write the 'Elegy on Captain Cook'.[118]

There was a further editing problem with the biography, this time with the publisher, Joseph Johnson, who felt that the candid biography contained unfavourable references to one of his most influential customers, one Mr Philips, who was an author of some reputation, the stepfather of the writer and philosopher Thomas Day. In her biography, Seward tells the story of Day's attempts to 'train' a wife. Aside from her obvious amusement at the episode, she made a serious attempt to find some justification for Day's unorthodox behaviour and examined the root causes of his unhappy childhood. Here she found his stepfather Philips to be culpably responsible by having ill-treated Day as a child. It was this criticism

---

[116] Charles Darwin, *Charles Darwin's Life of Erasmus Darwin*, ed. by Desmond King-Hele (Cambridge: Cambridge University Press, 2003), pp. 75–76.

[117] Darwin, *Life of Erasmus Darwin*, p. 76.

[118] Darwin, *Life of Erasmus Darwin*, p. 65.

which offended the 'over-scrupulous' Joseph Johnson, and he refused to publish the sections of the work that concerned Day. As Seward knew that these passages were among the most interesting parts of the work, she stood her ground and was prepared to go the extent of finding a new publisher if necessary. Her friends intervened and persuaded her to revise the offending sections. The passages remained with just a few minor revisions, but her respect for Johnson ended. From her wrangles with Johnson, who had also delayed the copyright fees of sixty guineas, to the Darwin family's anger about the disrespectful portrayal of their illustrious relative, to the reviewers' contempt for the work's lack of conformity, the memoirs proved to be problematical from start to finish and were Seward's final publication. They are an invaluable source of information for us and provide the most comprehensive record of the period Darwin spent at Lichfield. And, unlike the juvenile letters and letter books, the memoirs survive intact, untouched by the censors.

Chapter 6
Final Words:
The Last Will and Testament

'Poor Miss Seward is expecting her own death every day', wrote Hester Thrale Piozzi in March 1805.[1] Despite her poor health, Anna Seward continued to keep her letter books in good order, and the autobiographical content was their main value. 'There is no greater vanity in publishing one's letters, than one's essays or poems', she argued.[2] Tortured with the pain from rheumatism, her breast injury, a broken kneecap, occasional haemorrhages, dizziness, and violent headaches, she was still able to escape the metaphorical 'hard day's travel over wastes of writing paper' to visit the Lancashire and Yorkshire coasts and the fashionable spas at Matlock and Buxton in Derbyshire to take the water cures.[3] She describes the pleasure she took in a visit to an old friend in Warwickshire in 1808. The forty-mile journey of seven hours was a delight in itself, giving her the time to read Scott's *Marmion* and Southey's *Madoc* on the way. Once there, her mornings were spent leisurely reading poetry, and her evening's entertainment was a rubber of whist with her host, James Mitchel, who was one of her last remaining contacts with her youth.

Back home at the Palace, she fought off her various ailments to continue her correspondence, now writing double-length letters whenever she had the strength and continuing to copy many of them into her letter books. She explained her aims to Scott:

> Fortunate for you that, that I, who never know how to lay down my pen when it has been taken upon to address you, am obliged, by malady, and by much writing, to avoid intruding often on any individual Friend. Therefore I pray you to consider each letter of mine, when it arrives, as *two*, and read it piecemeal at short intervals of leisure.[4]

She wrote compulsively until the pen slipped from her hand and she fell into a fatal coma. On her death, there was one final piece of literature waiting to be read: her remarkable twenty-two-page last will and testament.

Dated 15 February 1808, the year before her death, Seward's will illuminates many of the obscured aspects of her life and her works and provides an apt

---

[1]   Thrale Piozzi, 'Letter to Lady Keith' (31 January 1810), *The Piozzi Letters*, vol. II, pp. 60, 264.

[2]   Seward, 'Letter to Rev. — Berwick' (6 October 1788), *Letters*, vol. II, p. 165.

[3]   NLS, MSS, 865, fols 25–28, Seward, 'Letter to Walter Scott' (20 June 1803).

[4]   NLS, MS 3875, fols 186–89, Seward, 'Letter to Walter Scott' (25 June 1806).

illustration of her compulsive drive to control her reputation for posterity. She starts with the confirmation that her name is Anne, or Anna Seward, as she was usually known, and continues with a simple request for a frugal and private funeral, 'without any other needless expense', she writes, 'than that of a lead coffin to protect my breathless body'.[5] This modest directive opens a remarkably complex document comprising over twenty pages of specifications for the disposal of her literary and financial legacy. It is a remarkable manuscript in its comprehensive summation of her life and its disclosure of her self-definition as a writing woman. It also provides a fascinating insight into how she used the will to structure a form of continuity through portraiture in the absence of natural heirs. It exposes the limitations constructed by gendered conventions that restricted her control over her posthumous reputation and even over her financial portfolio. The scope of the will is to offer a valuable additional source of information in the form of an unedited manuscript.

Like Clarissa Harlowe's will, which was an articulate record of Richardson's character's life achievements in the form of a legal document, Seward's will has a narrative that sits comfortably alongside her literature.[6] And as she was aware that the document would be read aloud and discussed in detail after her death, it has a flamboyant eloquence. It would have made an impressive reading. Transgressing conventional form and content, the will is extensive and complex. In its own time and for several years afterwards, it was accorded an almost mythical status, with rumours of an 'enigma' designed by its author and secreted among the pages, with a supposed substantial reward for solving it.[7] The bequests, which include her collection of portraits and paintings, her literary works and a substantial financial portfolio, bring to light her desire to leave some form of familial succession in addition to an enduring reputation. It is also clear that she wanted to retain a tight control of her financial bequests in perpetuity. She expresses her own sense of genealogy through portraiture by giving the portraits of those dearest to her a provenance and a line of descent. In financial matters, having personally administered her considerable fortune for many years, she deliberately breaks the common law of *couverture* in order to leave money, revenues, shares and stocks to the personal possession of married female friends.

The conventions surrounding the law and its application to women came under Seward's scrutiny. The legal system held that in marriage, a husband and wife comprised a single unit, and although individual families made their own arrangements, in principle a married woman had no legal rights over property, money, or even her children. This notion is expressed eloquently by the influential

---

[5]   Lichfield RO, Seward Family MSS, D262/1/35, p. 1.

[6]   Richardson, *Clarissa*, pp. 1412–20. Seward's will can be seen to display several parallels to Clarissa's will, where it has little precedence in the field of actual wills.

[7]   Lichfield Record Office holds a letter dated 23 January 1818 from Peter Tennion of London enquiring whether the reward for a solution to the enigma by Anna Seward had been given yet. (Seward Family MSS, D 262/2/11). See Appendix II.

legal scholar Sir William Blackstone in his series of lectures, which were later published as *Commentaries on the Laws of England* of 1765–69, and particularly in *The Laws Respecting Women* of 1777.[8] Blackstone observes that a woman's property passed to her husband's authority on marriage, stating that 'she can't let, set, sell, give away, or alienate anything without her husband's consent'.[9] In Blackstone's interpretation, a married woman could expect to be protected by her husband yet would not have any legal rights. As a single woman, Seward was in the fortunate position to control her own finances without intervention, particularly since her father appointed her as the sole trustee and 'executrix' of his own estate; his male relatives had no rights over her inheritance. But the law for married women was different. By the common law of *couverture* it was within a husband's rights to use his wife's inheritance to pay his own debts, for example, or to borrow against. It was perfectly legal to break *couverture* by making a specific stipulation in a will, and this is exactly what Seward did. She also wrote her own form of an entail into the will in her attempt to control the devolution of her estate.[10] In the sense of limited ownership there was a further complication. Most women legatees had to rely on the trustees' integrity, as the capital could be used for their own financial investments if they so wished.

There is a point of comparison to be made with Thomas Seward's now barely-legible last will and testament.[11] This document is typically short and succinct, and he leaves his entire estate except for a few minor bequests to his daughter, Anna. What proves to be the most interesting aspect of the document is the revocation of a will he made previously. His new will, dated October 1781, appoints Seward as his sole trustee and 'executrix'. He refers to her as a 'woman of business' who is fully capable of handling his affairs with ease. In this appointment he was not only placing his absolute trust in her competence, but was allowing her an unusual authority and control that she clearly intended to carry forward to her dealings with her own estate. His only stipulation concerning the distribution of his estate

---

[8]   William Blackstone, *Commentaries on the Laws of England* (Oxford: Clarendon Press, 1765–69); *The Laws respecting Women, as they regard their natural rights, or their connections and conduct; also, the obligations of parent and child, and the condition of minors, &c.* (London: J. Johnson, 1777).

[9]   William Blackstone, *The Laws respecting Women*, p. 65.

[10]   The head of a wealthy family was considered to be solely a custodian of the family estates, and the assets of lineage were fixed in unbreakable entails. Land, property and money passed to the eldest son by the convention of primogeniture. In his comprehensive study, Lawrence Stone explains how the other children were economically reliant on their father or elder brother, and although they could be granted parts of any un-entailed estates, they had no claim on the entailed land and property (Lawrence Stone, *The Family, Sex and Marriage in England, 1500–1800* (London: Penguin, 1979), p. 71). In her complicated will Seward attempts a similar system, with most of her estate held in trust. The chain of inheritance links, in some cases, several generations.

[11]   The Prerogative Court of Canterbury, Bishop Quire Numbers 192–238, PROB 11/1191, 1780, Thomas Seward's will.

was an unwritten provision for his own relatives to receive the same proportion of Seward's fortune as she intended to leave her mother's relatives, with whom she had a much closer relationship. She honoured his request.[12] Thomas Seward's action served two purposes: first, he was able to ensure his own future security by placing his financial affairs in the hands of the person closest to him (his stroke in 1780 would have had a bearing on this), and, second, he presented Seward with the opportunity to put her formidable organisational skills into effect and to achieve the financial independence she valued so highly.

Following her opening pragmatic request for a simple funeral, Seward provides the details of exactly where she wanted her coffin to be interred. The family vault is situated inside Lichfield Cathedral beneath the aisle known as the Choir Pavement, and it was Seward's intriguing preference to be buried there, at the feet of her father, just as Clarissa Harlowe asked to be buried at the feet of her 'dear and honoured' grandfather, in her will.[13] Doubtful that the Dean and Chapter would be prepared to disturb the aisle, however, Seward had another solution which reaches even further back into her favourite literary history, to the story of Eloïsa and Abelard. She asked that she might be laid with her deceased companion, her 'faithful and excellent Friend thro' the course of Thirty-seven years', John Saville.[14] Because of the echoes of disgrace that reverberated around Seward's life, it is not surprising that the remaining family and executors wanted to avoid any further, posthumous scandal. The entry in the Seward family bible reveals her final resting place to be under the Choir Pavement with her family, rather than sharing a vault with her beloved Saville.[15] The fact that she requested to be buried with Saville shows her resilience to the scandal. To return to her angry letter to Erasmus Darwin, when he told her parents of the affair, she is clear in her life choices. She states that she was not prepared to be bullied into making sacrifices that might affect her happiness: 'I have found a satisfaction in lessening the cares, and adding to the comforts of that worthy creature that I would not exchange for the applause of a generally misjudging world.'[16]

---

[12]   Seward refers to this request in her will, stating, 'In the foregoing disposition of my property I have had in Remembrance of my dear Father's request, Viz, that whatever part of my said fortune I might chuse to bequeath to my Mother's Relations I should bequeath a nearly equal part to those of his family' (Lichfield RO, Seward Family MSS, D262/1/34, p. 17).

[13]   Richardson, *Clarissa*, p. 1413.

[14]   Eloïsa and Abelard were interred in the same grave in the monastery of the Paraclete. He died in 1142, she in 1163. (Alexander Pope, 'Eloisa to Abelard', in *The Twickenham Edition of the Poems of Alexander Pope*, general ed. John Butt, 3rd edn, 6 vols (London: Methuen & Co; New Haven: Yale University Press), 1962, repr. 1972), vol. II, *The Rape of the Lock and Other Poems*, ed. by Geoffrey Tillotson).

[15]   Mary Alden Hopkins, *Dr Johnson's Lichfield* (London: Peter Owen, 1956), p. 240.

[16]   Cambridge UL, MS DAR 227. 3: 24, Seward, 'Letter to Erasmus Darwin' (16 March 1772).

The burial place instructions lead on to a bequest of five hundred pounds for a sculptor to create a monument for Seward's family. She makes no mention of an epitaph for herself. The executors chose to pay Walter Scott £100 from the will's miscellaneous funds to compose a suitable verse and also to design the memorial. This was a generous amount which can be placed in perspective by a comparison with the sum of £500 which Scott was paid for the copyright of his hugely successful *Border Minstrelsy*. Robert Southey considered himself to be a great friend of Seward and voiced his views on this subject, believing that she had specifically requested a memorial for herself and that this would prove to be a monument to her egotism. Writing to Mary Barker, the friend who accompanied him on a visit to Seward in 1808, Southey describes the bequest as 'the only foolish part of her arrangements [...] a poor vanity: the very verger, when he shows the monument, will relate it to her discredit'.[17] His allegations reinforce the general outlook on the prevalent expectations of modesty in women's behaviour that Seward usually ignored. During her life and particularly after her death, she attracted various accusations of arrogance and egotism because she resisted the idea of virtuous feminine modesty in her writings and in her dealings with people. Codes of eighteenth-century virtue allowed for a certain amount of male vanity, but women were judged by radically different criteria. Chastity and obedience were important virtues, but, above all, modesty was the desired norm.

The literary vanity that played a significant role in poetry and other writings by men was strongly disapproved of in female writers. Neither Wordsworth nor Coleridge attracted much contemporary criticism for vanity when proposing theories of their own poetic immortality in the preface to the *Lyrical Ballads*.[18] They intended their work for posterity, and Seward viewed her own work in a similar light. Regardless of conventions, she was not modest about her achievements. When Francis Mundy sent her some of his verse for her critical opinion in 1799, she was flattered that he had quoted from 'Monody on Major André', but was annoyed at a reference to self-doubt which highlighted her youthful lack of confidence in her writing. The diffidence of youth, when she was apprehensive about her status as an uneducated woman, had gradually been replaced with a forthright confidence gained through years of literary study and the conviction that her poetry would endure. As a mature woman, she habitually wrote and acted without reference to gendered practice or to conventional standards.

Seward's complete indifference to codes of literary modesty is revealed specifically in her biography of Erasmus Darwin, where she sets out her aims and objectives clearly and without reserve in the dedication and the preface. Addressing the Earl of Carlisle in her dedication, she does apply the accepted diminutive term,

---

[17]   Robert Southey, 'Letter to Mary Barker' (13 May 1809), in *Selections from the Letters of Robert Southey*, ed. by John Wood Warter, 4 vols (London: Longman, Brown, Green and Longman, 1856), vol. II, pp. 137–38.

[18]   William Wordsworth and Samuel Taylor Coleridge, *Lyrical Ballads, with a few other poems* (London: J. & A. Arch, 1798).

'my little Tract', expressing the hope that it will 'interest and amuse a transient hour of his leisure'. Self-assurance radiates from her subsequent statement, however, where she asserts exactly what she wants, 'that approbation from him which must reward biographic integrity'.[19] In her preface, she emphasises her divergence from the traditional format of biography by explaining her reluctance to write of Darwin's time lived in Derby when she saw little of him, or of his early days before she knew him. She excluded his letters on the grounds that they were of no literary value and refused to be drawn into undeserved flattery of her subject, stating, 'Every man has his errors.'[20] Through her revealing anecdotes about Darwin and his friends, she claimed that she intended to offer an impartial and balanced representation, telling Scott that a biographer should always be 'willing to praise but not afraid to blame'.[21] She made few concessions to modesty, and by flouting the 'sacred duties' of biography, she confirmed her disregard for proper decorum. Seward's attempts at self-memorialisation through her writings challenged several aspects of conventional expectations of women's behaviour, and, as Southey's assessment confirms, she came to be judged as egotistical rather than intellectual, and as vain rather than ambitious.

Yet, the will stresses that the monument is for her 'late father and his family', and, contrary to Southey's observations, any other purpose for it is merely by implication.[22] If Seward intended to provide a memorial to celebrate her own achievements as well as for her family, she was of a mind with Samuel Johnson, who wrote that every man 'may expect to be recorded in an epitaph, and therefore finds some interest in providing that his memory may not suffer by an unskilful panegyrick'.[23] Southey was not aware of the letter from Charles Simpson to Walter Scott in which the solicitor puts forward the request for the inscription and monument design, at the same time expressing his reservations about the standard of the 'unskilful panegyricks' to be found in Lichfield. Simpson wrote, 'May we beg an inscription in English and a design for the monument. The inscriptions in our cathedral are very bad with few exceptions. The family consisted of Mr and Mrs Seward, Miss S. Seward who died about 25, and Mrs Seward our friend.'[24]

From the somewhat vague and inaccurate description provided by Simpson, who, as the family lawyer, should have had more precise details at hand, Scott had complete discretion to produce both the epitaph and monument design. The completed marble monument, which is now situated close to the entrance doors of

---

[19]   Seward, *Memoirs*, p. iv.

[20]   Seward, *Memoirs*, p. viii.

[21]   NLS, MSS, 865, fols 23–24, Seward, 'Letter to Walter Scott' (19 March 1803).

[22]   Lichfield RO, Seward Family MSS, D262/1/35, p. 1.

[23]   Samuel Johnson, 'An Essay on Epitaphs', *The Idler*. In Two Volumes, Volume II, The Third Edition, With Additional Essays, 1740, p. 288, *Literature Online*. http://lion. chadwyck.co.uk.

[24]   NLS MSS, 865, fols 143–44, Charles Simpson, 'Letter to Walter Scott' (1 October 1809).

the cathedral, shows a carving of a female figure weeping under a willow tree with an unstrung harp in its branches and the following words:

Amid these aisles, where once his precepts showed
The heavenward pathway which in life he trode,
This simple tablet marks a father's bier,
And those he loved in life, in death are near.
For him, for them, a daughter bade it rise,
Memorial of domestic charities.
Still would you know why o'er the marble spread,
In female grace the willow droops her head;
Why on her branches, silent and unstrung,
The minstrel's harp is emblematic hung;
What poet's voice is smothered here in dust,
Till waked to join the chorus of the just;
Lo! One brief line an answer sad supplies –
Honour'd, belov'd, and mourn'd, here SEWARD lies:
Her worth, her warmth of heart, our sorrows say:
Go seek her genius in her living lay.

Scott's verse makes clear that the epitaph's main concern is the memory of Anna Seward's life, rather than her father's or her family's, whose names are absent from the inscription. In Samuel Johnson's 'Essay on Epitaphs,' he explains that the purpose is to offer examples of virtue and that an inscription should clearly illustrate the person's characteristics and achievements: 'praise ought not to be general, because the mind is lost in any indefinite idea, and cannot be affected by what it cannot comprehend'.[25] Scott's single line containing the words 'Honour'd, belov'd, and mourn'd' provides the vague, indefinite idea that Johnson guarded against. Two qualities that Scott identified, Seward's 'worth' and her 'warmth of heart', have a tacit relationship with womanly attributes which is accentuated by their soft alliteration. They are reinforced by the 'female grace' of the carved weeping figure, implicitly placing Seward within a female poetic tradition, despite the benevolently flattering 'genius', a term conventionally used for men and which evokes another Johnson caveat: 'In lapidary inscriptions, a man is not upon oath.'[26]

Typically, Seward's own epitaph for John Saville, which is also situated in the cathedral, closes with the imagery of death and the afterlife with lines borrowed

---

[25] Samuel Johnson, 'An Essay on Epitaphs', *The Idler*, II, p. 297, *Literature Online*. http://lion. chadwyck.co.uk.

[26] Samuel Johnson, quoted in James Boswell, *Life of Johnson, Together with Boswell's Journal of a Tour to the Hebrides and Johnson's Diary of a Journey into North Wales*, ed. by George Birkbeck Hill, rev. by L.F. Powell, 6 vols (London: Oxford University Press, 1934), vol. II, p. 406.

from Johnson's epitaph on the musician Claudy Phillips ('Sleep undisturbed within this peaceful shrine / Till angels wake thee with a note like thine'[27]):

Sleep then, pale, mortal frame, in yon low shrine,
'Till angels wake thee with a note like thine!'[28]

Writers, naturally, have recourse to an alternative manifestation of living warmth; the poet may be dead but the poems remain. While allowing that the sepulchral dust has settled and smothered the poet's voice, Scott animates the epitaph with a conventional but rather dismissive closing address to the reader to 'Go seek her genius in her living lay'. In this way, he did not have to praise the poetry that he publicly conceded to be just a 'pleasing register of her sentiments, her feelings, and her affections'.[29]

Following the will's memorial details are the personal bequests. There is no detailed record of Seward's household organisation or of the servants she employed. She obviously had a sizeable staff to perform the necessary work in such a large house, and she practised economy where possible. She did not have her own coach, for example, but travelled out in a hired carriage and, later in life, around Lichfield in a sedan chair. Her servants are generously remembered in the will on the proviso that they remained with her and cared for her during her last illness. 'Proper mourning' and ten pounds each, together with their full quarterly wage, was their reward. There were a few exceptions. A servant known as John Fish was bequeathed an annuity of twenty pounds, as was Mary Wright, another favourite. Mary Atkins, the housekeeper, received a single payment of thirty pounds. Leaving money to servants could prove complicated. A few years previously, Samuel Johnson had deliberated on the appropriate amount for a gentleman to leave to a favourite servant. He was writing his will and he wanted to provide an annuity for Francis Barber, whom he treated more as an adopted son than as a servant. He sought advice from his physician, Dr Richard Brocklesby, and was told that a nobleman would be expected to reward a faithful servant with an annuity of around fifty pounds. Johnson left Barber a generous seventy pounds and later added a codicil making him the residuary beneficiary of an estate of almost fifteen hundred pounds.[30]

Seward's paid companion, Elizabeth Fern, was bequeathed a magnificent annuity of sixty pounds. 'Stout and nimble' Elizabeth was the much-loved friend,

---

[27]   Samuel Johnson, 'An Epitaph on Claudy Phillips, a Musician' in Anna Williams, *Miscellanies: Essays in Prose and Verse*, 1766, *Literature Online.* http://lion.chadwyck.co.uk.

[28]   Seward, 'For a marble tablet in Lichfield Cathedral sacred to the memory of John Saville, forty-eight years vicar-choral of that place', *Poetical Works*, vol. II, p. 195.

[29]   Walter Scott, 'Biographical Preface', *Poetical Works*, vol. I, p. xxxix.

[30]   Sir John Hawkins, *The Works of Samuel Johnson, LL.D.: Together with His Life, and Notes on His Lives of the Poets*, 11 vols (London: J. Buckland et al., 1787), vol. I, pp. 594–95.

nurse and companion of Seward's final years. Elizabeth travelled with Seward, acting as an amanuensis and reader during the times when she was too ill to engage in her best-loved activities of reading and writing.[31] Seward's description of Elizabeth Fern calls attention to her own finely-drawn but unfavourable observations of the marriage market. She was concerned with the attitude of men who were, she remarked, generally 'governed by only two motives in their wedding engagements; – by the pursuit of beauty or wealth'. Within the description is a far wider representation of the expectations of young women who had neither beauty nor wealth:

> Miss F[ern] had once beauty, but a cutaneous eruption on the face, though slight, soon tarnished and muddied her once radiant complexion. From that period, of fourteen years remoteness, she has lived without lovers, though her height and shape, as you know, are fine; her countenance expressive, and her features agreeable. Those who remember her beautiful, compare, to her disadvantage, the *has been* with the *is*; and men of her later acquaintance confess her agreeable, but her want of fortune ices their commendation. What has been will probably continue to be. I hope to Heaven she may recover [from a fever], but I think she will not marry.[32]

In his indignation about what he considered to be the vanity of Seward's memorial, Robert Southey poured further scorn on Elizabeth Fern's annuity, surely unaware of its generous extent. Southey raised a few objections to Seward's financial decisions: 'Everybody who has money to dispose of knows persons who ought to have it, and they are greatly to be censured who give any part of their property to those who have no claims to it; I include moral claims as well as those of kindred. Scott's legacy and her monument-money should have gone to Miss Fern.' However, Southey had more on his mind than Elizabeth Fern's welfare, and his thoughts reveal his bitterness about not being mentioned in the will. He wrote to Mary Barker expressing his disappointment: 'She might have left me a set of her works, or some piece of plate, and I should have shown such a token with pleasure.'[33]

Extraordinarily, there is no charitable bequest in the will; nothing is left to the poor of the parish. Seward's more generous consideration for her friends, godchildren and various relatives is shown with fifteen bequests of different sums of money, ranging from two to five guineas, for mourning rings. Her good friends who had an important influence on her later poetry, Lady Eleanor Butler and Sarah Ponsonby, each received five guineas, as did Eliza Smith, John Saville's surviving daughter. Eliza was also left the laces, together with an intriguing bequest of the contents of a locked bureau, but unfortunately the details of these contents were not disclosed.

---

[31]   JBM, MS 38/23, Seward, 'Letter to Mary Powys' (22 October 1808).

[32]   Seward, 'Letter to Charles Simpson' (19 September 1804), *Letters*, vol. VI, 191–92.

[33]   Southey, 'Letter to Mary Barker' (13 May 1809), *Letters of Robert Southey*, vol. II, p. 138.

Among this series of bequests is a generous five guineas for a mourning ring for Elizabeth Cornwallis, or 'Clarissa', as Seward always called her, the daughter of the Bishop of Lichfield. It was by Bishop Cornwallis's special concession that Seward was able to stay on at the Palace after her father's death, and he never missed an opportunity to point out resentfully how many wealthy prospective tenants for the Palace he regularly turned down. Seward believed that Cornwallis came to regret his promise never to evict her, and although she always paid a large rent advance and tried her best not to complain about his new building works that she thought looked like 'cowsheds', there was a constant fear of his disapproval. She even had a water closet installed at her own expense. 'I must [...] be most wary not to incence him', she wrote, and she cultivated her friendship with the excitable Clarissa, who is remembered in the will as a 'highly esteemed' friend.[34] In her poem 'Clarissa', Seward returns to an old theme, advising her to nurture wisdom and reap the 'fruits of knowledge' in order to counteract the effects of ageing, particularly the loss of beauty.[35]

As land and property were usually passed along a male line of inheritance, female testators tended to consider personal heirlooms as their line of continuity. This notion has a literary representation in Clarissa Harlowe's will, as she describes in fine detail her bequests of clothes, linen and laces, jewellery, family plate, pictures, musical instruments, books and framed needlework. The kind of material commodity which was poised between the past and the future had no place at all in Seward's will. If women's self-definition was positioned in terms of their possessions, Seward was far more concerned with her literary legacy to provide herself with the lasting imagery of a writer. The settlement and preservation of her property and financial portfolio were more important than her household effects and personal possessions. There is one reference to a personal item, an antique fan, which is left to Mary White, who was the wife of her cousin Thomas. Described as 'my curious Fan, of Ancient date, but exquisite Workmanship, and with a French Mount of Red Leather',[36] this is her solitary concession to personal artefacts, suggesting that it had a special association rather than being an individual thing of beauty. A fan was much more than an item of fashion or utility; it was often given as a present to a young woman by her admirer, or offered as a wedding gift to be carried by the bride. As a representation of feminine values with its own fixed, coded language of meanings, the fan possibly held a fascination as a symbol of hidden emotions and concealed feelings. Apart from the fan, the absence of any other description of the personal items typically associated with female heredity reveals the measure of Seward's self-definition. Most of the material artefacts she leaves do not relate to sentimentality or express a notion of social standing. Instead, they are casually described in the most perfunctory of terms: 'my best

---

[34] Johnson BM, MS 38/19, Seward, 'Letter to Mary Powys' (9 April 1805).
[35] Anna Seward, 'Clarissa', *Poetical Works*, vol. III, p. 344.
[36] Lichfield RO, Seward Family MSS, D262/1/35, p. 2.

laces', 'all the apparel I have worn', and 'my best diamond ring'.[37] These are the spare descriptions of nothing more than the minutiae of her life, set among the detailed and complex descriptions of the items designated as important to her self-construction.

The items which may have connected Seward with domesticity were sold off. Her household effects; furniture, plate and, remarkably, even her books, were sent to public auction to pay off trifling outstanding debts and funeral expenses. This is a forceful comment on the ephemeral nature of domestic property. However, it also provided a further opportunity for Seward to consolidate her posthumous reputation. As a public sale, it was liable to generate interest and excitement from admirers and souvenir hunters who wanted their own heirlooms from the Seward estate.

If Seward had no specific concerns about the destination of her household goods, her collection of portraits proved to be an expression of family history. In the absence of a genetic line of inheritance, the portraits conveyed a form of symbolic continuity, and her instructions for their preservation are clear-cut. Her remarkable talent for intricately drawn word portraits complements the painted images. Two portraits of Thomas Seward, one a miniature by Richmond and the other an unusually badly-executed portrait by Joseph Wright of Derby, are bequeathed to cousins. Seward indicates that one of the Palace's paintings, a portrait of her paternal grandmother painted by the famous Caroline artist Sir Peter Lely, belongs to her cousin, Susannah Burrows, and must be restored to her. The miniature portrait of John Saville, painted when he was aged thirty-four by the fashionable artist John Smart, is singled out for special attention. Seward gives this portrait a female line of inheritance, leaving it to Saville's daughter, Elizabeth Smith, who is asked to 'value and preserve it as a jewel above all price'.[38] The terms of the will state that in the case of Elizabeth Smith's previous demise, the precious miniature must pass to Smith's daughter, Honora Jager, rather than to her son, Saville Smith. Likewise, Honora Jager and her own future heirs are given special instructions for the portrait's protection. 'Guard it with Sacred care from the Sun and from damp,' writes Seward, 'as I have guarded it.'[39] Seward's terminology, specifically the adjective 'sacred', makes a clear connection between the portrait and a religious artefact, as she casts Saville's persona in a saintly mould.

Seward insists on preserving this particular image of John Saville, who is depicted in powdered and curled wig with a high-collared, buttoned coat, as she considered it to be an almost exact physical resemblance of him. More importantly, she thought it gave an accurate representation of his character. She explains her reasoning for her concern for the portrait's welfare:

---

[37] Lichfield RO, Seward Family MSS, D262/1/35, p. 2.
[38] Lichfield RO, Seward Family MSS, D262/1/35, p. 2.
[39] Lichfield RO, Seward Family MSS, D262/1/35, p. 2.

[…] that so the posterity of my valued Friend may know what in his prime was the form of him, whose mind thro' life, by acknowledgement of all who knew him, could discern the superior Powers of Talent and Virtue, was the seat of liberal endowment, warm Piety, and energetic benevolence.[40]

This representation of Saville's best qualities is the one that she intended to pass down the generations alongside the portrait.

Another painting that Seward wanted to preserve for posterity was a mezzotint engraving from a George Romney illustration entitled *Serena Reading*.[41] She thought that it resembled her dearly-loved, beautiful foster sister, Honora Sneyd, almost exactly in looks and posture when she was sixteen years old, even though Romney had never met Honora. Seward commissioned the artist to provide a copy for herself, and she explains in the will how she had a plaque made to sit above the frame with the words 'Such was Honora Sneyd'.[42] Seward preserved Honora's memory in a series of poems which portrayed her romanticised vision of her, and she intended the same for the portrait, which was placed in her bedroom so that it was the last image she saw each night.[43] The engraving's recipient is Honora's brother Edward Sneyd, or, she states, in the case of his previous demise, his 'amiable' daughter Emma. Again, Seward reinforces her sense of the importance of lasting visual imagery with the following instructions:

[…] value and preserve [the engraving] as the perfect, tho' accidental resemblance of her Aunt [Honora], and my ever dear friend, when she was surrounded by all her Virgin glories – beauty and grace, sensibility and goodness, superior intelligence and unswerving truth.[44]

She mentions another portrait of Honora Sneyd in the will, confirming it as a very poor resemblance.[45] It was one of a pair of miniature portraits sketched in the popular spa town of Buxton, Derbyshire in 1769 by Honora's eighteen-year-old, 'gallant, faithful and unfortunate lover', Major John André.[46] In Buxton, he gave one of the portraits to Seward as a memento, keeping the other for himself. When

---

[40]   Lichfield RO, Seward Family MSS, D262/1/35, p. 2.

[41]   *Serena Reading*, by George Romney, 1781, National Portrait Gallery. The illustration is from William Hayley's poem *The Triumphs of Temper* (William Hayley, *The Triumphs of Temper: a poem. In six cantos*, London: J. Dodsley, 1781), a didactic work which expresses the principle that a young woman must possess a good temper to acquire a husband.

[42]   Lichfield RO, Seward Family MSS, D262/1/35, pp. 2–3.

[43]   Seward, 'Letter to Mrs M. Powys' (22 September 1792), *Letters*, vol. III, pp. 174–75. Seward also had a silhouette portrait of Honora which she took with her on every journey. This portrait is not mentioned in the will.

[44]   Lichfield RO, Seward Family MSS, D262/1/35, p. 3.

[45]   Seward writes, 'That picture was his first attempt to delineate the Human face, consequently it is an unfavourable and most imperfect resemblance of very distinguished beauty' (Lichfield RO, Seward Family MSS, D262/1/35, p. 3).

[46]   Lichfield RO, Seward Family MSS, D262/1/35, p. 2.

André was imprisoned for spying in America, it is said that he had the miniature portrait of Honora hidden inside his mouth. Seward writes that André's miniature portrait is 'an unfavourable and most imperfect resemblance of distinguished beauty',[47] although in the monody she dedicated to him, she flattered his 'nice hand', which, 'caught ev'ry grace, and copied ev'ry charm'.[48] She wanted Honora to be remembered by others in the same way that she herself evoked her youthful image, and that was as 'Serena' in the Romney portrait. With Honora Sneyd set permanently within the imagery of her 'Virgin glories', an earlier harmonious time for Seward was encapsulated in that portrait.

Although she sat for portraits by Myers, Smart and Tilly Kettle, Seward's preferred portrait of herself was naturally the one painted by George Romney, who had been introduced to her by William Hayley, their mutual friend, on one of her visits to Sussex. Hayley had commissioned the portrait for himself, and later, Seward had her own copy painted. This portrait is left to her lawyer and executor, Charles Simpson. As it is the visual representation of the author and therefore an important part of her literary heritage, it is placed under Simpson's official protection for posterity. Seward left instructions for Scott to have an engraving made from the portrait by a top London artist of his own choice and to use this as the frontispiece to the volumes of poetry. However, Romney had painted Seward in 1786, when fashion determined a high, padded and pomaded hair style. The portrait shows her with her hair arranged elaborately, piled up on her head and topped with an ornamental laurel wreath and small veil. This was not comfortable imagery for her. She emphasises that the artist of the new engraving should repaint the hair to give her a more fashionable and dignified appearance. She writes in her 'posthumous' letter addressed to Scott, 'I wish that the heavy disposition of the hair, which the fashion of that period dictated, might in the engraving be altered to a more light and picturesque form, such as is now worn, and which can never appear over-charged or ungraceful.'[49] At the time of the writing of her will, hair fashion was simpler and derived from ancient Greek sources, which was much more in keeping with her literary self-image.

Charles Simpson wrote to Scott that he preferred not to send the valuable portrait to London for fear of damage on the journey, but that he knew of a good artist who would come to Lichfield and make a copy of it for around twenty or thirty guineas. Simpson offered to have an engraving made of Thomas Seward from the Joseph Wright portrait at the same time. Scott, however, decided to turn down these offers. He appeared to be making his own arrangements, but in fact he did nothing. When the executors and family discovered that there would be no

---

[47]   Lichfield RO, Seward Family MSS, D262/1/35, p. 3.

[48]   Seward, 'Monody on Major André', *Poetical Works*, vol. II, p. 71.

[49]   NLS, MSS, 870, fol. 14, Seward, 'Posthumous Letter from Anna Seward to Walter Scott' (17 July 1807).

portrait, they expressed their anger at his slipshod attitude, clearly believing that its absence would affect book sales.[50]

Harry White wrote angrily to Scott to express the family's dismay, and, at the same time, he offered a glimpse into the significance of Seward's visual image to her friends and to the reading public: '[W]e are all astonished, disappointed, hurt, that no copy has been taken of Romney's fine portrait – it would naturally have aided the sale. – In truth, I know some friends who would have purchased the volumes merely for its sake.'[51] It was some time before Scott replied, eventually writing to Simpson with the casual comment, 'I have given up all idea of the portrait, having been indifferently served by the artist whom I wished to have made the copy from your picture.'[52] Despite her intention to construct her visual image for posterity, ultimately there was no portrait at all of Seward to preface her poetry volumes. Archibald Constable printed the unflattering Tilly Kettle portrait as the frontispiece for the correspondence volumes, and this was certainly not Seward's favourite image of herself. Many of the later engravings of her are based on the Romney portrait and repeat the ornamental hairstyle. This, of course, is the image that remains.[53]

According to one observer, the splendid rooms of the Bishop's Palace were conspicuously 'ornamented with Paintings and well chosen Prints', some on loan from relatives.[54] Together with literature and music, they point out Seward's cultural preferences. Two key features of her descriptions of the portraits are their monetary worth and her own appreciation of art and of fashionable artists. Using expressive language, such as 'fine', 'beautiful', 'exquisite', 'value' and 'valuable', she names the individual artists, repeating the term 'celebrated'.[55] Her appreciation of art is also noticeable when she makes her bequests for her remaining collection of paintings. Amongst these are two paintings which were given to her as gifts by John Saville, and these were bequeathed to Thomas White. Seward names them as 'the Mezzotint print of the dying St Stephen by West' and 'the Exquisite French Engraving, Instruction Paternelle'. Saville's choice of artwork adds substance to Seward's representation of him. *The Martyrdom of St Stephen*, depicting the first Catholic martyr, is one of the less recognised works of the successful history painter Benjamin West, and its powerful spiritual imagery emphasises the dominant points of Seward's description of Saville's spiritual nature, his 'Virtue [...] liberal endowment, warm Piety, and energetic benevolence'.[56]

---

[50]   NLS, MSS, 865, fols 153–54, Henry White, 'Letter to Walter Scott' (2 July 1809).

[51]   NLS, MSS, 865, fols 153–54, Henry White, 'Letter to Walter Scott' (2 July 1809).

[52]   NLS, MSS, 9609, fol. 8, Scott, 'Letter to Charles Simpson' (27 June, 1810).

[53]   Many engravings based on the portrait were made in the following years, including *Miss Anna Seward*, by Woolnoth after George Romney [no date]. See Figure 1.

[54]   Galbraith, *The Journal of the Rev. William Bagshaw Stevens*, p. 66.

[55]   Lichfield RO, Seward Family MSS, D262/1/35, p. 2.

[56]   Lichfield RO, Seward Family MSS, D262/1/35, p. 2.

Fig. 1   *Miss Anna Seward*, by Woolnoth after George Romney [no date]

The second work, an ambiguously narrative piece, *Instruction Paternelle*, represents a shared personal expression of the emotional turmoil of their enduring relationship and the family conflict it caused. The engraving shows a group of three figures within a predominantly red background: a seated middle-aged couple and a standing young woman in a striking satin dress, seen from behind with her head averted. The older woman also looks down passively, drinking from a glass, and the man raises his hand, seemingly in admonition. Later, in 1809, the German writer Goethe, who was a favourite of both Seward and Saville, put forward an interpretation of this painting in his *Elective Affinities*, describing the well-known engraving and the attitudes of its figures:

> A noble and chivalrous-looking father, seated, one leg thrown over the other, is addressing his daughter, with what seems to be the utmost seriousness. She herself, a splendid figure in a wonderfully pleated white satin gown, is only seen from behind, but her whole being seems to indicate that she is taking his words to heart.[57]

It is easy to see why the couple identified themselves with the imagery of the painting. The restrained and dignified figure of the reproached daughter is one that corresponds to Seward's description of her conflict with her parents during the early time of her relationship with Saville. Seward also owned a series of small pictures described as 'beautiful Drawings' by William Bree, and these were left to Harry White. She uses the Bree drawings to express the association between her love of art and of literature by writing connective poems on the backs of the drawings.[58]

With the careful attention Seward paid to the disposal and after-care of her portrait and painting collections, it is extraordinary that her library of annotated and inscribed books was not similarly distributed to her friends or cousins, but was sold in the public auction. There is a record of one book with an interesting provenance surviving the sale, which was held in May 1809. Honora Sneyd's brother, Edward, attended the sale and bought Seward's heavily annotated copy of Godwin's *Caleb Williams*. In the volume, her flyleaf inscription addresses the reader directly: 'Reader, behold in three volumes three characters of the male sex, each drawn with equal force.' She continues with a plot synopsis and an analysis of the novel's 'general moral'. The annotations extend to the pages and include marginalia such as 'Awkward' and 'Strange, that expressions so vulgar should stain at intervals a style so generally eloquent', with each notation signed 'AS'.[59] The extensive note on the flyleaf reveals that she intended her literary critiques to reach a small but receptive audience in the form of her books' new owners. The critique progresses throughout the novel, and it supplements her published letters on Godwin's works.[60] With this removal from her usual literary critique in the form of epistolary exchange or journal articles, she expanded her coterie beyond the realm of correspondence and quite literally into her books.

---

[57]   Johann Wolfgang von Goethe, *Elective Affinities*, trans. by David Constantine (Oxford: Oxford University Press, 1994), p. 148. Seward, Saville and Goethe would not have known that originally the figure of the seated man held out a coin, which had been omitted in the engraving. What appeared then to be a domestic scene is now generally accepted to be either a brothel scene or a proposal. Edward Snow, *A Study of Vermeer*, 2nd edn (Berkeley: University of California Press, 1994), p. 196.

[58]   Seward, *Poetical Works*, vol. III, pp. 329–39.

[59]   William Bates, 'Godwin's Caleb Williams Annotated by Anna Seward', *Notes and Queries*, Second Series, 9 (24 March 1860), pp. 219–20.

[60]   Seward, *Letters*, vol. IV, pp. 208–14, 223–29.

Seward's choice of Scott as her editor was mostly influenced by his network of Edinburgh publishing connections. She had lost faith in her own London publisher, Joseph Johnson, when he made the unsuccessful attempt to censor her memoirs of Erasmus Darwin. There was also the eight-volume edition of Dryden that Scott was working on, which incorporated a comprehensive account of the poet's life. The literary works are combined with details of Dryden's engagement with politics, his private life, his reputation during his life and after his death, and his merit as a dramatist, poet, philosopher, translator, prose artist and critic. Seward wrongly anticipated similar rigorous treatment for her own works.

Archibald Constable's bequest was the exclusive copyright for the twelve volumes of letters. In the two years before her death, Seward had been in discussion with the Edinburgh bookseller about the publication of her works. Scott, of his own volition, assisted with negotiations for the sale of the copyrights, acting as intermediary with Constable. At this time, Constable was occupied with opening a London office, and he delayed the negotiations, quibbling over the payments. His London friend and business colleague, John Murray, had cautioned him against the heavy financial commitment necessarily involved in the purchase of Seward's copyrights, predicting that the works would not sell well. He wrote to Constable, warning him 'not to betray his usual circumspection' by advancing a large sum of money for the sake of 'the mere honour of carrying the publication of an English poetess into Scotland'.[61] Profits were clearly crucial to both sides in the negotiations, and Seward demanded one thousand pounds for the perpetual copyright of the works, which were proofed and ready for publication. She knew the market and thought this reasonable, having kept a close eye on comparable copyrights, such as William Hayley's:

> My former friendship and correspondence with Hayley instructed me as to the sums he obtained for the copy-right of his separate Works, wch were perhaps not better writing than mine. The recollection of those sums convinces me that Mr C. [Constable] in giving me a thousand pounds for the perpetual property of my whole works of prose and verse now ready for the Press wou'd have an infinitely cheaper purchase than Hayley's Bookseller ever obtained from *him*.[62]

She had never had to chase after a publisher in the past and she was not prepared to push herself forward at this stage:

> None shall have either a part, or the whole of my Collection on lower terms than I have offered them to our Friend [Constable] and if any others shou'd be the Purchaser he must seek *me*. I may stand behind a counter with my poetic wares spread upon it, but I will never be an Itinerant, and carry a pack from door to door.[63]

---

61 John Murray, 'Letter to Archibald Constable' (2 June 1807), in *Archibald Constable and his Literary Correspondents. A Memorial*, ed. by Thomas Constable, 2 vols (Edinburgh: Edmonton & Douglas, 1873), vol. I, pp. 375–76.

62 NLS, MSS, 865, fols 126–30, Seward, 'Letter to Walter Scott' (8 August 1808).

63 NLS, MSS, 865, fols 126–30, Seward, 'Letter to Walter Scott' (8 August 1808).

The negotiations wavered and waned until Seward's death. Her last letter, which was written in a delirious scrawl to Walter Scott in the week before she died, has a postscript complaining about Constable, and, most interestingly, it contains a reference to previously unknown letter books dating from 1780 and 1781:

> Mr Constable has not done right in making no reply to my proposals – If he did not chuse to accept them he should not have left me a year in uncertainty not that it signifies in my present state but Leigh and Matthews of the Strand have urged me twice to treat with them and if my health had not been so hopeless, I should [have] demanded of Mr C. final determination: and because I had [word obscured] with him than any man I had purposed to add two or three volumes of my letters written in 1780 and 1781 to increase what I must think, the cheapness of the copyright, but it is all over now! It is Thursday and each intervening day since I closed my letter has taken large death-strides upon me.[64]

Alarmed by the morbid inevitability of the letter's sentiments, Scott responded immediately with an encouraging letter begging Seward to 'take heart [...] and do not let us lose you'.[65] Scott was not used to expressing his affection for his friends, and he apologised for the awkwardness of his words, adding that Constable had promised to take up the copyright negotiations again. But by the time his letter reached Lichfield, Seward was dead. Her instructions in the will regarding her correspondence were reiterated in a posthumous letter for Constable, dated 17 July 1807, assigning him the following brief:

> I wish you to publish two volumes annually, and by no means to follow the late absurd custom of classing letters to separate correspondents, but suffer them to succeed each other in order of time, as you find them transcribed.[66]

The literary legacies were by no means uncomplicated. In the case of the letter books, Archibald Constable proved to be an unfortunate choice of editor and publisher. There is no satisfactory explanation why Seward decided to keep the unreliable bookseller as the appointed editor of her correspondence. She does state clearly in her will that she had not asked Scott to edit the letters because she believed that their different political perspectives would make it impossible for him to be objective with her work. She was not to know that most of her political debate would be excised from the letters before publication. According to Robert Southey, who took a personal interest in the publication of the correspondence, Constable's greed and personal interests transcended his professional integrity:

> By not printing the whole which she designed for publication, he has given some of her hastiest and most violent expressions, which now pass for her settled

---

[64]   NLS, MSS, 865, fols 131–32, Seward, 'Letter to Walter Scott' (13 March 1809).

[65]   NLS, MSS, 854, fols 11–11ᵛ, Scott, 'Letter to Anna Seward' (19 March 1809).

[66]   NLS, MSS, 910, fol. 73, Seward, 'Posthumous Letter to Archibald Constable' (17 July 1807).

judgement, because the letters in which they were qualified or retracted do not appear. In another point she has been ill-used. It was her design that they should be published in portions, at intervals of two years between each: the reason of this certainly was that by the time the latter portions were published, some persons there spoken of would in the natural course of years have dropped off [...] But she left the letters to a Scotch bookseller and he, as might have been foreseen, had no other thought than how to make the most immediate profit, in utter contempt of the conditions that accompanied it.[67]

Seward had arranged for her letters to be published in twelve volumes with two volumes being printed annually and not, as Southey suggests, biennially and most certainly not concurrently. Completely disregarding her instructions, Constable published the letters in six synchronous volumes in 1811, even though he knew they would not sell well in this format. Southey implies that Constable used political tactics in editing the correspondence. In his letter, he claims that the publisher was uneasy about a series of letters between Scott and Seward that contained derogatory comments about Lord Francis Jeffrey. Lord Jeffrey was the influential founding editor of the leading Whig periodical, the *Edinburgh Review*, and both Constable and Scott were wary of offending him. Scott claimed disingenuously that he and Jeffrey were good friends.[68] They had been companions at the Bar, and Jeffrey regularly accepted Scott's articles and reviews for publication. Their friendship was centred on 'mutual confidence and gratitude',[69] according to Lockhart, but Scott confided to Seward that Jeffrey's harsh reviews of his works bothered him. He was furious that Jeffrey had publicly reproved him for editing the works of Dryden rather than concentrating on his own creative writing. Scott was pragmatic and needed the money: 'I have neither the time nor inclination to be perpetually making butterflies that he may have the pleasure of pulling their legs and wings off,' he countered.[70]

Robert Southey had received hostile reviews for his own works and was well aware as a frequent reviewer himself of the liabilities of the undertaking. He explained his dislike of Jeffrey's unfair reviewing technique to his friend, Charles Danvers:

Jeffrey came back in the stage with us, to visit the Lakes, and supped here; so you see we are good friends. What I condemn in him is, a habit of speaking of books worse than he thinks of them, [...] because ill-natured things are said with better effect than good-natured ones, and liked better; and for the sake of

67 Southey, 'Letter to Walter Savage Landor' (5 June 1811), *Letters*, vol. II, p. 226.
68 NLS, MSS, 854, fol. 13, Scott, 'Letter to Anna Seward' (10 August 1806). In a letter to Seward dated 1806, Scott jokingly refers to Jeffrey as 'my little friend', continuing, 'Many good-natured Country Tories (myself for example) take great pleasure in coursing and fishing without any impeachment to their amiabilities and probably Jeffrey feels the same instinctive passion for hunting down the Bards of the day.'
69 Lockhart, *Memoirs*, vol. II, p. 27.
70 NLS, MSS, 854, fols 9–10ᵛ, Scott, 'Letter to Anna Seward' (23 March 1808).

selling his Reviews he often abuses books in print which he makes no scruple to praise in conversation. But his praise and his censure are alike haphazard and worthless.[71]

Seward had absolutely no fear of crossing swords publicly with Jeffrey, as she was not directly involved with the Edinburgh publishing houses at this time. Accusing him of ignorance and envy, she referred to him as 'Judge Jeffreys' in her letters.[72] She contested Jeffrey's negative review of Scott's *Marmion* by using her influence with the editor of the *Critical Review* to publish her own highly complimentary review. Most of the deprecating comments about Jeffrey in Seward and Scott's exchange of letters were light-hearted, but obviously Scott did not want to see them in print. He wrote, for example, that Southey had the ideal opportunity to retaliate during a Lakeland boat trip with Jeffrey, 'when it would have cost the poet nothing but a wet jacket to overset the critic and swim triumphantly to shore […] this very day the Review of *Madoc* was published.'[73]

According to Lockhart, Scott took matters into his own hands, deleting all references to Jeffrey from the correspondence:

> He requested the bookseller to allow him to look over the manuscripts and draw his pen through passages in which her allusions to letters of his own might compromise him as a critic on his poetic contemporaries. To this request Constable handsomely acceded, although it was evident that he thus deprived the collection of its best chance of popularity.[74]

Constable and Scott scoured through the letters books, removing anything that made them feel uneasy. The executors, too, took the opportunity to remove political comments and local anecdotes. 'At most only one half shall be published', declared Charles Simpson.[75] To add to Southey's indignation, Constable then passed the remaining correspondence to Jeffrey's brother-in-law, Morehead, 'that the selection might be made as agreeable to Gog [Southey's nickname for Jeffrey] as possible'. Southey also claimed resentfully that Morehead purged 'her best letters to me' and, indeed, only two of Seward's letters to him are printed. Southey's ego was fragile, and he thought his literary reputation might have been harmed. 'Special care has been taken to keep in all that could injure me', he complained, 'and omit as much as might serve me', even though most of Seward's comments

---

[71]   Southey, 'Letter to Charles Danvers' (7 November 1805), *Letters*, vol. II, p. 346.

[72]   Seward was referring to the notorious chief justice of the seventeenth century who was responsible for the 'Bloody Assize', which resulted in the transportation and hanging of hundreds of followers of the Duke of Monmouth.

[73]   NLS, MSS, 854, fol. 13, Scott, 'Letter to Anna Seward' (10 August 1806).

[74]   Lockhart, *Memoirs*, vol. II, pp. 328–29.

[75]   NLS, MSS, 865, fols 140–41, Charles Simpson, 'Letter to Walter Scott' (16 April 1809).

on his work were in praise.[76] Approximately half the original collection of letters that Seward wanted Constable to publish was removed, and, consequently, her plans for a self-constructed literary image were seriously impaired.

It was not just the literary dealings that failed to comply with Seward's complex instructions. As the will takes on its statutory aspect, the language shifts in tone from literary to legal, and the properties, shares, bonds, annuities and monies are either distributed or placed in trust funds. Seward took her financial commitments seriously enough to administer her father's estate diligently, and she left a considerable fortune of her own. Together with many of her contemporaries, she was outraged by the initiation of income tax in 1798–9. To help finance the war, William Pitt levied a personal income tax at two shillings in the pound (i.e., 10%) on incomes of above £200 a year, and there was a graduating scale for the lower incomes of £60 to £200 a year. Her assessment of £90 in 1799 prompted her to write in dismay to her aunt, Jane Martin:

> Appealing upon my income last year from my assessed taxes, which were charged to me at ninety pounds per annum; the present tax is the same thing [...] it is a heavy affair and will induce all prudent people, who spent their income before this requisition was made, to abridge their expenses; to refrain from soliciting an influx of company; and to content themselves at home except where health requires the assistance of medical waters. May we rest assured from the belligerent spirit which prevails in the cabinet, and indeed pervades the hearts of a large majority of the nation, that our burdens will dreadfully increase.[77]

Her annual income was assessed at £900, and added to this was the revenue that did not attract tax: her shares, rents, trusts and navy bonds, which together yielded high returns, although it is not clear whether she chose to spend these or to re-invest them. As the Bishop's Palace was a tenancy, this reverted to the cathedral authorities after her death. There were, however, two other properties in her ownership. In 1801, she had bought a house on the Cathedral Close specifically for John Saville to live in, and she retained the freehold in her own name. For several years before his death, Saville had been too ill to travel to his performance venues. It was 'never in his power to save money', and Seward thought that his small, damp house was not good enough for him, so she bought him a new home, a 'pleasant mansion'.[78]

---

[76] Southey, 'Letter to Miss Barker' (4 November 1812), *Letters*, vol. II, p. 297. Seward's letter to Scott dated 26 March, 1806, contains her favourable review of *Madoc*. Scott did not publish this letter. NLS, MSS, 3875, fols 157–8, Seward, 'Letter to Walter Scott' (26 March 1806).

[77] NLS, MS 585, Seward, 'Letter to Jane Martin' (20 July 1799).

[78] Seward, 'Letter to T. S. Whalley' (16 August 1803), in Thomas Sedgewick Whalley, *Journals and Correspondence of Thomas Sedgewick Whalley, DD., of Mendip Lodge, Somerset*, ed. by Hill Wickham, 2 vols (London: Richard Bentley, 1863), vol. II, p. 234.

After Saville's death in 1803, she invited his estranged wife Mary to live there with her daughter, Eliza Smith. Saville had run up hefty debts amounting to £400 through spending most of his money on charity, on maintenance payments to Mary and Eliza and on his grandchildren, Honora and Saville Smith. In order to save him from being forced to sell his treasured collection of music and books, Seward paid off his debts, grateful that she was in a position to provide for him. On his death, she paid his funeral expenses and for the mourning, as well as buying the vault and commissioning a monument inscribed with her epitaph for him. At the same time, she gave Mary Saville and her family an annuity of £100 with the free tenancy of the house, which was later underwritten in her will. If this was a gesture driven by guilt, as much as a benevolent desire to insulate Saville's family from poverty, Seward's power to choose where to spend her money was gratifying. Her financial independence allowed her to provide for Saville during his life and for his family after his death, and it was a great disappointment to her that Mary and Eliza were never properly grateful.

So, in her will, Seward left the fine house together with its appurtenances to her executors to hold in trust for Mary, Eliza, Saville Smith and his descendants, for their own occupation or to rent out if they wanted. Her other property, a house in West Gate, was occupied by Eliza's daughter Honora, who was by then married to Robert Jager, with the tenancy agreement in his name. This house is also left to the executors to hold in trust for Honora Jager. In a later codicil, Seward changes her mind and asks that the house be sold to buy bonds, which would yield a higher return for Honora. Her bequests to Honora include a share in the Trent to Mersey Navigation Canal, and this is where Seward exercises her legal rights to provide for Saville's granddaughter. She makes it clear that she wants *couverture* overturned to provide all revenues for Honora's 'sole and separate use and with which or any part thereof her said husband shall not intermeddle notwithstanding coverture, nor shall the same be liable to his debts and engagements, but her receipt alone shall be good and sufficient discharge to any said executor and trustee.' The legal rescindment of the common law of *couverture* gave Honora a certain level of control of her own finances. Yet, as with the rule of entail, the properties and most of the shares remained part of the Seward estate in perpetuity. Honora may have received her dividends and with them a measure of independence, but she had no actual control of the capital.

Seward's frugality belied her vast fortune. A substantial portfolio of canal and turnpike shares is bequeathed to the executors, to be held in trust for two years in order to accrue enough interest to fund the beneficiaries' legacies and annuities, before they reaped the revenues. In the mid-1760s Erasmus Darwin, with his fellow Lunar Society members Josiah Wedgwood and Thomas Bentley, were among the entrepreneurs who began planning the construction of turnpike roads, inland navigation systems and waterways across the Midlands countryside. As these were private enterprises, investment was necessary to get the schemes under way. The widening consumer market and increasing pressure of traffic required improved communications. Roads became rutted from the traffic of heavy industry, and they were often reduced to little more than filthy tracks in between fields from the livestock droves that crossed them daily.[79] Erasmus Darwin dealt cleverly with this problem by training his horse, Doctor, to trot alongside his carriage. If the carriage became trapped in the mud, he continued his journey on horseback.[80] Early industrialisation needed a little more than a spare horse, however, and Turnpike Trusts were set up by local initiatives to take over the parishes' responsibility for road maintenance. Users were charged a toll which financed the maintenance of the turnpikes.

Waterways were a cheaper option for haulage, and canals, again mostly privately funded, were the natural extension to link rivers with national and regional networks. The consequence of such improved communications for Lichfield was that it became a major staging-post standing at the cross of the London to Chester road and the Bristol to Derby road.[81] Having no major water resource of its own, it was an area untouched by the Industrial Revolution, and so it retained its traditional architectural charm and ambience. Thomas Seward had invested wisely in the canals and Turnpike Trusts, and these proved exceptionally profitable, increasing in value almost immediately on issue and paying out regular large dividends. Money was raised in shares of £200, and investors were restricted to owning twenty shares. Seward's portfolio included a hefty ten shares in the Trent to Mersey Navigation scheme, six shares in the Staffordshire and Worcestershire Canal, several in the Birmingham and Fazely and the Chesterfield Canals, together with securities in the Lichfield, Chesterfield and Sheffield Turnpikes, which were bonded at a total of over £3,000 and, finally, navy and private annuities valued at £2,400.

Seward looked to the financial independence of her friend, Mary White, who was left the proceeds of a Navigation share. Again, she overturns *couverture*, insisting that this is for Mary's sole and separate use, 'free from the control of her husband for and during the term of her natural life and her receipt alone shall be sufficient discharge for the same'. But regardless of all her strategies and provisions, the will failed to achieve Seward's objectives on several counts. There is no way of knowing whether all of her financial requirements were put into action, or if the husbands did actually 'intermeddle' with their wives' inheritances, as there was no formal procedure for monitoring requests like these. A letter from Charles Simpson to William Seward Hall dated June 1809 reveals that some of the shares were disposed of before their designated date, breaking the original terms stipulated in the will. 'All parties are agreeable to sell', writes Hall, and although the terms of the will demanded that all shares and properties be held in

---

[79]   Roy Porter, *English Society in the Eighteenth Century*, 2nd edn, rev. edn (London: Penguin Books, 1991), p. 191.

[80]   Nicholas Redman, *The Whitbread Archive: Dr Erasmus Darwin and Breadsall Priory, Derbyshire* (London: for Whitbread PLC [n.d.]).

[81]   King-Hele, Desmond. *Erasmus Darwin: A Life of Unequalled Achievement* (London: Giles de la Mare, 1999), p. 25.

trust for two full years, Simpson was well within his legal rights to begin selling off the shares at his own discretion. [82] Saville Smith sold off his shares within three months of Seward's death.

Where this unique, complex last will and testament fails to provide the dynamic and forceful outcome that Seward intended, it does offer a self-defining narrative that reveals its author's relationships with her writing, her friends and family, her fortune and her literary peers. If her instructions had been followed as she wanted, her control over her literary reputation would have had a greater chance of success. It fell to her executors and literary legatees to interpret the contents and to protect the legacy on their own terms, no matter what the consequences to Seward's carefully organised design. Her literary reputation which she constructed over the period of her writing career, from her early juvenile letters to the correspondence addressed to her illustrious friends and colleagues, did not survive unscathed. When her volumes of letters were published together, two years after her death, the general reaction from the literary world was one of incredulity at her apparent egotism. However, Seward's favourite literary journal, the *Gentleman's Magazine*, led a small series of tributes, and although her work appeared sporadically in anthologies throughout the first half of the nineteenth century, it was usually described with increasingly pejorative terms. There was little critical analysis of Seward's letters at the time they were published or in the years afterwards, with just a few references to them.

Letters were losing their literary dominance, and women's correspondence in particular was no longer the ideal vehicle for self-expression. Seward imagined her correspondence as a unified text in which her life and her interaction with the fascinating and the learned would unfold over the course of almost thirty years of letters. Perhaps she hoped, as Rousseau had, that posterity would love her, if not for her poetry, then for her correspondence. The letters are always personal, despite their formality, always written from outside a feminine awareness, always expressed with confidence and authority. There is no capitulation to the limitations imposed on female authorship. The distinctive voice speaking in its poetic tone should stand as a complete testament to her achievements. Had the letters been published over the course of several years as she requested and had they been left uncensored, they would have opened up a new conception of Anna Seward.

Her last will and testament, the juvenile letters, the unpublished manuscripts and fragments, together add brilliant new facets to the received view of her life. Her will shows her resolve to control her reputation and financial assets into posterity, as well as leaving a lasting memorial in the form of literary and artistic works. She reveals that the independence she fought for and won in her youth was financed into maturity by the portfolio of shares, properties and monies. The contents of the letters to Emma, although veiled by several layers of editing, rewriting and censorship, still speak loudly of the bitter struggle to find a balance

[82]   Lichfield RO, Correspondence mainly of Charles Simpson and Thomas White, D262/2/5, William Seward, 'Letter to Charles Simpson' (14 June 1809).

between intellect and domesticity. The Powys and Sykes letters disclose Seward's strength of character as she withstood the hostility and cruel pressures exerted particularly by her parents but also by her Lichfield friends and neighbours, who turned against her because she refused to end her enduring relationship with John Saville. The 'Cat Letters' and Boswell's love letters indicate the turning point in Seward's life, when she realised her ambition to become more than a 'poetess', but an author who could stand equal with her male contemporaries. The unpublished letters to Walter Scott give an insight into her determination to achieve literary immortality.

In time, Anna Seward's literary voice may well appropriate a greater public esteem. Her poems may eventually reach a secure place in the literary canon. Yet, can they be read without a full understanding of the poet who wrote them? These manuscripts and fragments, forgotten and lying unread, give us a fresh insight into the vibrant life of the poet and ensure that her words are 'not inevitably perishable'.

Appendix 1

'Epitaph for John Saville', Anna Seward, 'Letter to Mrs Childers, Sen.' (23 September 1803), *Letters of Anna Seward: Written Between the Years 1784 and 1807*, vol. VI, p. 113. The epitaph is inscribed on a marble tablet in Lichfield Cathedral.

Sacred to the memory of John Saville
Forty-eight years Vicar-Choral of this Church,
Died August 2, 1803, aged sixty-seven.

Once in the heart, cold in yon narrow cell,
Did each mild grace, each ardent virtue dwell;
Kind aid, kind tears, for others' want and woe,
For others' joy, the gratulating glow;
And skill to mark, and eloquence to claim
For genius in each art, the palm of fame.
Ye choral walls, ye lost the matchless song
When the last silence stiffn'd on that tongue.
Ah! who may now your pealing anthems raise
In soul-pour'd tones of fervent pray'r and praise?
Saville, thy lips, twice on thy final day,
Here breath'd in health and hope, the sacred lay.
Short pangs, ere night, their fatal signal gave,
Quench'd the bright sun for thee – and op'd the grave!
Now, from that once fair form and beaming face,
Insatiate worms the lingering likeness chase;
But thy pure spirit fled, from pains and fears,
To sinless, – changeless, – everlasting spheres.
Sleep then, pale, mortal frame, in yon low shrine,
"Till angels wake thee with a note like thine!"

Appendix 2

Miss Seward's Enigma, 1855 (Lichfield Record Office, Seward Family MSS, D262/2/11)

1   The noblest object in the works of art;
2   The brightest gem which nature can impart;
3   The point essential in a Lawyer's lease;
4   The well known signal in a time of peace;
5   The Ploughman when he drives his plough;
6   The Soldier's duty, and
7   The Lover's vow;
8   The Planet seen between the earth and sun;
9   The Prize which merit never yet has won;
10   The Miser's treasure, and
11   The badge of Jews;
12   The Wife's ambition, and
13   The Parson's dues.

Appendix 3

A summary of the main provisions of Anna Seward's last will and testament, dated 1808–1809 and taken from a photocopy of the probate copy of the will (Lichfield Record Office, Seward Family MSS, D262/1/35, Anna Seward, 'Will and Codicils').

Executors: Charles Simpson and Thomas White

Miscellaneous Bequests

All clothes	Maid servant employed at the time of Seward's death
Laces and contents of bureau	Elizabeth Smith (John Saville's daughter)
Fan and best diamond ring	Mary White (wife of cousin Thomas White)
Mourning and £10	All servants employed at the time of death

£500 for a monument
Furniture, plate, books, pictures and drawings, household effects to public auction to discharge any small remaining debts and for funeral expenses.

Literary Works

Sole copyright for poetry and prose works	Walter Scott
Sole copyright for letter books 1784–1807	Archibald Constable
All remaining letters and papers	Executors and Trustees

Paintings and Portraits

Miers portrait of Anna Seward	Mary White
Richmond miniature of Thomas Seward	Susannah Seward Burrows (cousin, daughter of father's nephew)
Wright portrait of Thomas Seward	Henry White (cousin)
Collection of Bree drawings	Henry White
Romney portrait of Anna Seward	Charles Simpson (lawyer and executor)
West print and French engraving	Thomas White (cousin, also executor)
Romney engraving of Honora Sneyd	Edward Sneyd (Honora Sneyd's brother)

| André miniature of Honora Sneyd | Mary Powys (friend) |
| Smart portrait of John Saville | Elizabeth Smith |

Property (held in trust)

| House, inc. contents, on Cathedral Close | Mary Saville (John Saville's wife) |
| House, inc. contents, on West Gate | Honora Jager (John Saville's granddaughter) |

Mourning Rings (money for)

5 guineas	Lady Eleanor Butler (friend)
5 guineas	Sarah Ponsonby (friend)
5 guineas	Elizabeth Cornwallis (friend, Bishop's daughter)
5 guineas	Mary Powys (friend)
5 guineas	William Feary (friend,)
5 guineas	Thomas Lister (friend)
5 guineas	Dr William Hussey (friend)
4 guineas	Mr and Mrs Hussey (friends)
2 guineas	Mary White (wife of Thomas White)
2 guineas	Susanna Seward Burrows (cousin)
2 guineas	Mrs Hinckley (wife of cousin Thomas Hinckley)
2 guineas	Jane Martin (wife of cousin Thomas Martin)
2 guineas	Mrs Simpson (wife of Charles Simpson)
2 guineas	Mrs Ironmonger (friend)

Annuities

£50	Mary Saville
£50	Elizabeth Smith
£50	Elizabeth Fern (friend and paid companion)
£35	Robert Seward (cousin)
£30	Mary Atkins (housekeeper)
£20	Mary Wright (servant)
£20	Thomas White (cousin)
£20	William Roberts (cousin)

Legacies

| £260 | Charles Simpson |
| £150 | John Fish (servant) |

£100	Anna Seward (daughter of Lt. Col. Seward)
£100	Anna Rogers Stokes (friend, wife of botanist Jonathan Stokes)
£100	Anna Seward Stokes (goddaughter, daughter of Anna Rogers Stokes)
£100	Stephen Simpson (?son of Charles Simpson)
£100	Robert Seward (cousin)
£100	Henry Cary (friend, poet)
£50	James Cary (godson, son of Henry Cary)
£50	Edward Simpson (brother of Charles)
£50 each	3 Miss Ashwell sisters (friends)
£50	Mrs Short (friend)
£50	Robert Fellowes (friend, poet)
£50	Richard Hinckley (godson, son of Thomas Hinckley)
£50	William Mott (friend)
£30	Mary Fleming (friend)
£10	Mrs Oakley (friend)
£10	Ann Hickman (former servant)

Trent to Mersey Navigation (10 shares held in trust)

2 shares	Susanna Seward Burrows (cousin)
2 shares	Jane Martin (cousin)
1 share	Honora Jager (Elizabeth Smith's daughter)
1 share	Mary White (Thomas White's wife)
1 share	Saville Smith (Elizabeth Smith's son)
1 share	Children of the late Grace Roberts (who was Thomas Seward's niece)
1 share	Children of the late Mrs Hall (who was Thomas Seward's niece)
£500 bond	Thomas Burrows (husband of cousin Susanna Seward Burrows)
£150 bond	William Roberts (cousin)
£150 bond	Miss Roberts (daughter of Grace Roberts)

Staffordshire and Worcestershire Canal (6 shares held in trust)

1 share	Susanna Seward Burrows
1 share	Elizabeth Smith
1 share	Mary Saville
1 share	Saville Smith (Elizabeth Smith's son)
1 share	Honora Jager (Elizabeth Smith's daughter)
1 share	Henry White

Chesterfield Canal

£110 bond   Charles Holland Hastings (friend)

Birmingham and Fazeley Canal

1 share   Charles Simpson
Remainder   Executors

Lichfield Turnpikes Trust (£2,390 bond)

£500   Thomas Hinckley (cousin)
£200   Mrs Simmons (sister of Thomas Hinckley)
£200   Mrs Harper (wife of Robert Harper)
£50   Thomas White jnr. (godson, son of Thomas White)
£145   Thomas White
£100   Miss Roberts (daughter of Grace Roberts)
£597.10s   Children of Grace Roberts dec'd
£597.10s   Children of Mrs Hall dec'd

Sheffield and Sparrowpit Turnpike Trust (£340)

Thomas White (cousin)

Chesterfield Turnpike Trust (£320)

Thomas White (cousin)

Navy Annuities (£1,000)

£500   Payment for monument
£200   Charles Simpson
£200   Thomas White
£100   Walter Scott

Four percent Annuities (£1,400)

£500   Edward Sneyd (dividends to go to Lovell Edgeworth, Honora
                   Sneyd's son)
£900   Charles Hastings (friend)

Long Annuities

£20	Thomas White
£15	William Roberts

Residue

Taxes etc.   £200

Codicil 1 (8 March 1809)

Sale of house on West Gate to buy government or security bonds. Proceeds as before.

Mary Wright	extra £2 annuity
Mary Atkins	extra £3 annuity
Elizabeth Fern	extra £10 annuity
John Fish	legacy revoked, £20 annuity
Honora Burrows	£100 (goddaughter, Susanna Burrows' daughter)
Mary Powys	£100 (friend)

Codicil 2 (8 March 1809)

Children of Grace Roberts	legacy revoked, to receive half of the Hall legacy:
Children of Mrs Hall	half of legacy revoked
Elizabeth Smith	Annuity reduced by £50 (extra profits from canal to make up the deficit)

Bibliography

Archives

Cambridge University Library, Cambridge, Cambridgeshire Cambridge UL, DAR 227. 3: 24, The Darwin Family Letters

Derbyshire Record Office, Matlock, Derbyshire MS 381, vol. 2, Baptism Records, Eyam, 1742–1746

Huntington Library, San Marino, California, USA, HL, MSS JE754–780, Papers of Edward Jerningham, 1760–1812

Lichfield Record Office, Lichfield, Staffordshire Lichfield RO, Seward Family MSS, D262/1/1–34, Correspondence and other papers of the Seward Family, including the poetess Anna Seward, 1756–1809

Lichfield RO, D262/1/35, Copies of the will and codicils of Anna Seward, with extract of bequests, 1808–1809

Lichfield RO, D262/2/1–12, Correspondence mainly of Charles Simpson and Thomas White, 1767–1851

Lichfield RO, AS17, Letter of Elizabeth Seward to Anna Seward

National Library of Scotland, Edinburgh, Scotland

    NLS, MSS 854, 865, 870, 910, 1750, 1753, 2223, 2521, 3653, 3874–75, 3877, 9609, Catalogue of Walter Scott Correspondence

    NLS, Sir Walter Scott MSS, 879–80, The Sir Walter Scott Manuscripts; Parts Two and Three: The Scott Correspondence

    NLS, MS 585, Letter of Anna Seward to Jane Martin

    NLS, MS 2255, Letter of Anna Seward to F.N.C. Mundy

The Prerogative Court of Canterbury

    Bishop Quire Numbers 192–238, PROB 11/1191, copy of Thomas Seward's will

The Samuel Johnson Birthplace Museum, Lichfield, Staffordshire

    JBM, MS 35/1–20, Collection of autograph letters of Anna Seward to Joseph Sykes and his wife Dorothy

    JBM, MS 38/1–28, Letters of Anna Seward to Mary Powys

University College, London, Library

    The Pearson Papers, MS 577

Yale University, Beinecke Rare Book and Manuscript Library, New Haven, Connecticut, USA

    YUB, C 2467–75, Letters of Anna Seward

    YUB, L 1142–53, Letters of James Boswell

The Works of Anna Seward

'Elegy on Captain Cook' (London: J. Dodsley, 1780)

'Monody on Major André, by Miss Seward, to which are added letters addressed to her by Major André in the year 1769' (Lichfield: J. Jackson, 1781)

Poems, by Miss Seward, to which are added, letters addressed to her by Major André, in the year 1769 (Dublin: P. Byrne and C. Jackson, 1781)

'Poem to the memory of Lady Miller' (London: G. Robinson, 1782)

Louisa: A Poetical Novel, in Four Epistles (London: J. Jackson and G. Robinson, 1784)

'Ode on General Elliott's return from Gibraltar' (London: T. Cadell, 1787)

'An Adieu to the rocks of Lannow', written by Miss Seward and set to music by Dr Hayes (London: Thompson, 1789)

'Stormy Lannow', the words by Miss Seward in imitation of 'Seaton Cliffs', set to music by J. W. Callcott (London: T. Skillern, c. 1795)

Llangollen vale, with Other poems, ed. by Jonathan Wordsworth (London: G. Sael, 1796, repr. 1994)

Original Sonnets on Various Subjects: And Odes Paraphrased from Horace (London: G. Sael, 1799)

Memoirs of the Life of Dr Darwin; Chiefly During his Residence in Lichfield, with Anecdotes of his Friends, and Criticisms on his Writings (London: J. Johnson, 1804)

'O why my locks so yellow', a favorite recitative & air, the words by Miss Seward, composed by Mr Rauzzini (London: Goulding, Phipps & D'Almaine; Dublin: Goulding, Knevette & Co; Glasgow: James Stevens, c. 1805)

'Blindness, a poem, by Anna Seward, written at the request of an artist, who lost his sight by the gutta serena, in his twenty eighth year, and who was therefore obliged to change his profession for that of music patronised by the Duchess of Leeds, to whom this poem is, by permission, dedicated' (Sheffield: William Platt, 1806)

Poetical Works of Anna Seward, With Extracts from Her Literary Correspondence, ed. by Walter Scott, 3 vols (Edinburgh: John Ballantyne; London: Longman, Hurst, Rees and Orme, 1810)

Letters of Anna Seward: Written Between the Years 1784 and 1807, ed. by Archibald Constable (Edinburgh: Archibald Constable; London: Longman, Hurst, Rees, Orme, Brown, Miller and Murray, 1811)

Primary Sources

Addison, Joseph, *A Letter from Italy To the Right Honourable Charles Lord Halifax In the Year MDCCI* (London: H. Hills, 1709)

Allardyce, Alexander, ed., *Letters from and to Charles Kirkpatrick Sharpe, Esq.*, 2 vols (Edinburgh: William Blackwood, 1888)

Astell, Mary, *Some Reflections on Marriage Occasioned by the Duke and Duchess of Mazarine's Case; Which is Also Considered* (London: John Nutt, 1700)

Austen, Jane: see Kinsley

Bagshaw Stevens, William: see Galbraith

Bailey, Margery, ed., *Boswell's Column. Being his Seventy Contributions to the London Magazine under the pseudonym The Hypochondriack* (London: W. Kimber, 1951)

Balderston, Katherine Canby, ed., *Thraliana: The Diary of Mrs Hester Lynch Thrale (Later Mrs Piozzi), 1741–1821*, 2 vols, 2nd edn (Oxford: Clarendon Press, 1951)

Beaumont and Fletcher: see Thomas Seward

Blackstone, William, *Commentaries on the Laws of England* (Oxford: Clarendon Press, 1765–69)

—— *The Laws respecting Women, as they regard their natural rights, or their connections and conduct; also, the obligations of parent and child, and the condition of minors, &c.* (London: J. Johnson, 1777)

Bloom, Edward A. and Bloom Lillian D., eds, *Addison and Steele: The Critical Heritage* (London and Boston, Mass.: Routledge & Kegan Paul, 1980)

—— eds, *The Piozzi Letters: Correspondence of Hester Thrale Piozzi (Formerly Mrs Thrale), 1784–1821* (Newark, Del.: University of Delaware Press; London: Associated University Presses, 1991)

Birkbeck Hill, George, ed., *Life of Johnson, Together with Boswell's Journal of a Tour to the Hebrides and Johnson's Diary of a Journey into North Wales*, rev. by L. F. Powell, 6 vols (London: Oxford University Press, 1791; repr. 1934)

Blackwood's Edinburgh Magazine (1823; 1824)

Boswell, James, *The Journal of a Tour to the Hebrides with Samuel Johnson, LL.D* (London: Charles Dilly, 1785)

Boswell, James: see Bailey; Lustig; Reed

Brooke, Frances, *The History of Lady Julia Mandeville* (London: Dodsley, 1763)

Burdett, Richard: see Harley

Burney, Frances, *Memoirs of Dr Burney, arranged from his own manuscripts, from family papers, and from personal recollections*, 3 vols (London: Edward Moxon, 1832)

—— *Evelina*: see Cooke

—— *The Wanderer*: see Doody

—— *Journals*: see Hemlow

Butt, John, ed., *The Twickenham Edition of the Poems of Alexander Pope*, 3rd edn, 6 vols (London: Methuen and Co; New Haven: Yale University Press, 1962, repr. 1972)

Cardiff Corvey Articles, VI

Carroll, John, ed., *Selected Letters of Samuel Richardson* (Oxford: Oxford University Press, 1986)

Cavendish, Margaret, Duchess of Newcastle, *Natures pictures drawn by fancies pencil to the life. Written by the thrice noble, illustrious and excellent princess the lady Marchioness of Newcastle* (London: J. Martin, and J. Allestrye, 1656)

—— *Sociable Letters* (London: William Wilson, 1664)

Chapone, Hester Mulso, *The Works of Mrs Chapone*, 4 vols (London: John Murray, 1807)

Cibber, Colley, *An apology for the life of Mr Colley Cibber, comedian, and late patentee of the Theatre-Royal: With an historical view of the stage during his own time. Written by himself* (London: J. Watts, 1740)

Coleridge, S. T.: see Wordsworth; Zall

Constable, Thomas, *Archibald Constable and his Literary Correspondents*, 3 vols (Edinburgh: Edmonton & Douglas, 1873)

Cooke, Stewart, J., ed., Frances Burney, *Evelina or, The History of a Young Lady's Entrance into the World* (New York: Norton, 1998)

Cumberland, Richard, *The Observer: Being a Collection of Moral, Literary and Familiar Essays* (London: C. Dilly, 1785)

Curran, Stuart, ed., *The Poems of Charlotte Smith* (Oxford: Oxford University Press, 1993)

Darwin, Erasmus, *The Botanic Garden: A Poem in Two Parts*, pt. 1, 'The Economy of Vegetation' (1791); pt 2, 'The Loves of the Plants' (1789), 2 vols (London: J. Johnson 1789–92)

—— *The Conduct of Female Education in Boarding Schools* (Derby: J. Johnson, 1797; repr. London: Routledge/Thoemmes, 1996)

—— *Commonplace Book. The Diary of Erasmus Darwin with his Scientific Notes* (East Ardley: Micro Methods, c. 1970)

—— *Letters*: see King-Hele

Davie, John: see Kinsley

Defoe, Daniel: see Landa

Doody, Margaret Anne, Robert L. Mack and Peter Sabor, eds., Frances Burney, *The Wanderer; or, Female Difficulties* (1814; Oxford: Oxford University Press, 1991)

Dryden, John: see Scott

Duff, William, *An Essay on Original Genius; and its Various Modes of Exertion in Philosophy and the Fine Arts, Particularly in Poetry* (London: Dilly, 1767)

Dyce, Alexander, *Specimens of British Poetesses, selected and chronologically arranged by Alexander Dyce* (London, T. Rodd, 1827)

Edgeworth, Richard Lovell and Maria Edgeworth, *Memoirs of Richard Lovell Edgeworth, Esq., Begun by Himself and Concluded by his Daughter, Maria Edgeworth*, 2 vols (London: Hunter, 1820)

The Edinburgh Review (1804)

The Female Spectator (1744-46)

Fénelon, François de Salignac de La Mothe, *The Adventures of Telemachus, the son of Ulysses*, translation of *Les Avantures de Télémaque*, pt. 1 trans. by Isaac Littlebury; pts 2–3 trans. by Abel Boyer; pts 4–5 trans. by Alexander Olde, 2 vols (London: A. & J. Churchill, 1699–1700)

Fowkes, D. V.: see Harley

Fraistat, Neil and Susan S. Lanser eds., Helen Maria Williams, *Letters Written in France in the Summer of 1790 to a Friend in England; containing various anecdotes relative to the French Revolution* (Ontario: Broadview, 2002)

Galbraith, Georgina, ed., *The Journal of the Rev. William Bagshaw Stevens* (Oxford: Clarendon Press, 1965)

Genlis, Stéphanie Felicité Ducrest de St Aubin, Comtesse de, *Memoirs of the Countess de Genlis: Illustrative of the History of the Eighteenth and Nineteenth Centuries, written by Herself*, 8 vols (London: Henry Colburn, 1825)

The Gentleman's Magazine (1809)

Goethe, Johann Wolfgang von, *The Sorrows of Young Werther*, trans. by Michael Hulse (London: Penguin Books, 1989)

—— *Elective Affinities*, trans. by R. J. Hollingdale (London: Penguin, 1971)

Graham, Elspeth, ed., in *Her Own Life: Autobiographical Writings by Seventeenth-Century Englishwomen*, 2nd edn (London: Routledge, 1992)

Gray, Thomas: see Lonsdale

Greene, Donald, ed. *Samuel Johnson: The Major Works*, 2nd edn (Oxford: Oxford University Press, 1984)

Harley, J. B., Fowkes, D. V. and Harvey, J. C., eds, *Richard Burdett's Map of Derbyshire* (Derbyshire: Derbyshire Archaeological Society, 1975)

Hawkins, Sir John, *The Works of Samuel Johnson, LL.D: Together with His Life, and Notes on His Lives of the Poets*, 11 vols (London: J. Buckland et al, 1787)

Hayley, William, *The Triumphs of Temper: a poem. In six cantos* (London: J. Dodsley, 1781)

—— *Poems on Serious and Sacred Subjects* (Chichester: W. Mason, 1818, repr. London: Kessinger Publishing, [n. date])

—— The *life, and posthumous writings, of William Cowper, Esqr.*, 4 vols (Chichester: printed for J. Johnson, London, 1803)

Hays, Mary, *Female Biographies, or Memoirs of illustrious and celebrated women of all ages and countries*, 6 vols (London: R. Phillips, 1803)

—— see Ty

Hayward, Abraham, ed., *Autobiography, Letters and Literary Remains of Mrs Piozzi (Thrale)* (London: Longman, 1861)

Haywood, Eliza: see Spacks

Hemlow, Joyce et al., *The Journals and Letters of Fanny Burney (Madam D'Arblay)*, 12 vols (Oxford: Oxford University Press, 1972-84)

Holcroft, Thomas, *Caroline of Lichfield: A Novel*, translated from the French [of Madam de Montolieu], 3 vols (London: G. G. J. and J. Robinson, 1786)

The Hypochondriack (March 1783)

Johnson, Samuel, *A Journey of a Tour to the Western Isles of Scotland in 1773* (London: Hamilton, Adams & Co, 1786)

—— *Diary*: see Birkbeck Hill

—— *Letters*: see Redford

—— *Major Works*: see Greene

Kames, Lord Henry Home, *Six Sketches on the History of Man, containing, the progress of men as individuals and with an appendix, concerning the propagation of animals and their offspring.* 2 vols (Philadelphia: R. Bell and R. Aitken, 1776)

Kelly, Christopher: see Masters

Keymer, Thomas and Alice Wakely, eds., Samuel Richardson, *Pamela; or, Virtue Rewarded* (1740; repr. Oxford: Oxford University Press, 2001)

King-Hele, Desmond, ed., *The Letters of Erasmus Darwin* (Cambridge: Cambridge University Press, 1981)

Kinsley, James and John Davie, eds, Jane Austen, *Northanger Abbey; Lady Susan; The Watsons; Sanditon* (Oxford: Oxford University Press, 2003)

Kinsley, James, Jane Austen, *Mansfield Park*, 2nd edn (Oxford: Oxford University Press, 2003)

Kirkpatrick Sharpe, Patrick: see Allardyce

The Lady's Magazine (August 1770)

Landa, Louis, ed., Daniel Defoe, *A Journal of the Plague Year, being Observations or Memorials of the Most Remarkable Occurrences, as well Publick as Private, which happened in London during the last Great Visitation in 1665. Written by a Citizen who continued all the while in London* (Oxford: Oxford University Press, 1722; repr. 1991)

Lanser, Susan S.: see Fraistat

Lewis, Theobald: see Thomas Seward

Lincolnshire History and Archaeology (1997)

Lockhart, J. G., ed., *Memoirs of the Life of Walter Scott, Bart.*, 7 vols (Edinburgh: Robert Cadell; London: John Murray and Whittaker, 1837)

Lonsdale, Roger, ed., Thomas Gray, 'Elegy Written in a Country Churchyard', in *The Poems of Thomas Gray, William Collins, Oliver Goldsmith* (London: Longmans, 1969)

Lustig, Irma S. and Frederick Pottle, eds, *Boswell: The Applause of the Jury, 1782–1785* (New York: McGraw-Hill; London: Heinemann, 1981)

—— *Boswell: The English Experiment, 1785–1789* (New York: McGraw Hill; London: Heinneman; 1986)

Mack, Robert L.: see Doody

Masters, Roger D. and Christopher Kelly, eds, Jean-Jacques Rousseau, *Julie, or the New Héloïse: Letters of Two Lovers who live in a Small Town at the Foot of the Alps*, trans by Philip Stewart and Jean Vaché (1761; repr. Hanover and London: University Press of New England, 1997)

Miller, Lady Anne, *Poetical Amusements at a Villa Near Bath*, 2nd edn, 4 vols (London: Edward and Charles Dilly, 1776)

Modern Philology (1993)

Molière, Jean Baptiste Poquelin, *Les Femmes Savantes* [The Learned Women] (1672; Boston; D. C. Heath, 1896)

Montagu, Elizabeth Robinson, *An essay on the writings and genius of Shakespear, compared with the Greek and French dramatic poets, with some remarks upon the misrepresentations of Mons. de Voltaire* (London: J. Dodsley; Baker and Leigh; J. Walter; T. Cadell; J. Wilkie, 1769)

Monthly Mirror (1796)

Monthly Review (1786)

More, Hannah, *Essays on various subjects, principally designed for young ladies* (London: J. Wilkie & T. Cadell, 1777)

Mundy, Francis Nöel Clarke, *Needwood Forest and The Fall of Needwood. With Other Poems* (Derby: Thomas Richardson, 1830)

—— *The Fall of Needwood* (Derby: J. Dewry, 1808)

—— *Poems* (Oxford: W. Jackson, 1768)

Nichols, John, *Literary Anecdotes of the Eighteenth Century*, 9 vols (London: printed for the author by Nichols, Son and Bentley, 1812–1816)

Notes and Queries (1859; 1860)

Osborn, James M., ed., Joseph Spence, *Observations, Anecdotes and Characters of Books and Men. Collected from Conversation*, 2 vols (Oxford: Clarendon Press, 1966)

Pearson, Hesketh, ed., *The Swan of Lichfield: Being a Selection from the Correspondence of Anna Seward* (London: Hamish Hamilton, 1936)

Percival, Thomas, *The Third Part of a Father's Instructions: adapted to different periods of life, from youth to maturity* (Warrington: W. Eyres for J. Johnson, London, 1800)

—— *Biographical Memoirs of the late Thomas Butterworth Bayley* (Manchester: W. Shelmerdine, 1802)

—— *Medical Ethics* (Manchester: S. Russell for J. Johnson, London, 1803)

Percy, Thomas, *Reliques of Ancient English Poetry*, 2nd edn (London: J. Dodsley, 1767)

Piozzi, Hester Thrale, *Anecdotes of the Late Samuel Johnson, LL.D., During the Last Twenty Years of His Life* (London: T. Cadell, 1786)

—— *Letters to and from the Late Samuel Johnson, LL.D. to which are added some Poems, never before Printed. Published from the Original MSS. in Her Possession*, 2 vols (London: A. Strahan and T. Cadell, 1788)

—— *Observations and Reflections Made in the Course of a Journey through France, Italy, and Germany*, 2 vols (London: A. Strahan and T. Cadell, 1789)

—— see Bloom; Hayward

Pope, Alexander: see Butt

Pottle, Frederick: see Lustig; Reed

Reade, Aleyn Lyell, *Johnsonian Gleanings*, repr. edn. of London: Reade, 1909–1952, 10 vols (New York: Octagon Books, 1968)

Redford, Bruce, ed., *The Letters of Samuel Johnson, 1731–1772*, 5 vols (Oxford: Clarendon Press, 1992)

Reed, Joseph W. and Frederick Pottle, eds, *Boswell: Laird of Auchinleck, 1778–1782* (London: Heinemann; New York: McGraw-Hill, 1977)

Reeve, Clara, *The Progress of Romance, through times, countries, and manners: with remarks on the good and bad effects of it, on them respectively*, 2 vols (Colchester: Printed for the Author, by W. Keymer, 1785)

Repton, Humphry, *Variety* (London: Cadell, 1788)

Review of English Studies (1946)

Richardson, Samuel, *Pamela*: see Keymer

—— *Clarissa*: see Ross

—— *Letters*: see Carroll

Rogers, Ann, *The History of Miss Temple*, 2 vols (London: Printed for Rogers, 1777)

Ross, Angus, ed., Samuel Richardson, *Clarissa; or, the History of a Young Lady*, 2nd edn (1747; repr. London: Penguin, 1988)

Rousseau, Jean-Jacques: see Masters

Rowton, Frederic, *The Female Poets of Great Britain* (Philadelphia: Carey and Hart, 1849)

Sabor, Peter: see Doody

Scott, Walter, ed., *Minstrelsy of the Scottish Border: consisting of historical and romantic ballads, collected in the southern counties of Scotland; with a few of modern date, founded upon local tradition*, 2 vols (Kelso: printed for T. Cadell Jun. & W. Davies, London, 1802)

—— ed., *Sir Tristrem: a metrical romance of the thirteenth century; by Thomas of Ercildoune, called the Rhymer*, edited from the Auchinleck MS. by Walter Scott (Edinburgh: Archibald Constable, 1804)

—— ed., *The Works of John Dryden: Now First Collected in 8 Volumes, Illustrated with Notes Historical, Critical and Explanatory and A Life of the Author*, 8 vols (London: William Miller; Edinburgh: James Ballantyne, 1808)

—— ed., *The Works of Jonathan Swift: containing additional letters, tracts, and poems not hitherto published; with notes and a life of the author*, 19 vols (Edinburgh: Archibald Constable, 1814)

—— *The Lives of the Novelists* (London: Dent, 1825)

—— *The Life of Napoleon Buonaparte, Emperor of the French*, 9 vols (Edinburgh: Archibald Constable, 1827)

—— *Life*: see Lockhart

Seward, Thomas; Sympson of Gainsborough and Lewis, Theobald, eds, *The Works of Mr F. Beaumont and Mr J. Fletcher, Collated with all the Former Editions, and Corrected with Notes by Mr Theobald, Mr Seward and Mr Sympson, etc. and with a Preface by Mr Seward*, 10 vols (London: J. and R. Tonson and S. Draper, 1750)

—— 'The First Conjugal Ode', *The Poetical Register, and Repository for Fugitive Poetry for 1810 (–11) with Criticisms of Various Works*, 8 vols, 2nd edn (1805; London: F. and C. Rivington, 1803–1815)

—— 'The Female Right to Literature': see Suarez

Seward, William, *Anecdotes of Some Distinguished Persons: chiefly of the present and two preceding centuries. Adorned with sculptures*, 8 vols (London: Cadell & Davies, 1795–1796).

Smith, Charlotte: see Curran

Southey, Robert, *The Poetical Works of Robert Southey* (London: Longman, Brown, Green, and Longman, 1845)

—— *Letters*: see Warter Wood

Spacks, Patricia Meyer, ed., Eliza Haywood, *The Female Spectator* (Oxford; Oxford University Press, 1999)

Spence, Joseph: see Osborn

Stevens, William Bagshaw: see Galbraith

Suarez, Michael F., ed., Thomas Seward, 'The Female Right to Literature, in a Letter to a Young Lady from Florence', in *A Collection of Poems by Several Hands: compiled by Robert Dodsley* (London: J. Dodsley, 1782; repr. London Routledge /Thoemmes,1997)

Sympson of Gainsborough: see Thomas Seward

A System of Vegetables, translated from the thirteenth edition of the *Systema Vegetabilium of Linneus* by a Botanical Society at Lichfield, 2 vols (Lichfield: J. Jackson, for Leigh and Sotheby, London, 1783)

Tomaselli, Sylvana, ed., *A Vindication of the Rights of Men; with, A Vindication of the Rights of Women; and, Wollstonecraft* (Cambridge: Cambridge University Press, 1995)

Town and Country Magazine (1786)

Ty, Eleanor, ed., Mary Hays, *Memoirs of Emma Courtney* (Oxford: Oxford University Press, 1996)

Wakely, Alice: see Keymer

Warter, John Wood, ed., *Selections from the Letters of Robert Southey*, 4 vols (London: Longman, Brown, Green and Longman, 1856)

Wickham, Hill, ed., *Journals and Correspondence of Thomas Sedgewick Whalley, DD., of Mendip Lodge, Somerset*, 2 vols (London: Richard Bentley, 1863)

Williams, Anna, *Miscellanies in Prose and Verse* (London: T. Davies, 1766)

Williams, Helen Maria, *Letters Written in France, in the Summer 1790, to a Friend in England; Containing Various Anecdotes Relative to the French Revolution; and Memoirs of Mons. And Madame du F* (London: T. Cadell, 1790)

—— see Fraistat

Wollstonecraft, Mary, *Mary, a fiction* (London: J. Johnson, 1788)

—— see Tomaselli

Women's History Magazine (2005)

Wordsworth, William and Samuel Taylor Coleridge, *Lyrical Ballads, with a few other poems* (London: J. & A. Arch, 1798)

Zall, Paul M., ed., *Coleridge's 'Sonnets from Various Authors. Bound with Rev. W. L. Bowles' "Sonnets"'* (California: La Siesta Press, 1968)

Secondary Sources

Abrams, Lynn, *The Making of Modern Woman: Europe, 1789–1918* (London: Pearson, 2002)

Alexander, J. H. and David Hewitt, eds., *Scott and his Influence* (Aberdeen: Association for Scottish Literary Studies, 1983)

Ashmun, Margaret, *The Singing Swan: An Account of Anna Seward and Her Acquaintance with Dr Johnson, Boswell, and Others of Their Time* (New Haven: Yale University Press; London: Oxford University Press, 1931)

Armstrong, Isobel and Virginia Blain, eds, *Women's Poetry in the Enlightenment: The Making of a Canon, 1730–1820* (Basingstoke: McMillan Press; New York: St. Martin's Press, 1999)

Backscheider, Paula R., *Eighteenth-Century Women Poets and their Poetry: Inventing Agency, Inventing Genre* (Baltimore: Johns Hopkins University Press, 2005)

Barker, Hannah and Elaine Chalus, eds, *Women's History: Britain, 1700–1850. An Introduction* (London: Routledge, 2005)

Barney, Richard A., Plots *of the Enlightenment: Education and the Novel in Eighteenth-Century England* (Stanford, Ca.: Stanford University Press, 1999)

Bate, Walter Jackson, *Samuel Johnson*, 2nd edn (London: Hogarth Press, 1984)

Benstock, Shari, ed., *The Private Self: Theory and Practice of Women's Autobiographical Writings* (London: Routledge, 1988)

Bishop, Morchard, *Blake's Hayley: The Life, Works, and Friendships of William Hayley* (London: Victor Gollancz, 1951)

Blain, Virginia: see Armstrong

Breen, Jennifer and Mary Noble, *Romantic Literature* (London: Arnold, 2002)

Brewer, John, *The Pleasures of the Imagination: English Culture in the Eighteenth Century*, 2nd edn (Chicago: University of Chicago Press, 1997)

Butler, Marilyn, *Romantics, Rebels and Reactionaries: English Literature and its Background, 1760–1830* (Oxford: Oxford University Press, 1981)

Byatt, A. S., *Unruly Times: Wordsworth and Coleridge in their Time* (London: Vintage, 1997)

Castiglione Dario and Lesley Sharpe, *Shifting the Boundaries: Transformation of the Languages of Public and Private in the Eighteenth Century* (Exeter: University of Exeter Press, 1995)

Chalus, Elaine: see Barker

Clarke, Norma, *The Rise and Fall of the Woman of Letters* (London: Pimlico, 2004)

Classen, Constance, *The Colour of Angels: Cosmology, Gender and the Aesthetic Imagination* (London: Routledge, 1998)

Clifford, James L., *Hester Lynch Piozzi: Mrs Thrale*, 2nd edn (Oxford: Oxford University Press, 1987)

Coburn, Kathleen, ed., *Coleridge: A Collection of Critical Essays* (New Jersey: Prentice Hall, 1967)

Darwin, Charles: see King-Hele

Darwin, Erasmus: see Harris

Davidoff, Leonora and Catherine Hall, *Family Fortunes: Men and Women of the English Middle Class, 1780–1850* (London: Routledge, 1997)

Davies, Bertram H., ed., Sir John Hawkins, *The Life of Samuel Johnson, LLD* (London: Jonathan Cape, 1961)

Duff, David, ed., *Modern Genre Theories* (Harlow: Pearson Education, 2000)

Favret, Mary, *Romantic Correspondence: Women, Politics and the Fiction of Letters* (Cambridge University Press, 1994)

Fay, Elizabeth A., *A Feminist Introduction to Romanticism* (Oxford: Blackwell, 1998)

Firth, J. B., *Highways and Byways in Derbyshire*, 2nd edn (London: Macmillan, 1928)

Gill, Sean, *Women and the Church of England. From the Eighteenth Century to the Present* (London: SPCK, 1994)

Goldsmith, Elizabeth C., ed., *Writing the Female Voice: Essays on Epistolary Literature* (London: Pinter, 1989)

Graham, Elspeth and others, eds, *Her Own Life: Autobiographical Writings by Seventeenth-Century Englishwomen*, 2nd edn (London: Routledge, 1992)

Grundy, Isobel and Susan Wiseman, eds, *Women, Writing, History 1640–1720* (Athens, Ga.: University of Georgia Press, 1992)

Grundy, Isobel, *Lady Mary Wortley Montagu* (Oxford: Oxford University Press, 1999)

Guest, Harriet, *Small Change: Women, Learning, Patriotism, 1750–1810* (Chicago: University of Chicago Press, 2000)

Hall, Catherine: see Davidoff

Harman, Claire, *Fanny Burney: A Biography* (New York: Alfred A. Knopf, 2001)

Harris, Stuart, ed., *Cosmologia. A Sequence of Epic Poems in Three Parts comprising Part One: The Economy of Vegetation (1791) Part Two: The Loves of the Plants (1789) Part Three: The Temple of Nature (1803) by Erasmus Darwin* (Sheffield: Stuart Harris, 2002)

Hawkins, Sir John: see Davies

Hebron, Stephen: see Woof

Hewitt, David: see Alexander

Hibbert, Christopher, *The Personal History of Samuel Johnson*, 2nd edn (London: Pimlico, 1998)

Hopkins, Mary Alden, *Dr Johnson's Lichfield* (London: Peter Owen, 1956)

Kelly, Gary, ed., *Bluestocking Feminism: Writings of the Bluestocking Circle, 1738–1790*, 6 vols (London: Pickering and Chatto, 1999)

King-Hele, Desmond, *Erasmus Darwin: A Life of Unequalled Achievement* (London: Giles de la Mare, 1999)

—— ed., Charles Darwin, *Charles Darwin's Life of Erasmus Darwin* (1879; repr. Cambridge: Cambridge University Press, 2003)

Lee, Sir Sidney: see Stephen

Lonsdale, Roger, ed., *Eighteenth Century Women Poets: An Oxford Anthology* (Oxford: Oxford University Press, 1989)

Lucas, E. V., *A Swan and her Friends* (London: Methuen and Co, 1907)

Martin, Peter, *A Life of James Boswell* (London: Weidenfeld & Nicolson, 1999)

Martin, Stapleton, *Anna Seward and Classic Lichfield* (Worcester: Deighton and Co., 1909)

McCalman, Iain, *An Oxford Companion to the Romantic Age: British Culture 1776–1832* (Oxford: Oxford University Press, 1999)

McCarthy, William, *Hester Thrale Piozzi: Portrait of a Literary Woman* (Chapel Hill, North Carolina: University of North Carolina Press, 1985)

McMillin, Scott, ed., *Restoration and Eighteenth Century Comedy*, 2nd edn (New York: Norton, 1997)

Mellor, Anne K., *Mothers of the Nation: Women's Political Writing in England, 1780–1830* (Bloomington, IN: Indiana University Press, 2000)

Millgate, Jane, *Walter Scott: The Makings of the Novelist* (Edinburgh: Edinburgh University Press, 1984)

Mitford, Mary Russell, *Recollections of a Literary Life: Or, Books, Places, and People*, 3 vols (London: Richard Bentley, 1852)

Morse, David, *The Age of Virtue* (Basingstoke: Macmillan Press, 2000)

Murray, Venetia, *High Society in the Regency Period, 1788-1830* (London: Penguin, 1998)

Noble, Mary: see Breen

Nussbaum, Felicity, *The Autobiographical Subject: Gender and Ideology in Eighteenth-Century England* (London: John Hopkins University Press, 1989)

Olney, James, *Memory and Narrative: The Weave of Life-Writing* (Chicago: Chicago University Press, 1998)

Picard, Lisa, *Dr Johnson's London: Life in London, 1740–1770* (London: Weidenfeld & Nicolson, 2000)

Porter, Roy, *English Society in the Eighteenth Century*, 2nd edn, rev edn (London: Penguin Books, 1991)

—— *Enlightenment* (London: Penguin Books, 2000)

Raven, Ronald W., *The Theory and Practice of Oncology: Historical evolution and Present Principles* (New Jersey: Parthenon, 1990)

Redman, Nicholas, *The Whitbread Archive: Dr Erasmus Darwin and Breadsall Priory, Derbyshire* (London: for Whitbread PLC [n. date])

Roe Nicholas, ed., *An Oxford Guide to Romanticism* (Oxford: Oxford University Press, 2005)

Sharpe, Lesley: see Castiglione

Sisman, Adam, *Boswell's Presumptuous Task: Writing the Life of Dr Johnson* (London: Penguin, 2001)

Snow, Edward, *A Study of Vermeer*, 2nd. edn (Berkeley: University of California Press, 1994)

Stone, Lawrence, *The Family, Sex and Marriage in England, 1500–1800* (London: Penguin, 1979)

Swain, Margaret, *Embroidered Georgian Pictures* (Haverfordwest: Shire Publications, 1994)

Swinnerton, Frank, *A Galaxy of Fathers* (London: Hutchinson, 1966)

Todd, Janet, *Sensibility: An Introduction* (London: Methuen and Co., 1986)

—— *The Sign of Angellica: Women, Writing and Fiction, 1660–1800* (New York: Columbia University Press, 1989)

—— ed., *A Dictionary of British and American Women Writers 1660–1800* (London: Methuen, 1987)

Uglow, Jenny, *The Lunar Men: The Friends who made the Future, 1730–1810* (London: Faber and Faber, 2002)

Vickery, Amanda, *The Gentleman's Daughter: Women's Lives in Georgian England* (New Haven: Yale University Press, 1998)

Wilson, A. N., *A Life of Walter Scott: The Laird of Abbotsford*, 2nd edn (London: Pimlico, 2002)

Wiseman, Susan: see Grundy

Woof, Robert and Stephen Hebron, eds, *Romantic Icons* (Kendal: The Wordsworth Trust, 1999)

Wu, Duncan, ed., *Romanticism: An Anthology*, 2nd edn (Oxford: Blackwell, 1998)

Articles and Essays

Atkin, Wendy J., ' "A most ingenious Authress": Frances Brooke (1724–1789) and her Lincolnshire connections', in *Lincolnshire History and Archaeology*, 32 (1997), pp. 12–20

Batchelor, Jennie, 'Re-clothing the Female Reader: Dress and the *Lady's Magazine* (1770–1832)', *Women's History Magazine*, 49 (2005), pp. 11–21

Bates, William, 'Godwin's Caleb Williams Annotated by Anna Seward', *Notes and Queries*, 9 (24 March 1860), pp. 219–20

'Biographical Sketch of the late Miss Seward', *The Gentleman's Magazine*, LXXIX (1809), I, 378–79

Boswell, James, 'On Diaries', *Hypochondriack*, 66 (March 1783), reprinted in *Boswell's Column. Being his Seventy Contributions to the London Magazine under the pseudonym The Hypochondriack*, ed. by Margery Bailey (London: W. Kimber, 1951), p. 331

Brewer, John, 'This, that and the other: Public, Social and Private in the Seventeenth and Eighteenth Centuries', in *Shifting the Boundaries: Transformation of the Languages of Public and Private in the Eighteenth Century*, ed. by Dario Castiglione and Lesley Sharpe (Exeter: University of Exeter Press, 1995), pp. 1–21

Chapman, R. W., 'Mrs Piozzi's Omissions from Johnson's Letters to the Thrales', in *Review of English Studies*, 22 (1946), pp. 17–28

'Cibber's Apology', *Blackwood's Edinburgh Magazine*, 8 (January–June 1823), pp. 22–30

'Colley Cibber', *Notes and Queries*, 2, 8, (1859), p. 317

Crecelius, Kathryn, 'Authorship and Authority: Georges Sand's Letters to her Mother', in *Writing the Female Voice: Essays on Epistolary Literature*, ed. by Elizabeth C. Goldsmith (London: Pinter, 1989), pp. 257–72

'Editorial', *The Lady's Magazine*, 1 (August 1770), p. 170

Frye, Northrop, 'The Mythos of Summer: Romance', reprinted from Northrop Frye, *Anatomy of Criticism: Four Essays* (Princeton: Princeton University Press, 1957), in *Modern Genre Theories*, ed. by David Duff (Harlow: Pearson Education, 2000)

Fullagar, Kate, 'Caroline Lucretia Herschell', in *An Oxford Companion to the Romantic Age: British Culture 1776–1832*, ed. by Iain McCalman (Oxford: Oxford University Press, 1999), p. 541

Graham, Elspeth, 'Introduction', in *Her Own Life: Autobiographical Writings by Seventeenth-Century Englishwomen*, 2nd edn (London: Routledge, 1992), pp. 1–27

Greenhut, Deborah Schneider, 'Anna Williams', in *A Dictionary of British and American Women Writers 1660–1800*, ed. by Janet Todd (London: Methuen, 1987), p. 323

Harding, Anthony, 'Biography and Autobiography', in *Romanticism: An Oxford Guide*, ed. by Nicholas Roe (Oxford: Oxford University Press, 2005), pp. 445–55

Heiland, Donna, 'Swan Songs: The Correspondence of Anna Seward and James Boswell', in *Modern Philology*, 90: 3 (1993), pp. 381–91

Jordan, Frank, 'Scott, Chatterton and Byron, and the Wearing of Masks', in *Scott and his Influence*, ed. by J.H. Alexander and David Hewitt (Aberdeen: Association for Scottish Literary Studies, 1983), pp. 279–89

Mandell, Laura, 'Hemans and the Gift-Book Aesthetic', in *Cardiff Corvey Articles*, VI, 1, p. 6

Mee, Jon, 'William Hayley', in *An Oxford Companion to the Romantic Age: British Culture 1776–1832*, ed. by Iain McCalman (Oxford: Oxford University Press, 1999), p. 537

Nussbaum, Felicity A., 'Eighteenth-Century Women's Autobiographical Commonplaces', in *The Private Self: Theory and Practice of Women's Autobiographical Writings*, ed. by Shari Benstock (London: Routledge, 1988), pp. 147–71

Pratt, Lynda, 'Epic', in *An Oxford Guide to Romanticism*, ed. by Nicholas Roe (Oxford: Oxford University Press, 2005) pp. 332–49

Robinson, E., 'The Derby Philosophical Society', in *Annals of Science*, 9 (1953), pp. 359–67

Rubenstein, Jill, 'Sir Walter Scott as Literary Biographer', in *Scott and his Influence*, ed. by J. H. Alexander and David Hewitt (Aberdeen: Association for Scottish Literary Studies, 1983), pp. 189–98

Shuttleton, David, ' "All passion Extinguish'd": The Case of Mary Chandler, 1687–1745', in *Women's Poetry in the Enlightenment: The Making of a Canon, 1730–1820*, ed. by Isobel Armstrong and Virginia Blain (Basingstoke: McMillan Press; New York: St. Martin's Press, 1999), pp. 33–49

Waldron, Mary, ' "This Muse-born Wonder": the Occluded Voice of Ann Yearsley, Milkwoman and Poet of Clifton', in *Women's Poetry in the Enlightenment: The Making of a Canon, 1730–1820*, ed. by Isobel Armstrong and Virginia Blain (Basingstoke: McMillan Press; New York: St. Martin's Press, 1999), pp. 113–26

White, Henry, 'Memoir of Anna Seward', in *The Monthly Mirror*, 2 (January and February 1796), pp. 239–42

Wilson, Kathleen, 'British Women and Empire', in *Women's History: Britain, 1700–1850. An Introduction*, ed. by Hannah Barker and Elaine Chalus (London: Routledge, 2005), pp. 260–84

Online Publications and Articles

Bowerbank, Sylvia, 'Anna Seward (1742–1809)', *Oxford Dictionary of National Biography*, Oxford: Oxford University Press, 2004 <http://www.oxforddnb. com /view/ article/25135>

Braby, Peter, 'Letters of a Badsey Family, 1735–36', in *Vale of Evesham Historical Society Research Papers*, 1971 <file://A:\BadseyArticlesbypeterbraby.htm>

Eyam Hall, <http://www.eyamhall.com>

Furness, Peter, *On the Bradshaws and Staffords of Eyam, with a Notice of the Old Hall*, 1861–2, transcription by Paul Bradford, 2001 <http://www.wish fulthinking.org.uk/genuki/DBY/Eyam/Stafford/Bradhall.html>

Johnson, Samuel, *Prefaces, Biographical and Critical, to the Works of the English Poets*, VII, 43, 1779–1781, in *Literature Online* <http://www.lion. chadwick. co.uk>

—— 'The Rambler', Sections 1–54, from *The Works of Samuel Johnson*, sixteen vols, Electronic Text Centre, the University of Virginia Library, No. 15, Tuesday 8 May 1750; No. 35, Tuesday 17 July 1750; No. 18, Saturday 19 May 1750; No. 39, Tuesday 31 July 1750; No. 45, Tuesday, 21 August 1750 <http:// www.etext.lib.virginia.edu>

—— 'An Essay on Epitaphs in the Idler, By the Author of the Rambler. In Two Volumes. Volume II. The Third Edition. With additional Essays' *The Idler*, 1740, in *Literature Online* <http://www.lion.chadwick. co.uk>

Lichfield City Council, <http://www.lichfield.gov.uk/events.ihtml>

'The Martyrdom of William Seward', in *The Reformer*, July/August 1992, Ottery St Mary Reformed Church <file://A:\Themartyrdomofwilliamseward.htm>

Miller, James, *The Humours of Oxford: A Comedy* (1730), Act V, Scene 1, p. 79 <http://lion.chadwyck. co.uk>

Palaeography, The National Archives <http://www.nationalarchives.gov.uk/ palaeography/quick_reference,htm>

Roman, Alexander, 'Anchored in Christ: A Celebration of Ukraine's Pope', in *Ukranian Orthodoxy* <http://www.unicorne.org/orthodoxy.html>

Tilley, Joseph, *The Old Halls, Manors and Families of Derbyshire*, Volume 1, *The High Peak Hundred* <http://www.genuki.org.uk/big/eng/DBY/Tilley/ Volume1/LearnFoolowEyamHalls.html>

Warton, Thomas, 'The Pleasures of Melancholy', in *Miscellanies and Collections, 1660–1750: A Collection of Poems*, 1763 <http://www.caxton.stockton.edu>

Warton, Thomas, 'Of the Origin of Romantic Fiction in Europe. A Dissertation', in *The History of English Poetry*, 1774–1781, in *Literature Online* <http://www. lion.chadwick.co.uk>

White, William, 'History, Gazetteer and Directory of Staffordshire', 1851 <http://www.genuki.org.uk/big/eng/STS/Lichfield/Cathedral/index.html>

Williams, Anna, 'Essays in Verse and Prose', in *Miscellanies;* 'An Epitaph on Claudy Phillips. A Musician.' by Samuel Johnson, in *Literature Online* <http://lion.chadwyck.co.uk>

Wood, William, 'The Manor of Eyam' in *The History and Antiquities of Eyam, Derbyshire*, 1842, 1845, 1860, transcription by Andrew McCann, 1999 <http://www.genuki.org.uk/big/eng/DBY/Eyam/Wood/Manor.html>

Index